SOME DAY

SOME DAY
The Literature of Waiting
A Creative Writing Course With Time on Its Hands

ROBERT EIDELBERG

This is not a work of fiction. It is, in effect, a textbook example of the special topics courses offered by the English Department of Hunter College of the City University of New York.

On the evening of Tuesday, January 28, 2020,
thirty undergraduate students showed up in Room 404 Hunter West for the first class ever, anywhere, of "The Literature of Waiting."
What were these students waiting for?

What were they expecting?
Whatever it was, who knew it could be a book.
This book. Their book.

To order additional copies of this book, contact:
Xlibris
1-888-795-4274
www.Xlibris.com
Orders@Xlibris.com
811433

DEDICATION

Epigraph from New York Times Columnist David Brooks:
We have entered the endurance phase of this pandemic. We are slowly mastering this disease, but we have not yet done so. And so we wait – and endure. Endurance is patience.... Endurance is living through unpleasantness.... Endurance is fortifying.... Above all, endurance is living with uncertainty.

Epigraph from American author Armand M. L. Inezian:
Waiting was something he disliked these days because it made him realize how much time he had on his hands.

This book is dedicated to all of us with time on our hands who endure.

WAITING INSIDE:
OUR CONTENTS

An Introduction (Wait for It!) ix

Chapter 1   Take Your Waiting Places 1

Chapter 2   Waiting May Not Be Hard, But It Isn't Easy! 11

Chapter 3   Sing a Song of Some Day As We Merrily Roll Along 23

Chapter 4   They Also Serve Who Sit and Wait 34

Chapter 5   They Also Serve Who Wait on Those Who Wait 40

Chapter 6   With Patience You Can Learn to Wait 45

Chapter 7   "The Dumb Waiter" or The Dumb "Waiter"? 54

Chapter 8   "Growing Up," as in Russell Baker's 1982 Memoir:
             Is It a Kind of Waiting? Just Ask Any Kid! 65

Chapter 9   Are You on My Current Calendar – And Am I on
             Your Past Ones? 70

Chapter 10   On Hold for – and Holding On to – Dorothy
             Parker's 1928 Short Story "A Telephone Call" 74

Chapter 11   Waiting for Love in Ha Jin's 1999 Novel "Waiting" 84

Chapter 12   When in the Course of Daily Pre-Pandemic Human
             Events: Making Time – and Marking Time – for a
             Personal Waiting Journal 96

Chapter 13   Paging Playwright Clifford Odets: What Is It We
             Are Left Waiting for in 1935 When We Are Left
             "Waiting for Lefty"? 106

Chapter 14   Who Are the Barbarians Whose Arrival We Await
             in J. M. Coetzee's 1980 Novel "Waiting for the
             Barbarians"? 123

Chapter 15   Can't Wait to Read Charles Dickens' 1861 Novel
             "Great Expectations" And Five Other Works of
             "Waiting" Literature? 138

Chapter 16   Fearful Waiting in the 1967 Hollywood Movie
             "Wait Until Dark" and in Noel Coward's 1960 Play
             "Waiting in the Wings" 165

Chapter 17   Waiting Out (Enduring!) the 2020 Coronavirus
             Pandemic While Sheltered Off-Campus and
             At-Home with Giovanni Boccaccio's Waiting Work
             on the Black Plague of 1348 – "The Decameron" 169

Chapter 18   The Pro and Con Wizard of "The Wizard of Oz," in
             L. Frank Baum's Classic 1900 Novel of Hope 194

Chapter 19   What Exactly Is There Just Enough Room for in
             Those Rooms We Call a "Waiting Room"? 201

Chapter 20   Of Course Time Flies – But It Also Travels in Other
             Fantastic Ways (Especially in Alan Lightman's 1993
             Novel "Einstein's Dreams") 207

Chapter 21   All This Time Waiting and Waiting and Waiting for
             Samuel Beckett's 1953 Play "Waiting for Godot" 224

A Conclusion (Timely But Unexpected) to SOME DAY 261
About the Author 283

AN INTRODUCTION (WAIT FOR IT!)

How This Creative Writing Book and the Some Day Literature Course It's Based on Came About

Now wait.

Now.

Wait.

You do it all the time. Time and time again.

You're doing it right now: waiting on our every word.

So here goes: before there was this book SOME DAY on writing creatively about a world of waiting, there was a special topics Hunter College English course on "The Literature of Waiting" that featured a selection of novels, plays, and short stories by some rather world famous authors.

But wait: even before that time-sensitive college course there were, well, the elevators – particularly the ones in the North Building of Hunter College of the City University of New York. Elevators that you always had to wait distressing long for when they were apparently working and eternally long for when they were "out of service."

There was even that infamous elevator repair sign. Picture it: a photoshopped female student with her right hand flat out in the stop-and-wait position, her compressed lips silently conveying that any wait on your part for an elevator to come would be entirely futile. And did we mention that the repair sign would inevitably remain up even after that elevator had been fixed? Now that made a certain sense since it was only a matter of time before the sign was, like a broken clock, accurate again.

Then one day the wording of the sign looked somehow different (although "Hildy" the Hunter elevator girl remained essentially the same in pose and posture). But now here is what students were reading, instead, alongside Hildy's planted position:

> Now wait: does your life seem to be on hold? Will your time come "some day"? "The Literature of Waiting," a brand-new English Department course (English 25146, taught by Robert Eidelberg), explores the existential relationship between human life and time, hope, and endurance. Read and write creatively about how and why we wait and what it is we are waiting for – connection, love, success, happiness, power, life's meaning, death.
>
> For the spring 2020 semester, come Tuesdays and Thursdays from 5:35 pm to 6:50 pm and experience such classic and contemporary works (many of them with "waiting" in their titles) as: Waiting for Godot, by Samuel Beckett; The Dumb Waiter, by Harold Pinter; Great Expectations, by Charles Dickens; Waiting for the Barbarians, by J. M. Coetzee; Waiting, by Ha Jin; The Iceman Cometh, by Eugene O'Neill; Waiting for Lefty, by Clifford Odets; Robinson Crusoe, by Daniel Defoe; Merrily We Roll Along, by Stephen Sondheim; The Age of Innocence, by Edith Wharton; Rosencrantz and Guildenstern Are Dead, by Tom Stoppard; Waiting in the Wings, by Noel Coward.
>
> If you are intrigued by the relationship between human life and time, duration, expectation and endurance, "The Literature of Waiting" may just be the course you have been waiting for.

Registration for Hunter College's single section of "The Literature of Waiting" was officially capped at 30 students, and exactly 30 students – from honors upper freshmen to finally-about-to-graduate seniors – arrived by 5:35 pm (early or on time) for the course's first session on Tuesday, January 28, 2020.

And, yes, appropriately for a course entitled "The Literature of Waiting," at late registration there was a waiting list.

Historical and pedagogical note from author and educator Robert Eidelberg: our course had its last face-to-face, mouth-to-mouth on-campus session on Tuesday, March 10, 2020, after which the worldwide Coronavirus Pandemic threw us into what the City University of New York termed "distance learning." Chapters 1 through 13 of this book represent the intellectual and imaginative workings of "The Literature of Waiting" course "B.C." (Before Coronavirus); Chapters 14 through 21 represent a course that by necessity became less personally interactive and more written-response-oriented "A.D." (After Distancing).

My 27 Hunter College collaborators and I would love to hear from readers of SOME DAY not only about their reactions to this book's mandated teaching and learning division but also about how well SOME DAY, the whole book, worked for you as an intellectual do-it-yourself reading, thinking, and creative writing course on the literature of waiting – as a "book with a built-in teacher."

If, for whatever reason (social isolation from others, sheltered-in-place schooling, pandemic pedagogy), you, like us, had "time on your hands" and couldn't wait to exercise your mind by learning on your own about "waiting" in literature, please share your experience with us at "The Literature of Waiting" course email: glamor62945@mypacks.net.

CHAPTER 1

Take Your Waiting Places

If you think about the act of reading and the act of writing (and I hope you are doing that right now in anticipation of what I'm going to say next), both of these very human behaviors are acts of "waiting." And, as the illustrated children's book by Mo Willems tells us in its emphatic title: WAITING IS NOT EASY! Nor, apparently, was a Hunter College English Department creative writing and literature study course on "The Literature of Waiting" that listed the following required "waiting" works (many with the word "waiting" in their title):

Waiting Is Not Easy! by Mo Willems
The Dumb Waiter by Harold Pinter
My Mother's Calendars by Carol J. Adams
Waiting by Ha Jin
Waiting for Lefty by Clifford Odets
Waiting for the Barbarians by J. M. Coetzee
A Telephone Call by Dorothy Parker
The Wizard of Oz by L. Frank Baum
Einstein's Dreams by Alan Lightman
The Iceman Cometh by Eugene O'Neill
Waiting for Godot by Eugene Beckett

Plus a choice of one of the following six "waiting" works for independent reading and collaborative group work:

Great Expectations by Charles Dickens
The Age of Innocence by Edith Wharton

Robinson Crusoe by Daniel Defoe
Rosencrantz and Guildenstern Are Dead
    by Tom Stoppard
The Haunting of Hill House by Shirley Jackson
Eleanor Oliphant Is Completely Fine by Gail Honeyman

Plus a COURSEPACK assortment of "waiting" poems, songs and essays, and excerpts from:

Passing Time by Andrea Kohler
On Waiting by Harold Schweizer
Mythos by Stephen Fry
The Hebrew Bible: Jacob's 14-Year Wait for Rachel's
    Hand in Marriage
The Odyssey by Homer
The Trial by Franz Kafka
Letter from Birmingham Jail by Dr. Martin Luther King Jr.
Growing Up by Russell Baker
The Wings of the Dove by Henry James
Merrily We Roll Along composed by Stephen Sondheim
Waiting in the Wings by Noel Coward
The Decameron by Giovanni Boccaccio

The writing in the course was also extensive. And intensive. And incredibly, at times, insane. Yes, some of it was analytically "academic" (particularly after we all had to go online and teach and learn from one another from a distance), but most of it was crazily "creative" – imaginative writing *inspired* by all the literature the students were reading, and thinking about, and – for real – keeping scribbled notes on about their observations, their ideas, their perceptions, their confusions, their questions, their annoyances, their criticisms, and – especially – their delights.

You can imagine (or maybe you can't) how time flew when we all came together to talk in class in the early evening for an hour and fifteen minutes twice a week (with many students coming straight from a full-time job and "dinner" on the subway). We had a clock on our classroom wall that I was thrilled to note on Day 1 was broken. When it got fixed by our second meeting (I certainly wasn't the one who reported it!), my displeasure was palpable. As was my joy when (and I think the word actually is "fortuitously") it looked broken again (now and forever the time is 10:09) at the start of Session #3 (I didn't know whom to thank – and didn't want to know!).

Students were also provided with a page consisting of "waiting words and phrases" that they might, quite naturally, find themselves using in the academic and creative writing that the course would require of them. Or that they might want to glance at from time to time to help jump-start their writing. That page of "waiting words and phrases" looked something like this:

While waiting...
Just you wait...
I was waiting for...
I'm going to have to put you on hold...
Waiting on...
Waiting in...
Waiting at...
Finding the time...
I was being waited on...
Now wait!
During...
Not worth waiting for!
Where did the time go?
Easy come, easy go...
Now and then...
Waiting through...
I was expecting...
I was hoping...
Dream on!
I can't wait to...
Time to...
Growing up...
Can't wait!

Wait till...
The dumb waiter...
Hold on now!
Time and again
As I was waiting...
Hoping to...
I had some time on my hands...
Anticipating that...
Wait a minute!

Meanwhile…
-ing and waiting…
Busy waiting…
If not now, then when…
Waiting while…
Waiting with…
Waiting without…
And so on.

So, "with time on our hands," it was mostly out of all the creative thinking and writing we did in "The Literature of Waiting" course that this book came to life. Not only was the creative writing more fun for students to do than the periodically assigned conventional writing of academia – and more fun for me as the course's instructor to read on my B.C. subway ride home (not a minor consideration, let me tell you) – but students quickly came to believe that it was more real and lasting for them to "apply" their insights into an author's themes and artistry by creatively building a newly structured home for those themes and literary techniques.

I had formally stated in the printed requirements of our course of study that students would "indirectly demonstrate their textual understandings of a literary work by applying them imaginatively to the creation of magazine-type publishable pieces." Fun! (Or better than fun: late in our pandemically dark off-campus days, one student emailed me that "the reading and thinking about this course have both been a light in this time; I hope reading our assignments brings you a similar light." Oh, yes!)

Students were also informed that they would be keeping a "Personal Waiting Journal" for noting the daily occurrences of "waiting" in their lives and the lives of those they came in contact with – and that from these "noted" entries they would from time to time select one to take inspiration from, expanding and reconstructing the germ of the entry into a "CW/HW" – a piece of "creative writing homework"; later, when our course went "distant" because of the Covid-19 virus, many students found that "waiting for the pandemic to end" became the recurrent theme of their personal journal entries.

In the back of my mind I had the thought that the best of my students' writing might possibly flow stream-like into a trade-size softcover book of about 100 pages. I had even put together a working title: "NOW WAIT: An Assortment of Creative Writing from a Hunter College Course in The Literature of Waiting." That "pamphlet" (with a different title and almost three times the projected size – because the best of my students' writing became an undammable deluge) is the book you are holding in your hands right now (in either paperback or "e" form) with the *now* "waiting" title of "SOME DAY: The Literature of Waiting – A Creative Writing Course With Time on Its Hands." My publishing "plan" was for the book to have, toward the end of its first chapter, the earliest possible sample I could get of my students' writing – and what could be earlier than an in-class piece of writing on Day 1 of "The Literature of Writing" class?

So here is a SOME DAY assortment of those Day 1 pieces of writing. And what were these early evening (and probably fairly hungry; it was already 6:40 pm) college students to write about? The immediate assignment was to produce, legibly, in less than ten minutes, and in whatever form they cared to (prose, poem, list, definition, sketch, cartoon) whatever now came into their minds when they saw or heard or thought of the word "waiting."

Not only was I interested in seeing how well my students wrote (or drew), but I was seriously curious about – yes, I will say it: I could hardly wait for – what they had in their heads and on their minds about the idea of "waiting," which was, after all, the subject of our common and collegial course.

From Andrea Pinzon
There is a lot of doing in waiting; when we wait, we want time to be fast in order to receive what we are expecting.

From Anne-Lilja Rentof
One of the most frustrating aspects of day-to-day life is the intertwining of time, or rather the passage of time and stream of consciousness. The more one is conscious of the passage of time, which is often a result of idleness, the slower time seems to move.

From Bianca Correa
As the days turn into weeks and the weeks into months,
I find myself wondering where you are.
Are you waiting for the moment to come –
the moment in which the universe allows us to meet once again?
I will forever wait for you;
I will not stray.
Even if waiting is my downfall.

From Fawzi Saleh
Standing in line on Black Friday
Rice cooker timer

From Christina Louie
Sitting
Tapping my feet.
    Tap. Tap. Tap.
Glancing up at the clock,
    I sigh.
Once.
Twice.
Over and over…
    until this time is finally over.

From Chyna Chung
Waiting for love, peace, death, a ride from a friend, acceptance.
Waiting in silence
at the doctor's office,
waiting in line,
waiting on people.
Waiting for the wait to be over.

From Gamal Amin
Waiting patiently to be happy with who I am and what I do.
A never-ending journey with no guaranteed results.

From Gabriella Tuchman
Waiting is impatience. It is holding an ice cream cone full of your favorite flavor, watching each droplet melt to the floor. Waiting is anticipation – blinking back tears as you receive your graduation cap. It is dunking under water and holding your breath until you feel your lungs ready to implode. Waiting is boredom. It is standing on line, or tying your shoe.

From Hester Milford
It's a lot of pressure when teachers ask us to start writing in the first few moments of class. In my last class, I had to decipher the Goddess Diana and her curse on an unknowing hunter. "Waiting." What does that even mean? You don't want to write something generic – you know, like "minutes ticked by as I watched the clock." You want to stand out. Something original?

From Carolyn Reyes

If you live your life just "waiting" for something, life will just happen to you. You need to take action before you forget to live.

From Liala Ahmad

I've drawn a medical waiting room with three seated patients in quite different but probably equally uncomfortable positions. At the front deak, one of two receptionists calls out (but to whom?): "The doctor will see you now."

From Jason Chetram

Expecting or anticipating an event to occur at a time that is not the present.

From Wardah Malik

Staying someplace for a long time.

From Massiel Sanchez

I recently watched the movie "20th- Century Women" where one of the characters gets diagnosed with cancer, so I'm attempting to draw a waiting room.

From Michael McClenahan

Waiting makes me think of contemporary politics. Currently it feels as though we are in the midst of a grand realignment of the political landscape, with a number of different political horizons that seem possible. With political power relatively stratified along economic lines, it feels sometimes like the most one can do is wait with varying degrees of horror and hope for whatever the future will bring.

From Maxine Lim

A sketch of a person standing near the curb of a sidewalk in between an ornate streetlamp and a sign saying "No loitering, No Parking."

From Paige Thorne

I've drawn a young person standing at a bus stop. Her mouth is turned down, but the word "sigh" can still make it out and be heard.

From Henry Janani

Waiting for the train; waiting on line to get food; waiting to find "the one."

From Nathalie Chazoule

My fingers, they're so pruned it hurts and the water's not even wet anymore – the candle has long gone out – but challenging gravity will be beyond me. I'll tongue at the seed in my teeth instead of taking it out because it's comforting to think someone might come by to embarrass me for it. I should have turned the oven off. I'm not so sure of anything so I feel guilty when I think I am. Mostly, I am scared of hoping that physics' laws might be as fake as our own. I dread having to do it myself.

From Nattapat Karmniyanont

This is one of the two latest classes that I've enrolled in so far, and so I am a bit tired; hopefully, fatigue will not coax me into sleeping. Hmm, this seems like an interesting class so far. Hmm, oh yeah, what time will I be home today? Probably 7:30 or 7:40. At least tomorrow will be a relatively light day.

From Nicole Sanchez

Patience. Sympathy. Boundaries. Respect.

From Rabeya Rahman

graduation
end goal: happiness
microwave
blizzard / snowstorm
London
my boyfriend
bed
poor cellphone data
MTA buses
weekend

From Ryan Langan

By the time the sun rose on February 1st, I had been lying in bed awake for nearly twelve hours. I had wanted to be relaxed and confident when I submitted my MFA application, but that is not the nature of writing, a truth I've run from since the dire discovery of my primal need to wrangle language. Most of it is merely time passing – the internal clock running and accumulating knowledge and mnemonics to be used, regurgitated, exploited. That's all I've ever done. Now, while that action hangs in the balance of judgment – well, now I'm really waiting. I'm waiting for the waiting to return to me.

From Patrick Diaz

The New York City subway system represents many kinds of waiting and not uniquely moving along while waiting. Sitting, waiting for your stop, you're often completing other tasks or procrastinating. In the case of the latter, you're double waiting.

From Shanya Hopkins

Standing in line. Sweat dripping from the back of my neck. Watching the clock. Firmly gripping my ticket. When will they call my number? Thirst. All I can think of as I listen to the persistent plop of the water hitting the floor from the rancid spot on the ceiling. ... "Number 447." Her voice, loud and unwelcoming, breaks my delirium. I'll never lose ID again.

From Trever Polk

Even though it's sunny out, I'm lying on the couch in the living room; it's dark because of the wood-panel walls, so the light coming through the windows makes it feel like I'm in a jail cell, even though I could technically just go outside. But my head still hurts, and I don't have anything to do, anyway. So why bother putting in the effort to actually get up, walk outside, and adjust my eyes?

From Valeria Diaz-Huertas

Waiting for things to get better: time moves slowly, days go by and one begins to wonder when change will come; time is so precious – too precious to waste it.

Three weeks into our combined literature study and creative writing course on "worldwide works of waiting," Kila, the seven-year-old cousin of our classmate **Shanya Hopkins**, asked Shanya to *read with her* from the book OH, THE PLACES YOU'LL GO! by Dr. Seuss. Shanya couldn't wait to share that experience with our class:

> It struck me almost immediately – and I thought about everything we'd discussed so far in the course – and I found my cousin's reaction to "waiting" to be very wise. She told me that every place was "the waiting place" for little kids because she waited everywhere she went and before everything she did. She said that little kids live "waiting lives" because their parents control their time all the time.

Here's the part of Dr. Seuss's book that got that rise out of Shanya's cousin:

> *Headed, I fear, toward a most useless place.*
> *The Waiting Place...*
> *for people just waiting.*
> *Waiting for a train to go*
> *or a bus to come, or a plane to go*
> *or the mail to come, or the rain to go*
> *or the phone to ring, or the snow to snow*
> *or the waiting around for a Yes or No*
> *or waiting for their hair to grow.*
> *Everyone is just waiting.*
> *Waiting for the fish to bite*
> *or waiting for the wind to fly a kite*
> *or waiting around for Friday night*
> *or waiting, perhaps, for their Uncle Jake*
> *or a pot to boil, or a Better Break*
> *or a string of pearls, or a pair of pants*
> *or a wig with curls, or Another Chance.*
> *Everyone is just waiting.*
>
> *NO!*
> *That's not for you!*
>
> *Somehow you'll escape*
> *All that waiting and staying.*

We invite you all – as a matter of course – to escape with us now into waiting places far from useless. Oh, the places we can and will go!

CHAPTER 2

Waiting May Not Be Hard, But It Isn't Easy!

Dr. Seuss was right about waiting (Dr. Seuss was mostly right about pretty much everything). And so was Shanya Hopkins' worldly wise seven-year-old cousin when she blurted out that little kids live waiting lives because "their parents control their time all the time." One of the ways parents control the lives of their toddler children is by choosing which books they will learn from when they are read aloud to by their mother and father.

One of the most popular of these books is Mo Willems' illustrated children's book about how we all – all of us! – live our lives waiting; the book is called WAITING IS NOT EASY! and was published in 2014. My college collaborators and I recommend that you get your adult self a copy in order to truly *see* what waiting consists of through the fifty-three pages of Willems' own illustrations. The facial expressions and body language of Willems' two featured characters – Gerald, the elephant, and Piggie, the, well, piggy – literally show the reader what waiting looks like and feels like to these two four-legged friends (and, of course, to us humans, as well).

And the words Willems sparingly uses to accompany Gerald's and Piggie's actions and reactions?

Well here they are, in sequence, with all their punctuation marks, their italicized letters, their capital letters, their repetitions, their font changes, and their tones of voice. Say them aloud. Listen for rhythms within the prose of Willems' strictly limited vocabulary. And – wait for this – look for possible poems about "waiting" that may be lurking in and between Willems' words.

In short, do what several of our college collaborators have done: find a poem that is there just waiting for you.

(in upper case) GERALD!
I have a (in italics) *surprise* for you!
Yay! What is it?
The surprise is a (in italics) *surprise*.
Oh.
Is it big?
Yes!
Is it pretty?
Yes!
Can we share it?
Yes!
(all in upper case) I CANNOT WAIT!
You will have to.
Wait? What? Why?
The surprise is not here yet.
So I will have to...(in italics) *wait* for it?
Yes.
(in upper case) GROAN.
Oh, well. If I have to wait, I will wait.
I am waiting. Waiting is not easy...
(in italics) *Piggie!* I want to see your surprise now!
I am sorry, Gerald. But we must wait.
(in upper case) GROAN!
I am (in italics) *done* waiting! I do not think your surprise is worth all this waiting.
I will not wait anymore!
(in smaller type size) Okay. I will wait some more.
It will be worth it.
(in upper case) GROAN!
(in upper case) EEK!
(in italics). *Piggie!* We have waited too long!
It is getting dark.
It is getting darker.
Soon we will not be able to see each other!
Soon we will not be able to see anything!
(all in upper case) WE HAVE WASTED THE WHOLE DAY!
We have waited and waited and waited and waited and waited!
And for (in upper case) WHAT!

(Piggie, looking up at – and pointing to – what will be shown on the final two silent pages of WAITING IS NOT EASY! as the starry night) For (in italics) *that!*

How to Inflict Pain and Jumpstart the Process of Internal Conflict in Your Colleagues
By Shanya Hopkins

So, will I have to...

wait for it?

Yes.

The Anxiety (& Subsequent Frustration) of Waiting
By Shanya Hopkins

What is it?
Is it pretty? Is it BIG?
What is it?
Eek!
I CANNOT WAIT...
***Wait**?*
And for what?
For that?
Yay?

Waiting Is Long
By Fawzi Saleh

I am waiting,
I do not want to wait,
The day is long,
I want it soon,
The day is wasted,
Is waiting worth it?

I will do anything
But wait,
I cannot wait,
I will not wait,
Waiting is dark,
Waiting is long.

Why do I wait?
How long do I wait?
Is it done?
I want it now,
Where is it?
I am waiting.

GROAN
By Anne-Lilja Rentof

Why must we wait so long?
GROAN – Oh, what is worth the wait?
I wait and wait, and yet I see
It is not yet here

Why must you wait so long
To show me what you have?
I want to see
I want it now
GROAN – why is it not yet here?

I must see what you have,
For now I cannot wait
GROAN – the day is done, this is too long

Is it worth the wait?

?
By Nathalie Chazoule

is worth worth waiting for?
why, I cannot have too much
but your worth
is too easy
wasted too soon

for what?
more?
more what?

To Share
By Gabriella Tuchman

I am alone.
 Wait.
Done!
 Wait, we will be worth it. We can be anything.
Groan, okay.
 Surprise!
Wait, what?
 A surprise...
Why?
 To share!
I am done.
 Why? Wait.
Groan, okay.

 I have waited and waited to be your anything.
Okay.
 I waited for what?
I am sorry.
 I waited and waited. I waited to be worth it. I am done.
Wait!
 I am done waiting.
Okay.

FOR WHAT?
By Gamal Amin

GROAN! GROAN! GROAN!
I will not wait!
I am sorry.
I am DONE!
GROAN! GROAN! GROAN!
We have waited... FOR WHAT?
We have waited too long.
I am done waiting.
GROAN! GROAN! GROAN!
A surprise?
It will be worth it?
GROAN! Okay! I will wait...

And Now, From Finding "Waiting" Poetry In A Simply-Worded Illustrated Book That Parents Can Read Aloud to Their Children to Finding "Waiting" Poetry In a Convoluted Novel by Henry James That These Same Adults Might Have to Read Out Loud Several Times To Themselves In Order to Make Sufficient Sense of

By the time you get to the last word of Henry James's complex 700-page novel THE WINGS OF THE DOVE (published in 1902), you can be forgiven for not remembering that its opening sentence begins with the straightforward words "She waited, Kate Croy, for her father to come in...."

Talking about long novels with long sentences, novelist Sally Rooney said in a 2020 Sunday New York Times Book Review interview: "I used to find lengthy paragraphs without line breaks difficult and boring, and now I enjoy them. Come to think of it, I found Henry James almost unreadable five or six years ago, and now I love him!" The undergraduate students in Hunter College's "The Literature of Waiting" course were *not* asked to read James's truly intimidating novel, THE WINGS OF THE DOVE, in its entirety. In fact, they did not even have to make it all the way through the twenty-two pages that comprise the opening chapter of "Book First." All they had to do was make it past the moment when Kate's imperious "father at last appeared," ending what amounted to five pages of Kate's anxiously and reluctantly awaiting his arrival (*he* had summoned *her*, and was "unconscionably" – James tells his readers as his opening sentence continues – intentionally making her bide her time).

And the purpose of the assigned foreshortened reading? Nothing more than to find the "making-time poem" that Henry James had buried in his complex and convoluted prose. Our college collaborators actually found several such poems – all depicting the various "waiting ways" of Kate's visible behavior, all revealing her attitude toward her not yet-present pater familias.

So here is what "waiting" looks like if you are Kate Croy in a novel by Henry James at the same time that you are Kate Croy in found poems by four of our college collaborators.

She waited, Kate Croy ...
By Trever Polk

She waited, Kate Croy, for her father to come in:
in the glass over the mantel
positively pale
with the irritation that had brought her to the point of going away.

she remained
changing her place
moving from the shabby sofa to the armchair

She had looked
she had above all
from time to time
taken a brief stand on the small balcony

If she continued to wait it was really
that she might not add the shame of fear,
of individual, personal collapse
to all the other shames.
To feel the street, to feel the room,
to feel the table-cloth
and the centre-piece and the lamp
gave her a small, salutary sense
of neither shirking nor lying.

She tried to be sad, so as
not to be angry;
but it made her angry that
she couldn't be sad.

And yet where was misery,
misery too beaten for blame and
chalk-marked by fate
like a "lot" at a common auction,
if not in these merciless signs of mere
mean,
Stale
feelings?

She stared into the tarnished glass
too hard indeed to be staring at her beauty alone

She readjusted
Retouched.

stature without height,
grace without motion,
presence without mass

Slender and simple,
frequently soundless,
somehow always in the line of the eye.

When her father at last appeared
she became, as usual, instantly aware
of the futility of any effort to hold him to anything.

She waited, Kate Croy ...
By Jason Chetram

She waited, Kate Croy, for her father to come in,
Changing her place, moving from the shabby sofa to the arm-chair
She had looked at the sallow prints on the walls and at the lonely magazine
Taken a brief stand on the small balcony

Each time she turned in again, each time,
her impatience, she gave him up
She tried to be sad, so as not be angry;
but it made her angry that she couldn't be sad

She stared into the tarnished glass too hard
indeed to be staring at her beauty alone
She readjusted the poise of her black, closely-feathered hat;
retouched, beneath it, the thick fall of her dusky hair

There was a minute during which,
though her eyes were fixed,
she quite visibly lost herself in the thought
of the way she might still pull things round had she only been a man.

She waited, Kate Croy ...
By Christina Louie

She waited, Kate Croy, for her father to come in,
She showed herself, in the glass over the mantel,
A face positively pale with the irritation that brought her to the point of going away
Without sight of him.
She remained;
Changing her place, moving from the shabby sofa to
The armchair upholstered in a glazed cloth that gave at once –
She tried it – the sense of the slippery and of the sticky.
She looked at the sallow prints on the walls and
At the lonely magazine.
She above all, from time to time, took a brief stand on the small balcony.
Each time she turned in again,
Each time, in her impatience,
She gave him up,
While she tasted the faint, flat emanation of things.
She felt
The street, the room, the table-cloth and the centre-piece,
And the lamp, giving her a small, salutary sense, at least,
Of neither shirking or lying.
She prepared herself;
She came for the worst.
She tried to be sad,
So as not to be angry;
But it made her angry
That she couldn't be sad.
The girl's repeated pause before the mirror
And the chimney-place might have represented
her nearest approach to an escape from them.
Was it not in fact the partial escape from this "worst"
In which she was steeped to be able to make herself out again as
Agreeable to see?
She stared into the tarnished glass too hard indeed
to be staring at her beauty alone.
She readjusted the poise
of her black, closely-feathered hat;
Retouched, beneath it, the thick
Fall of her dusky hair;

Kept her eyes, aslant,
No less on her beautiful averted than on her
Beautiful presented oval.
Outside, on the balcony, her eyes showed as blue;
Within, at the mirror, they showed almost as black.
There was a minute during which,
Though her eyes were fixed,
She quite visibly lost herself in the thought of
The way she might still pull things round
Had she only been a man.

And to Conclude What Someone's "Waiting" Looks Like: the Powerful "When You" Prose From the Reverend Dr. Martin Luther King Jr.'s Letter from Birmingham Jail (Waiting While Black)

No document of American history better shows what several lifetimes of "waiting" look like than "Letter from Birmingham Jail" by the Reverend Dr. Martin Luther King Jr. And it is not an easy piece of writing to make your way through. As one Hunter College undergraduate student commented, "My goodness, did reading this letter take a lot of patience, and I am not even an African-American! God knows how much patience African-Americans needed – and continue to need – in facing racism and discrimination."

In his rhythmically resonating conclusion to "Letter from Birmingham Jail," Dr. King speculates that "perhaps it is easy for those who have never felt the stinging darts of segregation to say, 'Wait.'" But Dr. King doesn't stop there: "When you are forever fighting a degenerating sense of 'nobodiness' – then you will understand why we find it difficult to wait."

In between those two sentences Dr. King dramatically forces us to empathetically see more than a century of historical examples of "when you" – and to become those "you." College collaborator **Gamal Amin** calls these examples "blatant racial violence against black people," while college collaborator **Christina Louie** argues that "the Reverend Dr. Martin Luther King Jr. gives us in 'Letter from Birmingham Jail' ten different examples of waiting for just one thing: the rights of African-Americans to be treated as human beings. Dr. King describes all the ways that black people must navigate their white-dominated society and are waiting for rights such as the right to sit at a lunch counter and be accepted, the right to go to an amusement park such as Funtown, and even the right to not have to internalize racism through particular names and attitudes." Or, in Dr. King's own rhetorically powerful closing words:

> But when you have seen vicious mobs lynch your mothers and fathers at will and drown your sisters and brothers at whim;
>
> when you have seen hate-filled policemen curse, kick and even kill your black brothers and sisters;
>
> when you see the vast majority of your twenty million Negro brothers smothering in an airtight cage of poverty in the midst of an affluent society;
>
> when you suddenly find your tongue twisted and your speech stammering as you seek to explain to your six-year-old daughter why she can't go to the public amusement park that has just been advertised on television, and see tears welling up in her eyes when she is told that Funtown is closed to colored children, and see ominous clouds of inferiority beginning to form in her little mental sky, and see her beginning to distort her personality by developing an unconscious bitterness toward white people;
>
> when you have to concoct an answer for a five-year-old son who is asking, "Daddy, why do white people treat colored people so mean?";
>
> when you take a cross country drive and find it necessary to sleep night after night in the uncomfortable corners of your automobile because no motel will accept you;
>
> when you are humiliated day in and day out by nagging signs reading "white" and "colored";
>
> when your first name becomes "nigger," your middle name becomes "boy" (however old you are) and your last name becomes "John," and your wife and mother are never given the respected title of "Mrs.";

when you are harried by day and haunted by night by the fact that you are a Negro, living constantly at tiptoe stance, never quite knowing what to expect next, and are plagued with inner fears and outer resentments;

when you are forever fighting a degenerating sense of "nobodiness" –

then you will understand why we find it difficult to wait.

College collaborator Shanya Hopkins writes:

I counted a total of twenty-seven examples in the conclusion of Dr. King's "Letter from Birmingham Jail" of what "waiting" has looked like and consisted of in the socio-political and economic history of the United States.

I appreciated Dr. King's repetition of a form of the phrase "when you" as the use of repetition helped to heighten his argument emotionally. Using the word "you" allowed the audience to feel personally connected to his message by affording them the opportunity to visualize themselves as active participants in this hard crash course of waiting. The cascading "when you" examples also served the purpose of making the idea that African-Americans should "wait" out segregation completely absurd. I think this letter has had a profound impact since it was composed in the 1960's because it not only verbalizes the painful experience suffered by blacks over time but also connected to people of all backgrounds by grasping at human empathy and relating the two.

CHAPTER 3

Sing a Song of Some Day As We Merrily Roll Along

So how did this collaborative book based on creative writing inspired by lots of "waiting" works of literature come to be called SOME DAY? Well, in an English Department college course thematically about duration and endurance there came a point (in time!) that we just knew we had more than a "now wait" pamphlet in progress. What we had was an enlightening and, we hoped, entertaining book that could be publishable … some day.

Great expectations on our part? Not really. We had all heard and many had come to believe that "some day" our prince would come, that there was, indeed, "a time for us, some day a time for us," and that there was deep in our hearts – particularly toward the end of our endeavors during a worldwide coronavirus pandemic – a faith that we would "overcome some day." From Walt Disney's SNOW WHITE AND THE SEVEN DWARFS to Stephen Sondheim's WEST SIDE STORY to the black gospel WE SHALL OVERCOME, the expectation of and the waiting for "some day" has always been a major, perhaps timeless, part of the American songbook. No question about it: some day soon our book would also sing its song of some day.

And it was not surprising to me that when asked to find a selection of songs that spoke to them about hopeful waiting and the arrival of a fulfilling "some day," our undergraduate students in Hunter College's "The Literature of Waiting" course had a pretty easy time of it. "Some day" songs are just waiting to be heard. A sample from dozens of titles? Well, from "Waiting" by Green Day to "Waiting for a Girl Like You" by the rock band "Foreigner" to the "someday" of "Mean" by Taylor Swift.

To make it a little bit harder and somewhat more challenging, I asked the students to narrow the range of their "some day" songbook to those songs that not only spoke meaningfully to them but could serve as the inspiration for a personal letter of reconnection to a certain someone they had lost touch with in recent years. And then, of course, to write that letter, reintroducing themselves to that person by telling how the lyrics of their chosen song expressed either the kind of person they were back then, or are now, or soon intend to become.

Here are some of the letters that crossed land masses, time zones, and other realities.

From Anne-Lilja: All the best to Mia,

Hi Mia,

I know we haven't spoken in a long time. I miss all the wonderfully ridiculous stuff we used to get up to; and I miss your company. Do you remember all those musicals I was in? The first one I was ever in was *Annie* (I can't believe that was all the way back in second grade). One of my favorite songs from that show has always been "Tomorrow":

> *"Tomorrow, tomorrow, I love you, tomorrow; you're only a day away."*

I've always loved how plucky and optimistic Annie is, despite everything that happens to her. I strive to be like that. A lot of stuff has happened since the last time I saw you; and I know for a fact I'm not the same person I was, even from a couple of years ago. I'm definitely not that bright-eyed eight-year-old, anymore; but I'd like to think she's still there, just become more mature, while waiting for another tomorrow to come. Not all of the tomorrows—well, I guess now they're yesterdays—I've had since high school have been that great. But isn't that the wonderful thing about bad yesterdays? They're in the past. And there's always a chance for a brighter tomorrow. Not all of them have been bad, either. I've learned a lot, and become more comfortable in my own skin. I hope one of my tomorrows involves seeing you at some point; or, at the very least, that all of your tomorrows are filled with happiness.

All the best,

Your friend,
Anne-Lilja

From Valeria Diaz-Huertas: To all the little girls wishing they could just grow up,

Growing up I was constantly thinking about the "someday." "Someday I will be all grown up, I will have my own life where I could do what I want when I want. The first moment I can I'm out of here" I would think to myself. Now that someday has arrived, I cannot help but wish that I had stopped thinking about the someday and enjoyed my life as a child, as a daughter, and as a sister more.

When I turned 16, my mother threw me a small party to celebrate the fact that her little girl was growing up. For the father-daughter dance (for which I danced with both of my parents) I picked the song Never Grow Up by Taylor Swift (I know it's embarrassing, I'm sorry but I was a 16-year-old after all). I thought that the song was a perfect representation of what my parents and I felt at that exact moment, like time was fleeting. When I listen to that song, I am reminded of all these moments in my childhood, when my father would come home from work, all the fights I had with my mother, and the moments I shared with my brothers listening to music or playing games. I now wish that I had listened when she sings "I just realized everything I have is someday gonna be gone," because in a way it will be.

I often think about the stories my mother tells me, stories of when I was a baby, stories of when she was expecting me, my life was so different back then. My mother tells me stories of the trouble I would get myself in because I was always in a hurry to grow up, speaking out of turn or demanding to be treated like a "big girl" and fighting with my parents all the time because I wanted to stay out late and live my life! I think about how life has gotten so complicated since then.

And as I got older and entered adolescence, I was already impatiently waiting to enter adulthood. I was in such a hurry to grow up that I missed the moment I actually did. All of a sudden, I'm worrying about rent, groceries and bills, when I have to get to my next scheduled appointment, work or class. Sometimes I stop and think to myself, "where has the time gone?" and I worry about the day my parents won't be around anymore and I wish that somehow, someday time will stop. This is where I am now, living my life as an adult, anxious about time passing and the fact that I can do nothing to stop it. Trying to enjoy every single little moment with my parents and my siblings hoping that I won't grow up.

And that's not to say that I am not enjoying my life at this very moment, I am. I'm about to graduate college in a few months, I have a loving husband who is excited about this life we have started together, and my relationship with my parents hasn't ever been better. It's just that I wish that I had more time, I wish that I'd never grown up.

From Ryan Langan: Dear Stanley, With love and patience,

Dear Stanley,

It's funny the way time works – in the same moment that I feel years and years removed from you, I also feel like it's been a day or two since I've seen you. I hope you're at peace these days. I know I've found mine, although I didn't have quite the same journey to it as you did. I came close to where you are now – terrifyingly close – but I made it back through. You, however, were gone all at once, no turning back. Death is the all-moment. Life expands and contracts, but death is singular. I just hope that, whatever it is out there, it's something that can keep you in better spirits than you were here.

Anyway, I'm writing because as of late, I've been giving a lot of thought to waiting. I had always hated waiting, the fuse of my impatience slowly creeping toward a breaking point whenever I found myself at the subway station or the bus stop or the health clinic. My main problem was that I believed there to be nothing at the end of those waits that would justify its maddening character. So, rather than looking forward to something, I was simply stagnating. I'm sure you know the feeling – shit, you couldn't wait to get out of class in high school, couldn't wait to get out of work, couldn't even wait for life to open up another door, so you closed them all at once. But I found love a few months ago, a love I didn't even know I had been waiting for my whole life. And when she got to me, all the waiting I'd ever done in any capacity all at once became worth it. Waiting isn't torture or futility, as much as it may often seem. Waiting is what creates the worth of something good when it comes.

I couldn't articulate any of this, of course, without the words and insights and creations of others, from which we all learn everything. This particular line of thought comes from a Red Hot Chili Peppers song, "Animal Bar." The band did interviews about every song on their 2006 album, and in the one dedicated to "Animal Bar," the lead singer and writer, Anthony Kiedis, explained that the Animal Bar is a real place in a small town in Australia called Karumba. There, for almost the whole year, about ten months, there is no rain at all. It is just bone-dry and deathly, the landscape starving, the trees thirsty. Then, finally, the wet season comes, the skies open, and it pours for two months straight – just in time to save all the life there, and for just enough time to sustain it until the next wet season. And the people that live there spend almost all their time waiting. They stay there and wait for their whole lives. Why? Because what comes at the end of that wait is life-giving, is hope – even though they are brought to the brink, they know the wait will eventually end, and the water will come and wash it all away, an annual baptism. So, I don't mind waiting so much anymore, Stanley. I wish I could've told you all this while you were still here. Since I can't, I'll wait until I come across someone who needs it. My rainy season arrived in the form of love – maybe my words will someday be someone else's rainy season.

With love and patience,

Ryan

And Now, "Not a Day Goes By" That It Isn't "Our Time"

Legendary composer Stephen Sondheim celebrated his 90th birthday during the time that "The Literature of Waiting" course was sheltered in place because of the coronavirus pandemic – and so, somehow both in contrast to and in keeping with the mood of those many off-campus weeks, the students and I returned to examining – but backwards this time! – the "some day" connection between the American songbook and the theme of friendship.

The assignment went out along these lines online: we are going to read and think about three songs from legendary Broadway composer Stephen Sondheim, part of a fourteen-song score for Sondheim's 1982 musical MERRILY WE ROLL ALONG. One of the fascinating things about MERRILY WE ROLL ALONG is that its story is told in reverse time (backwards chronologically) as was the original 1934 non-musical play it is based on by the famous writing team of George S. Kaufman and Moss Hart.

College collaborator **Valeria Diaz-Huertas** has pointed out that one of her favorite musicals, THE LAST FIVE YEARS, composed by Jason Robert Brown, also plays with time: this 2002 off-Broadway love story – and 2015 movie musical – starts at the end of a couple's marriage for one of the individuals and proceeds at the beginning of their relationship for the other, and as real time goes by each person winds up at the other end of it. In the play and movie, the two characters never really meet except during the very middle of the musical with a song called "The Next Ten Minutes," with those words meant to allude to the idea of "forever."

But back to MERRILY WE ROLL ALONG, let's read in our COURSEPACK folder the pages that detail this backwards chronology – 1962, then 1960, then 1959-1958, then October 1957, then 1955 / 1980 – so that we have a sense of how the story of the friendship of Frank and Charley and Beth and their careers in and out of show business end, had developed over time, first began. If any of this seems a bit confusing (and why wouldn't it since their personal and professional lives are told backwards, like "forward to the past"), we might make better sense of the evolution/ devolution of their lives by next reading these dated paragraphs in reverse order – forward in time starting with 1955 / 1980, then October 1957, then 1959-1958, then 1960, and finally 1962.

Now let's talk about the creating of Sondheim's "roll along" songs – which, of course!, go along ("merrily") with the backwards story-telling and, according to Sondheim's brief "Composer's Note" (also to be found in COURSEPACK) – presented Sondheim "an opportunity to invent verbal and musical motifs which could be modified over the course of the years, extended and developed, reprised, fragmented, and then presented to the audience in reverse: extensions first, reprises first, fragments first.... In fact, if the score is listened to in reverse order - although it wasn't written that way – it develops traditionally."

Lastly, read the three songs that have also been included in your COURSEPACK folder – the "Merrily We Roll Along" for 1964-1962, "Our Time," and the framing (both first and last) song "The Hills of Tomorrow," which, interestingly, was doubly omitted in a 2020 off-Broadway revival of the show.

Here is how three college collaborators – **Carolyn Reyes, Nattapat Karmniyanont,** and **Chyna Chung** – responded to the course's more academic assignment to briefly state the "waiting" essence of each song.

Carolyn on the Sondheim song "Merrily We Roll Along": I think the essence of the song "Merrily We Roll Along" is about chasing your dreams and having patience when trying to achieve them because, as a line in the song says, "Before you know where you know where you are, there you are." And no matter how unattainable your dreams may seem to you now, if you keep rolling along (keep trying), then you will reach there one day, and faster than you think. Just keep a happy attitude, no matter whether the journey is easy or tough – and don't let the time slip away from you because, you know, it can pass so quickly.

Nattapat on the Sondheim song "Merrily We Roll Along": The essence of this song to me is that you might have a dream and you might chase it, but that does not guarantee your dream staying the same, nor does it mean you will enjoy the end of the journey, so enjoy the path there. I came to this conclusion from lines like "Some roads are soft / And some are bumpy" amongst others and from sections where the song talked about regretting or wondering how.

Chyna on the Sondheim song "Merrily We Roll Along": I think this song is more about notifying others that time waits for no one. While time is moving on, do not place your dreams on the backburner, for it will be too late to follow them ("time goes by and dreams go dry"). This is not a fairytale song but a realistic one that that says that you need to maintain your dreams and carry them with you on your life's journey, not wait for them to come to you.

Carolyn on the Sondheim song "Our Time": I think "Our Time" is about a person feeling that it's their time for success, to achieve something big in their life. The song is literally about two people's time to shine: they are at a point in their lives, right before that major change, that is full of happiness, excitement, and anticipation – and they're only thinking about the positive. The line "Worlds to change" can mean either their own individual worlds as they view them, or it can mean that they will have such an impact that they literally touch and change the lives of others worldwide.

Nattapat on the Sondheim song "Our Time": This song has a tone very similar to "The Hills of Tomorrow," but the key difference being that "Our Time" is filled with more expectations rather than waiting – in essence, more about looking to the far future and all of its promises. The line "Give us room and start the clock / Our dream coming true" is what drew me towards this conclusion.

Chyna on the Sondheim song "Our Time": This song tells us about leaving the past behind you ("yesterday is done") and seizing the moment you have in the present to take full advantage of your life. This is definitely a motivational song, and it is understandable why Charley and Frank play the song when they are full of optimism and hope for their future – and why it is told in 1957, at the beginning of their entertainment journey. This song speaks the hope they have for themselves and others.

Carolyn on the Sondheim song "The Hills of Tomorrow": I think the use of "The Hills of Tomorrow" nicely correlates with the songs "Merrily We Roll Along" and "Our Time." It speaks to dream-chasing, to overcoming obstacles as you continue on your journey, and to getting so close to your goal that you can see it in the near distance (the hills of *tomorrow*).

Nattapat on the Sondheim song "The Hills of Tomorrow": This song is more about the blazing hearts that many people possess at the peak of their life – a heart filled with hope and easy patience. I thought this because of the song's very hopeful tone, all about starting their journeys, eyes wide and voices loud, ready to light up their own path and ready for the beauty that tomorrow must bring.

Chyna on the Sondheim song "The Hills of Tomorrow": "If I can make you understand today that life is not about doing the best; it is about doing the best you can" speaks volumes – and everyone can take that message personally. It sounds like someone of age is speaking back on what they once used to believe but has come around to correct it. Frank is telling others that it isn't about being number one or going to the highest this or being the highest that. Life will teach you about effort, and effort is more practical than being number one. This song is, to me personally, the best of the three because it gives insight into what really matters in life coming from someone who has experienced a large part of it.

Students in "The Literature of Waiting" were also asked, in a CW/HW (creative writing homework) assignment, to use their imaginations and create the lyrics to a song of their own – one that could legitimately be entitled "Merrily We Roll Along," *or* "Our Time," *or* "The Hills of Tomorrow" *or* (and these are some of the other time-themed song titles from the MERRILY WE ROLL ALONG score) "Not a Day Goes By," *or* "Now You Know," *or* "Like It Was," *or* "Old Friends," *or* "Opening Doors." And, oh yes, they were advised: Have fun with all aspects of this "merry" assignment! Roll along with it!

Three students went ahead and did – and now you know.

My version of "Now You Know" by Valeria Diaz-Huertas

Wrong again
Why do you never learn?
You know who's to blame
Just another scar to earn

Now you know
You should have known better
Now all that's left is to grow

Made the same mistake
When will you learn?
When will you wake?
Nothing left to burn

Now you know
You should have known better
Now all that's left is to grow
What did you think?
That this time would be different?
So close to the brink
Nothing left but lament

Now You know
You should have known better
Can't come back from it this time

My version of "Now You Know" by Chyna Chung

Seniors,
They told you this is it
They told you this will be the very last bit
Fortunately for you
You took the bait!

And I'm here to tell you
There's so much more
More long nights

More fights
More lamp lights
More pencil shavings
More vending-machine cravings
More long lines
More words to define

More friends and good times
More time to live in your prime
More life-changing moments
More early morning glazed donuts
More sightseeing
All for your better well-being

There's so much more
There is
SO
MUCH
MORE!

My version of "Our Time" by Gabriella Tuchman

It is our time
Dontcha know it
It is our time
To show 'em what we got
Not just a bunch of kids
But adults ready willing and able to take care of ourselves
College doesn't scare us
We're ready to move on
Nothing can deter us
For long
Classes are exciting
Dorms are uninviting
But doesn't matter
Cuz
It is our time
Dontcha know it
It is our time
To move on
Not just a bunch of kids

But adults ready willing and able to take care of ourselves
Enrolling in interesting classes
Then passing
Into an even more adult life
Where all of our teenage strife
It is our time
Dontcha know it
It is our time
To move on
Not just a bunch of kids
But adults ready willing and able to take care of ourselves
Not having to rely on anyone else
But what if we still need help?
With all of the burdens we must schlep
It's a little scary to go at it alone
It is our time
Dontcha know it
It is our time
To move on
Not just a bunch of kids
But adults ready willing and able to take care of ourselves?
Thank you for always being there
We know we were not always fair
We know you will stand by our side
As we move along in stride
Classes are exciting
Dorms are uninviting
But doesn't matter
Cuz
It is our time
Dontcha know it
It is our time
To move on
Not just a bunch of kids
But adults ready willing and able to take care of ourselves

CHAPTER 4

They Also Serve Who Sit and Wait

One of literature's most renowned "waiters" – someone who literally stays behind and sits and waits – is Penelope, wife of Odysseus in Homer's epic poem THE ODYSSEY.

Penelope (probable widow?) is a status catch for any man and, thus, the prey of anxious suitors with marriage on their mind. However, Odysseus's wife is not a willing bigamist; she both loves her world-traveling husband and believes him to be but missing in action. What to do until Odysseus's actual too-long-delayed return?

Here's what: Penelope gets her suitors to agree to wait out Odysseus's reappearance by promising them that as soon as she finishes the weaving of a shroud for Laertes, Odysseus's elderly father, she will give one of them her hand in marriage. However, there is a calculating catch behind Penelope's fabrication: she will outwit and outwait every last one of the suitors by dutifully weaving the shroud by day and then unweaving that day's work by night. Truly, Penelope has "time on her hands" as she goes about her waiting game in the woof and warp of weaving and unweaving.

Penelope's wily ways come about not only as a result of all the macho pestering of her suitors (their form of "waiting") but also because Odysseus's long absence and penchant for adventure give a good bit of credence to the suitors' belief that he is "dead on non-arrival." Still, Penelope bides her time, weaving and unweaving and successfully creating a holding pattern that lasts a full three years (until the moment she is betrayed by a servant soon after Odysseus's secret return).

The poet T. S. Eliot, seeing Penelope's way of waiting as archetypically female, comments in his 1943 "Four Quartets" that "the telling bell" is:

> Older than time counted by anxious worried women
> Lying awake, calculating the future,
> Trying to unweave, unwind, unravel
> And piece together the past and the future,
> Between midnight and dawn, when the past is all deception,
> The future futureless.

Some American feminist critics find Penelope to be actually or subliminally "furious" about the situation in life that her husband has put her into. Here's American writer Dorothy Parker's 1982 poetic take on "Penelope" – the dramatically different life roles of adventurous world traveler Odysseus and his stay-at-home wife:

> He shall ride the silver seas,
> He shall cut the glittering wave.
> I shall sit at home, and rock;
> Rise to hear a neighbor's knock;
> Brew my tea, and snip my thread;
> Bleach the linen for my bed.
> They will call him brave.

Hunter College collaborator **Hester Milford**, who found Parker's poem for our course, believes that Parker's particular Penelope is filled with "thinly veiled anger alongside her willingness to wait." Hester will shortly present her own indirect take on Penelope in a letter from one of Penelope's suitors. But first, here is another college collaborator, **Nicole Sanchez**, giving us Penelope up close and personal.

From Nicole Sanchez, a wife with her hands full:

I often ponder Odysseus's arrival. My fingers sometimes grow tired as they weave yarn by day, and unweave the same string by night. This has become a daily practice for me, a repetitive process that has helped at least two years go by. Strange men who I don't care to meet call for my company and wait on the day I may reconsider, the day I may lose hope and give up. But me, I wait for the one I yearn for, Odysseus. This has not been easy, I feel my loyalty is being put through trials as Odysseus faces his very own in war. While Odysseus will receive public praise when he returns, I speculate what will be of our intimacy, us. I am not certain of what the future may hold, my endurance will tolerate the passing of days as they have. Still, I am bothered, my patience is tested every time the sun rises and falls. It's tested when I weave and unweave this shroud which seems will never reach completion.

From Hester Milford, a humble suitor writes a revealing love letter:

Dearest Penelope,

I, alone, have uncovered your truth. Late at night when the other men were fast asleep, I scurried into the room where your weaving takes place to peer upon the fine shroud suitable for a mournful king's father. I have long admired your weaving, though I lately have been pondering the longevity of the work at hand. I always considered myself a patient man, persisting for your hand in holy matrimony.

You can imagine how shocked I was when in the glimmer of the pale moonlight, I saw your fair skin glistening, as your nimble fingers picked apart the elegant garment you had worked so long to create. I rubbed my eyes, not once but many times. Though sensible as you are, you did not notice my lingering presence.

Years I have waited for you, Penelope. Grown accustomed to your ways, biding my time, living in this Kingdom, waiting for you to choose a new husband. I now recognize, dead or alive, you will not cease rest until Odysseus returns. And I cannot fault your fidelity for it is the very quality I seek in my own wife.

So I offer you this: allow me to stay, and enjoy my small comforts. I shall keep your secret, and shall wed my own bride in a far distant land. But for now, while this war rages, I far prefer my life of ease at hand. So pluck away.

Yours truly,

Your humble servant

From Christina Louie, suitor Maximus Argentine writes a revealing love letter:

Dear Penelope,

You are a woman of immense beauty, charm, status, and cunning–such cunning for a woman. I am humbled by your dutiful actions for your elderly father-in-law and I am sure that the shroud you are weaving will be a magnificent sight to behold. That is, when you finish your weaving … and BOTH you *and I* know of your *intelligence*. O Penelope! How you make us suitors wait and wait to even have a chance for your hand in marriage! An outsider looking in would pity us as fools, but not I: for I understand your heart. You are also plagued with this endless waiting – Odysseus has caused your suffering with his absence! You must work every day to keep the scoundrels from taking his place, and even more hastily at night to undo your work, but to this, I say, is the true pity. As your heart yearns for him, I am present. I am present and understand your wily ways, even accept them for you have no other choice. Faithful. Faithful and hopeful. This is something we both share as I remain of a hopeful heart that I will have your hand and your heart as time goes on. I will be at your side, to protect and admire, for as long as my heart shall beat. If there comes a day that you finish your weaving, I shall be waiting by the wayside for you.

Maximus Argentine

From Anne-Lilja Rentof, a third suitor, and an admirer in more ways than one,

Dear Madam,

We are not, all of us, as oblivious as you would wish to your nightly activities as you unravel not only the honorable duty you discharge for your father-in-law but our hopes and dreams as well. You need not fear, however, further discovery on my account as your loyalty and sharpness of mind do you justice.

However much I believe your devotion to be in vain, I cannot help but be impressed. As frustrated as at first I was – and, admittedly, still am – I find it makes the wait all the more meaningful: that someday I might have the opportunity to properly court a lady of such loyalty, dutifulness, resourcefulness, and keen understanding soothes the blow to my ego and calms a certain measure of growing impatience.

I can see, now, that it would do little to repeat the entreaties you hear every day – other than to simply fix you more firmly in your plan. We must all grieve in our own way, and I only hope that some day you will see that you are able to come to terms with the misfortunes that have so unhappily befallen you and your family – for your sake, if not for ours. Until such time, I will continue to wait and watch with interest (perhaps even amusement) to see your next strategy take form.

Ever yours,

A.

And They Also Serve Who Wait Biblically

In the beginning there was the waiting. In the Hebrew Bible, God does not create the world in one fell swoop: Boom!, and God looked – and saw that there now was an entire world where before (can we even say "before"?) there was an earth without form, and void.

Instead, the Bible tells us (The Book of Genesis, Chapter 1) that God takes his time (a total of six biblical days). And after each day's creation, the Lord God looks at his work in progress ("let there be" and what "was so") and pronounces what he has accomplished that day as "good." God has done his daily deeds: He stops. He looks. He names. He evaluates. He waits. Or as college collaborator **Henry Janani** colloquially and literally characterized it one day in "The Literature of Waiting" class: "God called it a day!"

And because God's "waiting" was both within the work and between God's worldly works, on the seventh day (The Book of Genesis, Chapter 2, Verses 1 through 4) "God ended His work which He had done, and He rested on the seventh day from all His work which He had done." Shabbat!

Biblical waiting also occurs quite famously further on (The Book of Genesis, Chapter 29) in the story of Jacob's love for the beautiful shepherdess Rachel (whom he met and assisted at the well) and of how Jacob told Laban, Rachel's father, how he would wait (and work!) in order to be betrothed to Rachel (who had an older and unmarried sister, Leah): "I will serve you seven years for Rachel your younger daughter."

But when the seven years of waiting and working are up, Laban tricks Jacob into marrying the still unmarried Leah because, as Laban explains to his new son-in-law: "It must not be done so in our country, to give the younger before the firstborn" – and so Jacob agrees to work (and wait!) another seven years to finally get to marry the love of his life.

College collaborator **Massiel Sanchez** writes on some of the reasons this story is canonical:

For starters, the story of Jacob and Rachel sets the precedent for patriarchy, upholding the idea of male dominance with Laban, the family patriarch, having complete power over the fates of his two daughters. But the story also illustrates the grueling nature of "waiting" itself (it's fitting that Jacob's waiting is literally "laborious") and the possibility that all of one's waiting may ultimately be futile. Waiting itself does not guarantee a reward; attached to waiting is uncertainty. From a Jewish perspective, Jacob's waiting can be compared to the Jews' wait for the messiah, but it also clearly illustrates the ways in which waiting, with all its pains, can be worthwhile: Jacob's waiting communicates and celebrates the Jewish people's dignified determination to continue to wait for the messiah that you can believe in. In contrast, from a Christian perspective, the arrival of Jesus signifies that all that initial waiting has been rewarded, while the Muslim perspective is similar to that of the Jews: Jacob's waiting an additional seven years serves as a guide for Muslims on how to do their own waiting.

CHAPTER 5

They Also Serve Who Wait on Those Who Wait

Waiting is not only not easy but it also can be a "trying" experience. As in Franz Kafka's 1925 novel THE TRIAL. Published a year after Kafka's death, THE TRIAL is a parable of modern alienation that, in its "Before the Law" section, showcases an unnamed young man (a "countryman" or citizen) and an equally anonymous gatekeeper stationed a ways away from the building housing the mindless bureaucracy charged with administering justice under the law. Here's how it goes (or doesn't) in an absurdist but all-too-believably-real world we today call Kafka-esque:

> Before the Law stands a gatekeeper. To this gatekeeper comes a countryman who asks to gain entry into the law. But the gatekeeper says that he cannot grant him entry at the moment. The man thinks about it and then asks if he will be allowed to come in later on. "It is possible," says the gatekeeper, "but not now." At the moment, the gate to the law stands open, as always, and the gatekeeper walks to the side, so the man bends over in order to see through the gate into the inside. When the gatekeeper notices that, he laughs and says: "If it tempts you so much, try it in spite of my prohibition. But take note: I am powerful. And I am only the most lowly gatekeeper. But from room to room stand gatekeepers, each more powerful than the other. I can't endure even one glimpse of the third."

> The man from the country had not expected such difficulties: the law should always be accessible to everyone, he thinks,

but as he now looks more closely at the gatekeeper in his fur coat, at his large pointed nose and his long, thin, black Tartar's beard, he decides that it would be better to wait until he gets permission to go inside. The gatekeeper gives him a stool and allows him sit down at the side in front of the gate. There he sits for days and years.

The man, who has brought many provisions along uses everything, however valuable, to bribe the gatekeeper. And while the latter accepts everything, he always says: "I only accept it so as to make sure that you don't think you haven't tried everything."

As the years go by, the countryman forgets about the other gatekeepers, and this first one appears to him as the only obstacle to his entry into the Law. He curses the unlucky circumstance, in the first years thoughtlessly and out loud; later, as he grows old, he still mumbles to himself. He becomes childish and, since in the long years studying the gatekeeper he has come to know the fleas in his collar, he even asks the fleas to help him persuade the gatekeeper.

Finally, his eyesight grows weak, and he does not know whether things are really darker around him or whether his eyes are merely deceiving him. But he recognizes now in the darkness an illumination which breaks inextinguishably out of the gateway to the law. Now he has no longer much time to live. Before his death, he gathers in his head all his experiences of the entire time up into one question which he has not yet put to the gatekeeper. He waves to him, since he can no longer lift up his stiffening body:

"Isn't it true that everyone strives for the Law?" he asks the gatekeeper. "How come, then, that in all these years no one else has requested entry to it?" To which the gatekeeper responds: "Nobody else could have been granted entry here, for this gate was made for you alone. Now I will go and close it."

Our college collaborators considered not only the particular question the countryman asked of the gatekeeper (and the gatekeeper's answer) but such other questions as how it came about that the citizen appeared one day at the hall of justice; why he actually wanted entry to the law; why he sat down, stayed, and waited for his entire life; how, if asked, he would explain (or rationalize) what his waiting existentially meant to him; and what other options he might possibly have considered. We also tried to get into the head of the story's second "waiter," whose waiting existed in a kind of parallel universe to the waiting of the countryman.

From Massiel Sanchez, in the head and out of the mouth of the countryman:

How unlucky am I? This gatekeeper just won't budge. I've tried everything. I've given him everything I've brought. Well, I guess I'll just have to wait a bit longer. He'll let me in eventually. There's no way I'm getting past him without permission. Unless maybe others appear and help me convince him. But I'm certain there's no way I can take him on alone, so I'll just wait here. Everyone should have access to the law. He has received my gifts with gratitude – so there is hope. Soon I will pass those gates. I have to keep trying. It won't be long now. I'll just have to wait a little bit longer.

From Michael McClenahan, in the head and out of the mouth of the countryman:

I thought I had a hard time waiting for water to boil! That was before all of this happened. When I first arrived at the gate, I wasn't opposed to waiting. I wasn't exactly in a hurry, after all. Nobody wants to see the Law. But, I thought, when one is called for, one has to do his duty. I thought I was just being responsible. Never mind that the doorkeeper wasn't particularly polite. Never mind that, after having a secretary call to reschedule my appointment several times at the last minute, I arrived for this appointment early. I didn't expect a thank you. I didn't even expect a particularly warm welcome. I know that these are busy people. I only thought that I would meet the Law, take care of whatever business it had in store for me, and be on my way!

It's been several years now, and I still haven't met with the Law. That wasn't a mistake. Not hours, not days, not months. Years. For years I've been told, "Jetzt aber nicht." Now you may think, one or two years isn't so bad. But that would be before I told you that when I first arrived here I was a rather spritely young gentleman. Now I cannot even get out of this chair in which they have me waiting.

I've tried pleading and begging. You can be sure that I've tried bribing. I know that I am not much longer for this world, and so I asked, "Isn't there anyone else with an appointment?" And right off, the gatekeeper told me, "No, there isn't. The Law waits only for you." But, I had no reason to be here, other than the reason for which the Law called me, which can only mean that we were both waiting for nothing.

From Liala Ahmad, in the head and out of the mouth of the countryman:

I am in utter shock. No matter the bribe, the gatekeeper is unrelenting. I feel as though I have tried every possible thing. But in his eyes my actions were not actionable. Why, oh why, are I not worthy? What more can I do to prove my commitment to entering these gates? I have one wish in life and it is to enter these gates and be recognized as a citizen. Oh, I would do anything to earn my place! Why is it so terrible to be foreign? I am but a mere countryman and he, a mere gatekeeper. It is wondrous to think that two men could be born of the same flesh, occupy the same land, feast on the same foods, have the same virtues and vices and still be considered foreign and, therefore, unworthy. Oh I cannot wait to be familiar. But I must...surely my case will be heard. Surely humanity will align its views with mine. No world could be this cruel. I must be patient. I will be.

From Patrick Diaz, in the head and out of the mouth of the gatekeeper:

Countryman, you urgently needed access to the law, yet you wait a lifetime for it? This confuses me endlessly. In my years as a gatekeeper I have become accustomed to the attitudes of men who would and would not gain access to the Law. You are so unlike these men, who challenge me or run through when they are not met at the gate. I suppose your own challenge is this: your waiting is a contradiction – or the strength of your waiting is this contradiction. The urgency to wait. It puzzles the mind.

I suppose, in this regard, I am not your personal gatekeeper. Or perhaps a different kind of gatekeeper: I am the one who does not challenge your waiting, so, indeed, you wait. This gate is your unwillingness to move past this barrier – one that you may have set for yourself. While I patiently guard this gate as your gate's keeper, your gate is one of your own making. Your door will close soon – of your own volition.

From Jason Chetram, in the head and out of the mouth of the gatekeeper:

Your time is coming to an end. This, however, means my time is coming to an end as well. For without you to wait outside this gate of justice, I no longer serve any purpose. It was thanks to you that I was able to have purpose in my life as a gatekeeper, since what point is a gatekeeper if nobody desires entry to the gate?

Unlike me, a mere gatekeeper, you could have lived your life to the fullest; however, you chose to spend it here. No one else would've come, as this gate was made for you alone. Unfortunately, my friend, we both know the truth. You could've forced your way past me or devised ploys to evade me. We both know that in your heart you are too afraid to face the truth that lies behind this gate. As such, you used me as an excuse to not proceed onwards towards the truth. Because you are a coward – a coward through and through as you breathe your final breath. However, my friend, if you truly wish to use me as your reason to justify your cowardice up until the very end, then I will happily oblige. For it is my only purpose, after all.

From Nathalie Chazoule, poetically in the head and out of the mouth of the gatekeeper:

Countryman,
In watching you wait I have come to see a stubborn mirror of reason;
They seem unchallengeable, our goals here;
Surely, it is reason that has driven you to face the law, the source of the same reason that prescribes me to my post here;
But it seems we are both waiting for something to come of this,
And now I question the purpose of this reason.

Surely we are both seeking a resolve to this condition, that of waiting
(Maybe that's where the reason comes in)
And it seems to me that resolve would require a prescription of knowledge,
And so even though we do not know what it is that we want to know, now we mustknow it in order to feel resolved.

See, I am starting to find this quite unreasonable in and of itself.
How come, now, seeking knowledge seems to be an act against nature?

Perhaps the purest way to wait is without hopes of resolve
Of knowledge.

CHAPTER 6

With Patience You Can Learn to Wait
(And If Patience Can't Make Time for You, Find Fortitude)

Can you do with a lesson or two on how to be "a waiter" – not the kind that serves up food in a café or restaurant but someone – anyone, actually – who has mastered the fine art of playing the waiting game and living the waiting life? Over the course of our course on "The Literature of Waiting," our college collaborators came to know several literary characters who were either terribly terrific or just plain terrible when it comes to waiting – and it always comes to waiting. They, then, after the required Pinter pause, set out to create instructive tutorials on "how to be someone who has learned to wait well."

In Harold Pinter's 1960 one-act play THE DUMB WAITER, Ben and Gus are an experienced team of hitmen waiting for their next victim to arrive at the scene of the about-to-occur crime. Although they have time on their hands, Ben and Gus don't depend on "dumb luck"; instead, they wait – but in distinct and different ways – on their social betters to order up their next job. They also, in the second half of the play, answer to a higher authority via the mechanical apparatus named in Pinter's title (a "dumb waiter" or, in the language of the play's stage directions, a "serving hatch").

If you take your own Pinter pause to purposely pronounce the title of Pinter's play in two differently accented ways, THE DUMB WAITER could be referring to an actual "serving hatch" that absurdly figures in the plot of the play or be characterizing Ben's and Gus's levels of street smarts and intelligence or their ease and ability in communicating.

In Ha Jin's 1999 novel WAITING, the three key characters – Lin Kong, his first wife, Shuyu, and his second wife, Wanna Mu – begin the novel waiting in ways different from each other and end the novel waiting not only in different individual ways but in ways different from how they were waiting three hundred pages earlier.

So, get ready to learn how to become a master of waiting – in general and in particular – whether you are waiting for, or waiting on, or waiting till, or waiting in. What goes into waiting? What does it look like? What does it feel like? And if the world is replete with people who either don't know what they are waiting for or don't even know that they are, in fact, living a life of waiting, well, to be articulate about it, that's just dumb. You owe it to yourself to learn how to be a better waiter than you are right now.

We begin with some big-picture looks at coping with the waiting life, move on to ways to hope for more specific "great expectations," and end with the last word in how NOT to wait.

Ryan Langan on How to Wait – by the Numbers

1. Acknowledge the time. Anyone who is considered "waiting" must be aware of the passing time. A receptionist will tell you to wait a few minutes. A subway app will tell you that the next train is at 5:02. Recognize the time and, without accepting or rejecting it, know its relative span.
2. Now for the fun part – react to the time. For me, this is a reaction typically characterized by a slow, building psychosis. If this "how to" were the five stages of grief, this would be the anger and denial stages. You begin to be filled with the ego – how dare I have to wait? ME? Whose time is the most valuable commodity on the planet earth?
3. Fill the time. To prevent yourself from losing your ever-loving mind, prevent yourself from spiraling out of control and perchance exploding with rage and/or sobbing with disbelief, employ thought. Distract yourself. Read a book, watch reruns of "The Sopranos," make faces at the little kid who won't stop crying in the waiting room, squeeze in a few pushups to maintain the physique. I don't care what you do! *Just try to forget that you're waiting.*
4. Return to reality. Yes, sometimes you'll have to. This is a quick step often prompted by checking your watch or glancing at the clock. Am I still waiting? Have I been waiting here all my whole

life? Is this all there is? Is time real? Or was time invented by clock companies to sell more clocks?

5. Finally, arrive at the time you were waiting for. You're okay – you made it. But what's next? Repeat. I hate to be the bearer of bad news – who am I kidding? I actually enjoy saying this: you will do this forever. Have fun.

Valeria Diaz-Huertas on Exactly Seven Ways to Wait for a New York City Subway Train

Waiting for the train is something that people in New York spend a lot of their time doing; in fact we all spend so much time waiting for the train that most of the time we don't even notice it anymore.

Read a book: While waiting for the train one could enjoy the company of a good book, you'd be surprised how much you can read in one commute. Reading a book (of my choosing) is one of my favorite ways to pass the time on a train ride, I get so lost in my book that I don't notice time or the stops passing. But be careful not to miss your stop because you can't seem to put your book down!

Listen to music: Another of my favorite ways to wait for the train is to listen to music, I love to listen to all types of music, new music or old, music that I discovered on my own or music that I grew up with. Listening to music on the subway could be a great way to pump yourself up for the rest of your day or to relax and de-stress.

Do some work: One really useful way to use one's time during their commute is to get some work done; this one is a really popular one amongst students and teachers. Whether you have to do a reading (that's not of your choosing) or write a paper that's due in an hour sometimes the time you spend on getting that work done during your commute could make the difference between a passing or failing grade.

Scroll through social media and emails or maybe play a game. Now if you're lucky enough that your commute is on the trains that run above ground, you could spend some time catching up on tabloids or responding to emails. Or you could spend your commute getting to the next level of that really addicting game you started only yesterday.

Eat your lunch: Perhaps one of the more infamous ways that New Yorkers wait for the train is by eating their lunch. If one person is having a tuna fish sandwich with boiled eggs on the train everyone in that wagon will know, but hey, New Yorkers lead busy lives.

Look at the subway ads: Sometimes you just sit on the train and wait for your commute to end, and while you're waiting you can't help but read the strange ad in front of you that's trying to sell you the next best life-changing product.

Take a nap: New York is the city that never sleeps, so what do New Yorkers do, they nap on their way to work. And somehow, they seem to know when their stop is coming up because they always wake up right on time. If you're going to sleep on the train, make sure you don't end up sleeping on top of the person next to you, in New York that's rude.

Complete Instructions from Nathalie Chazoule on How to Not Be Kidding About Waiting

1. Identify your intention in reading this tutorial.
2. Find the humor in reading a "how-to" tasked not only with instructing one on how to **be**, but written by a twenty-one-year-old at that.
3. Use the sentiment of your intention to not laugh off the task.
4. Use the humor to make the waiting bearable.

   Caution: Do not abuse humor to the point of indifference or nihilism.

Paige Thorne's Loop-to-Loop Waiting Guide

1A. Recognize that you are waiting…go to 2
  B. In denial…go to 5

2A. Waiting by yourself…go to 3
  B. Waiting with a waiting buddy…go to 4

3A. Listen to an amazing playlist…go to 6
  B. Stare aimlessly at the scenery around you…go to 6
  C. Think wanted thoughts…go to 6
  D. Think unwanted thoughts…go to 6

4A. Initiate a conversation that will dissipate all boredom...go to 6
　B. Play a game of your choosing...go to 6
　C. Sit together in a comfortable silence...go to 6
　D. Sit together in uncomfortable silence...go to 6

5A. Waiting is an always
　B. We are always waiting...go to 2

6. Congratulations! You have waited!...go to1

Steps on Waiting from Nicole Sanchez

Let go of the frustration and stress that results from waiting. It's useless and won't change your wait time. This alone is probably the most difficult step in waiting: acceptance.

Ask yourself if you can do anything to shorten your wait time. If it doesn't put you or anyone else in danger, don't wait – just do it.

If there's nothing you can do – for example, situations in which you have to wait for a train, a class, an appointment, or a date – I suggest the following: think about things you need to get done, think about your favorite song; hum; close your eyes; lay your head down; write things down. For at least a moment, don't think; maybe stare off a little; look at your surroundings, look at the lines on the palms of your hands. Look things up. Draw something.

Time is essential to waiting. Seconds, minutes, hours are units we use to measure things. No matter how we measure time, or how close or how far it seems, time will always keep going – and that time that you're waiting for will eventually come.

Human beings have no control of time, but they do have control over themselves, their attitude towards waiting, and what they do during their wait time.

Hester Milford's Advice on How to Lose Weight Without Waiting

Now that you have read the title of my tutorial, you may have assumed the contents: eat carrots, develop a rigorous workout regimen, cease snacking after 8:00 pm. Unfortunately for the health conscientious gurus out there hoping to glean knowledge from my time-honed secrets, I prefer to cut corners. This weight loss tutorial is for the impatient – an impromptu guide on my swift descent into the fast-paced world of eating disorders. Enjoy!

So, you went to the Gym. You ate small meals meant for rabbits. You logged your daily calories in your ~Brand Spanking New~ Diet App. You blathered about your healthy choices and instagrammed salads for all of two weeks. All that hard work. Now you step on the scale. YOU ONLY WEIGH .25 OF A POUND LESS?!?

You may cry. Maybe you eat a chocolate bar (or six). (This behavior is highly counterproductive and will not aid you in the long run – until you've read step eight.)

You are sick of waiting to lose weight. You've scrolled through too many pictures of flawless stick-thin women on your timeline. Maybe you have a really hot friend that seems to eat whatever she likes and never puts on any weight. (But she always complains about her body. So effing annoying. No one wants to hear it, Jessica!)

So now we have reached the fork in the road. You can resume option 1 and repeat with varying degrees of success. Or you can begin your journey down a new (Woo! exciting!) and harrowing road that requires no waiting.

Welcome.

You rush to the bathroom, fling both covers off the toilet seat and shove a finger down your throat in a dramatic fashion, certain the action will induce vomit within seconds. (You aren't inept. You've seen actors throw up on TV!) But wait! Surprise! Jamming one finger down your throat WON'T cause you to expel those chocolate bars immediately. It seems you need the help of the all-knowing internet!

You stick your hand into your pocket, retrieving the cellular device that is all but glued to your body. Ignoring the calorie counter app which shouts an inspirational message you may have once found endearing, you open Safari and plug in "How To Throw Up." Instantaneously you are flooded with helpful resources. Select one. (I suggest Quora – it's filled with people telling you not to do something all the while providing explicit detail on exactly how to do said thing.)

So now you know. Leaning fully over the toilet and using two fingers – index and middle — you begin to trigger your gag reflex, eventually causing bile to rise in your throat before finally vomiting. (Also known as "pulling trig," the popular term for throwing up on college campuses, most commonly used when a student has drunk too much and must clear space for more alcoholic consumption.)

For beginners, this hard-pressed process takes around five to seven minutes. Once you get the hang of it, you'll be in and out of the bathroom in no time. (Caloric, yet yummy chocolate bars? Almost like it didn't happen.)

Now that you've learned how to cheat the system go forth and indulge, Young Padawan. You'll be losing weight in no time.

A Tutorial from Anne-Lilja Rentof on Being a Good Waiter

Hold on a second—
…
…
…
Okay, be patient with me.
Don't get upset, I'll get to the good stuff eventually.
…
…
Don't be annoyed. Just sit back, relax.

Hey! Don't count the lines.
Don't look at your watch!
I'll get to it, I'll get to it.

Isn't there something you can do besides glare at the page?
Read? Hum a tune? Check your email?

I'll get to you soon.

I'm sure there are some interesting posts on social media.
…
…
Well, all right, let's get start—

Wait! Hold that thought!

Trever Polk on How to Be a Supermarket Cashier
(Because, Yes, It Is a Kind of Waiting)

Pretend to be nice to everyone. Even if the customer is rude to you, you have to be as fake-nice as you can. Ask if they found everything and if the store had what they needed and had met their expectations.

Pretend to be cynical. All right, you probably are already cynical after having dealt with the job for a few days. But when the customer complains about paying five cents for a disposable bag, don't talk about the environment. Pretend you're annoyed too – although you probably *are* annoyed with the fee just because you need to count how many bags everyone takes. If the customer complains about a politician, just go along with them. There's no time to argue.

Be ready to be hated. You're going to get a lot of customers who are rude to you for absolutely no reason. Maybe they're angry that the line is too long or their beer will get warm or their ice will melt. Maybe the item they're trying to buy isn't what the coupon is for. Maybe they don't believe you swiped their coupon. Or maybe they want to use their EBT for something SNAP doesn't cover. Regardless of what it is, if something is frustrating them, they'll probably blame you.

Be patient with the elderly. Old people will take forever to get their payment method of choice out from their wallet. If they pay in cash they'll probably want to pay the change so they get back an even amount, and it'll hold up the line (see above: be ready to be hated).

The manager is always right. Your floor manager might be horrible – she might tell you what you were taught in training was wrong, announce to the other staff her annoyance at your medical needs, or just criticize you for being too nervous on your first day – but don't try to defend yourself. She'll just try to get you fired for HR violations.

Don't think about time. If you watch the time, you'll only realize that five minutes seems like an hour. Your manager probably won't let you look at it for more than a few seconds, anyway. Just get into the rhythm of scanning.

Pretend it's a comedy. Your manager won't let you do anything besides watch the till when there's no one on line. Just think back to the weird people you've seen in the last hour and wonder what their deal is.

Savor your break. Being on break is the most intense form of waiting you'll do during your shift. So pretend as hard as you can that you're not waiting. Set an alarm for the time you need to go back and then avoid looking at any form of clock.

Be ready to be fired. If you've been working for less than sixty days, you have no union contract, and you can be fired without notice. Don't bother trying to get the job back because your floor manager will just try to fire you again anyway.

Warn all of your friends. Stores hire everyone, so if one of your friends needs work, they'll probably apply. Warn them. They won't listen.

CHAPTER 7

"The Dumb Waiter" or The Dumb "Waiter"?
What Happens – Pause – After the Wait Is
Over in Harold Pinter's 1960 Play?

These are the critical thinking questions that our class on "The Literature of Waiting" focused in on while reading Harold Pinter's 1960 one-act play THE DUMB WAITER straight through:

- *How many different ways can you pronounce the title of this Pinter play so that what it might be "about" changes?*
- *How is THE DUMB WAITER a play with – not two – but three or more "major" characters? Name them all.*
- *Where does the playwright make you "wait for it" with his pregnant pauses? Why there? Why anywhere?*
- *Where does the play have something to say about the nature of human connection and communication?*
- *How does the play visualize and dramatize a life spent "waiting"?*
- *Who or what is "dumb" in their waiting? ... (Pregnant pause) ... Who or what isn't?*
- *Critics categorize Pinter's THE DUMB WAITER as an early example of "theater of the absurd" in the style of Samuel Beckett's WAITING FOR GODOT. Your thoughts?*

As the curtain falls ending Pinter's THE DUMB WAITER, the men who make up the hitman team of Ben and Gus confront and stare at each other during an extended silence. Out in the audience, others have been waiting; the atmosphere is tense and time seems to have stopped still. Is that it?

Is that how we are to leave Ben and Gus, never knowing what they do next (if there is a "next") and never knowing what to make of it?

Are there possibilities that Pinter has hinted at in his one-acter of under an hour? Will Gus ask another of his incredulous and annoying questions of Ben? Like: "Have I been selected as our team's next victim – and why is that?" Will Ben – seemingly dumbstruck – wonder, as he's not wont to do, why Gus has unexpectedly stumbled through the door stripped of his killer attire – "his jacket, waistcoat, tie, holster and revolver"?

Or will Ben get over his being gobsmacked with surprise and wait for some authority figure in the rooms above their basement dwelling to order him to use his revolver (now leveled at the door that Gus just stumbled through)? Will Ben stop to wonder why hitman teammate Gus is seemingly the next person to be killed that day?

Or will Ben automatically shoot Gus because that's what Ben is conditioned to do or because Ben has had his intimations confirmed that his partner in crime is, authoritatively, the next scheduled victim? But no, Pinter's play ends at it began – with Ben and Gus in silence, their eyes meeting, their minds waiting for something to happen. And waiting along with them, as it has been throughout the play, is the audience.

In her 2011 book PASSING TIME: AN ESSAY ON WAITING, author Andrea Kohler quotes Mephistopheles as warning Faust that "letting the right moment to act go by, you *call* letting things unfold on their own time." Our college collaborators decided that the last moment in Pinter's play was the right moment that they could not let passively go by (despite the playwright's structured plan to let things "unfold on their own time").

No, let that moment be the latest but not the last Pinter pause; let it be the pause that refreshes the play's action. So, several of our collaborators lifted Pinter's dropped curtain back up and took at second look at the show they wanted to go on. Ben's and Gus's mutual life of waiting – and Pinter's dramatic eternity of silence, uncertainty, indecision, and inaction – all come to a stop (or continue in waiting ways only to be imagined). But time marches on – and the rest is far from silence. Instead, stage directions, dialogue, and "Action!"

Students wrote codas to THE DUMB WAITER as they went from being readers and viewers of Pinter's play left waiting for actual resolution to being the makers of their own alternate but definitive endings (director's cut). Here are four such codas.

A Coda to Harold Pinter's Play THE DUMB WAITER
By Liala Ahmad

The curtain does not fall. Picking up on the final moments of Pinter's play.

GUS (*recovering himself*): I knew this didn't used to be a café.
BEN (*releases the safety device on his gun*): You're slacking, mate.
GUS (*to himself*): I waited all this time...
GUS (*to BEN, who fingers the trigger*): I waited all this time to die.
GUS (*directly to BEN*): There was no job.
BEN (*adjusts his stance*): You never wanted to do the job anyway, You couldn't. You won't have to. Not ever.
GUS (*breathing heavily*): Is that why you're gonna take me out?
BEN (*stiffly*): I'm just following orders. Something you've forgotten how to do.
GUS (*musing*): From Wilson? Is he the one with all the orders? Telling his dumb waiters to give him his...what was it? His goddamn "ormitha macarunada"?
BEN: KAW! Would you quit running your damn mouth? You never know when to stop. Never.
GUS (*hysterical*): Hah! Greek my arse!
BEN: This ain't easy, Gus. But it's not hard. Nothing's hard if you just get on with it, mate. Just do your damn job, that's all! (*pulls the trigger – BANG!*)
GUS – and the curtain – fall.

A Coda to Harold Pinter's Play THE DUMB WAITER
By Paige Thorne

Opening stage directions: A long silence. They stare at each other.

GUS: Ben?

Pause.

GUS: What is this job, Ben?
BEN: Let's make this quick, Gus.
GUS: We've been working together for so long.

BEN's hand holding the revolver begins to shake and yet remains leveled at the door.

GUS: So that's why you originally left out me having my gun out.
BEN: You were a great partner, Gus, truly.
GUS: Apparently not great enough.

BEN looks GUS in the eye, steadying his shot.

GUS: Do you believe there's a god?
BEN: Unbelievable! Even when faced with death, thoughts still manage to run rampant in your head.
GUS: Well, do you? I don't want to pay for what happened to that girl.
BEN: In this line of work? No.

BEN pulls the trigger, GUS falls straight down, his limbs becoming numb with fear. GUS opens his eyes in awe, for BEN had fired a blank. BEN places a finger to his lips. The whistle in the speaking-tube blows.

BEN: The job is complete.
To ear. He listens.

To mouth.
BEN: No, I will not need assistance disposing of the body.
To ear. He listens.

To mouth.
BEN: Good. Have a nice day.

Curtain.

A Coda to Harold Pinter's Play THE DUMB WAITER
By Jason Chetram

Opening stage directions: A long silence. They stare at each other.

Gus: Does it really have to be this way?
Ben: Yes, it does. Ever since that job with that girl you've been different.
Gus: How could you not?
Ben: This is what we signed up for, it's too late to go back now. And now that we are here, there is no going back.

A long silence.

Gus: Ben, I understand. But aren't you hurting too?
Ben: No.
Gus: Surely, you can't be unbothered, right? Right, Ben?
Ben: Stop saying my name, I've had enough of you.
Gus: That's right, Ben, no one who we've hit before knew who you were.
      Do you have it in you to kill your own partner, Ben?
Ben: I'll blow your brains out right now, fool! Is that what you want!?

Ben raises the revolver the exact level to Gus's head; Gus stares at Ben down the barrel.

Gus: Ben, you remember the match at the Villa that day? And back when
      we took our exams? Ben, we might be killers, but it's different when
      you kill your own friend.
Ben: You're not my friend, you clown! A man who can't even tie his own
      shoes properly has no right to be my friend! We work together that's
      all! But not for long!
Gus: You can lie to me but you know the truth don't you? If you kill me,
      it'll be the end of you Ben, how would you live with yourself? Not
      even Wilson could help you with that. He'll dispose of you just like
      how you'll do to me.
Ben: What the hell do you know!?
Gus: You'll end up just like me, Ben, because we're the same.

Ben's hand now very slightly trembling.

Ben: I've let you speak for too long, this is the end for you, fool.
Gus: It's a shame we couldn't have that last cup of tea together, huh?

Ben's trembling stops immediately, he's come to a realization, he lowers his gun.

Ben: Oi, you sly bastard. You knew what was going on all along?! All the
      bullshit you've been spewing was to throw me off?! All of it?!

On the floor above, frantic stomps echo all the way to the basement room that the two men reside in.

Gus: It's too late for the both of us, my friend. Drop the gun, if we cooperate with them we might get a better sentence.

Ben, with a wicked smile beginning to stretch across his face.

Ben: Gus you bastard, you set me up. To think I've been set up by a clown, you sonuvabitch!

Ben raises his gun up again, this time with conviction burning in his eyes; the sound of heavy boots are approaching the room, seconds from bursting through the door.

They stare at each other.

Curtain.

A Coda to Harold Pinter's Play THE DUMB WAITER
By Fawzi Saleh

Ben and Gus stare at each other. Gus slowly raises his body while his hands tremble at his side.

Gus (*hesitantly*). Ben?

Ben lowers his revolver and glares at Gus.

Ben. Well what are you staring at me for! Where the hell is your jacket and waistcoat? And your revolver? For god's sake how are you going to do the job without your bloody revolver?

Gus turns around and stares out the door. He then shuts the door and faces Ben.

Gus (*panting*). He wants me dead.
Ben. Who wants you dead?

Gus locks the door and goes and sits on the bed. He clutches his arms and droops his head while he stares at the floor.

Gus. All the games he's playing with us, sending us cigarettes when he knows there's no gas, sending us bogus orders when we are waiting for–

Pause.

Gus (*raises his head and squints at Ben*). You knew, didn't you?

Ben frowns and puts his revolver in his holster.

Ben. Knew what? What nonsense are you talking about?

Gus (*in a shrewd voice*). Those orders – Jam tart, bamboo shoots – or the
mouldy biscuits, you made all that up didn't you? And of course, I
knew no one said light the kettle.
Ben walks over to Gus and looks directly at him. He tightens his fists.
Ben (*angrily*). You walk in here stripped of your belongings and then start
accusing me of lying? *Ben grabs Gus by the collars and raises him up.*
Ben. One more word and I'll bash you!

Gus grabs Ben's arms and tries to push him away.

Gus. Then why was he giving us orders when he knew there's no restaurant
down here. Was he talking in code, giving you instructions on how
to kill me?

*Ben lifts Gus off the floor. He then flings him onto the bed. Gus's head
clambers against the wall.*

Ben. Kaw! You've lost your marbles, I'll do the job alone this time.

Ben takes out his revolver and goes to unlock the door.

Gus. WAIT!

*Ben jumps back from the door startled. He turns around to face Gus, who
sits up on the bed and rubs the back of his head.*

Gus. I'm the target, he wanted you to kill me.

Ben freezes. Their eyes meet and Ben quickly looks away.

Ben (*huffs and shakes his head*). You hit your head too hard. Go to the
bathroom and put some cold water on your head.

The lavatory flushes. Again they make eye contact. Gus rises.

Gus. When I went to get a glass of water, two men came up behind me and mugged me. One clamped my mouth while the other took my holster. They told me to take off my jacket and waistcoat or else they would shoot me. They then took me out the back and when we got to the front, they shoved me inside.

Silence.

Ben begins pacing the room back and forth.

Ben. No, that can't be right, that's not possible.

Pause.

Ben. We always do the job together, we always get it done. Why would he target you?

Gus sits on the bed and puts the pillow in his lap. He squeezes the pillow and thinks hard.

Gus. It was the girl. We made a mess. He probably thought I was responsible for it and so he expected me to clean up after it.

Ben shakes his head and continues to pace, now faster than before.

Ben. No, we never clean up. Besides, he would have–

Ben abruptly stops in his tracks. He then sits down on the bed and presses his palm against his forehead.

Ben. Oh no.

Silence. Gus lets go of the pillow.

Gus. You remembered something?

Pause.

Ben (*sighs*). It's my fault. For the past few jobs, we've been making a lot of mistakes and I've been blaming them on you.

Gus (*confounded*). Mistakes? What are you talking about, besides the girl, I don't remember any jobs we've messed up on.

Ben (*shakes his head*). There was that one involving the business man. We attracted too much attention and the police almost got involved. Then there was that journalist. We almost killed the wrong person because someone else came before him.

Gus (*nervously*). That was months ago, he doesn't remember that.

Ben. But after the last one, we were at a bar, I started drinking and I couldn't stop. He asked me how we made such a mess and I started ranting about you. He said he was getting tired of you.

Gus. Tired of me? He barely knows me!

The whistle of the speaking-tube blows. Silence.

They stare at each other and then look at the speaking-tube. Neither of them moves.

Gus (*terrified*). It's him.

Ben's legs feel heavy and his stomach is in knots. He reluctantly walks over to the speaking-tube, takes out the whistle, and listens.

Voice on the speaking-tube. Is the job done?

Ben's heart races and his breathing becomes heavy. His legs begin to tremble and he leans against the wall for support.

Ben (*stammering into the speaking tube*). Uhhh... yyesss, it's completed.

Speaking-tube. I like you Ben, you never disappoint me.

Ben relaxes.

Speaking-tube. I'll send over the cleaning crew right now.

Silence. Ben's stomach growls loudly.

Ben and Gus stare at each other.

Gus (*eyebrows raised, whispers*). Lavatory?

Ben (*hisses*). Shut up!

Speaking-tube. What?

Ben (*apprehensively*). Uh.... sorry sir.... the uhhh....kettle just whistled.

Speaking-tube. Ah, tea after the job, you're a younger version of myself.

Ben (*nervous chuckle*). Thank you sir, I'll put off the kettle.

Silence.

Speaking-tube. You mean turn off the kettle.

Ben glares at Gus, who quickly lowers his gaze to the floor, a sly smile on his face.

Ben (*to the speaking-tube*). Oh right, sorry sir.

Speaking-tube. Well actually, my mother—

Ben (*cutting him off unintentionally*). I'll turn it off, goodbye.

Ben (*to Gus as he hangs up*). We have to leave right now.

Gus. Where are we going? What will we—

Ben (*cuts off Gus*). I don't know, grab whatever you can and let's go.

Ben grabs his newspaper and then they both head to the front door. Just when he unlocks the door, there is a loud knock.

A Voice. Cleaning service!

Patrick Diaz reviews a British Broadcasting Company (BBC)
production of Harold Pinter's original "no coda version" of THE
DUMB WAITER

Experiencing the play THE DUMB WAITER in print, I felt that there were
many interactions that read as extremely comedic. Because of this, my
general impression of the play was that it was leaning more on the side
of comedy, but touched on some dark themes. The tone of the play, as
I read the lines in my head, was light. This was not the case for the BBC
production of THE DUMB WAITER that I viewed on YouTube, which took
a completely different approach to tone than I would have had I made my
own adaptation.

What I specifically want to focus on is a scene where Gus and Ben argue
over the validity and common usage of the phrase "Light the kettle."
The most interesting thing about this sequence is that it paints a perfect
picture of the dynamic between these two characters. On the page, in my
opinion, it is comedic in tone. This likely comes from the fact that while a
person reads, they dictate the pace themselves with their internal voice
and imagination. While watching a play or television production, however,
a deliberate choice is made regarding the tone and pace. The audience
is at the mercy of the director, the production staff, the actors, and the
cinematographers in the case of a film adaptation.

This is perfectly on display in the BBC production. The actor portraying
Ben chose to play the lines a lot more emphatically than I would have
imagined, which makes the moment feel a lot more tense than it does
comedic. In the play, it reads as a quick bit of banter where Ben's
frustration comes through and makes for a funny moment. The intention
of the BBC play may have been similar, but the end effect because of
the overly emphatic performance – where the actor's face goes stark red
and he raises his voice – changes the entire tone of the scene. This is not
necessarily a bad thing, but is a noteworthy choice made with the tone
of the teleplay.

Although the BBC production initially does seem to start in a way similar to
what I imagined it, with the actors playing off of each other and chuckling
while keeping the pace up, it soon builds to this tense moment, and that
tone then permeates the rest of the production, leading to a complete shift
in my perspective on the play. What started off as a semi-dark humorous
play, ended up FEELING a lot darker.

CHAPTER 8

"Growing Up," as in Russell Baker's 1982 Memoir: Is It a Kind of Waiting? Just Ask Any Kid!

Or ask Bruce Springsteen via college collaborator **Ryan Langan**, who wrote in response to a class assignment to find a poem or song that captured "growing up, growing older, growing old" as a kind of waiting: "What better song is there on the subject of growin' up than the Bruce Springsteen song called "Growin' Up"? This is one of my dad's favorite songs, and I heard it on one of the benefit call-in TV concert things for pandemic relief, so I figured that enough elements of fate had come together to send this one on to the class." Here's the opening stanza:

> Well, I stood stone-like at midnight, suspended in my
> masquerade
> And I combed my hair till it was just right, and commanded
> the night brigade
> I was open to pain and crossed by the rain and I walked
> on a crooked crutch
> I strolled all alone through a fallout zone and came out
> with my soul untouched
> I hid in the clouded wrath of the crowd, but when they
> said, "Sit down," I stood up
> Ooh … growin' up

Or you could ask college collaborator **Shanya Hopkins** (older cousin to seven-year-old Kila, who insisted, as you might remember from Chapter 2 of SOME DAY, that "growing up" was nothing but kids' doing a lot of waiting because parents control all their time).

I absolutely loved the extended excerpts we read from writer Russell Baker's book GROWING UP. After reading and rereading his 1982 memoir, I realized that Baker's childhood or "growing up" was truly waiting, not only for him but for his mother as well. Baker's entire childhood was the cumulation of acts of waiting for Russell to make something decent of himself (at least by his mother's standards). His brief foray into journalism was the most obvious instance of waiting in which he exhibited all of the usual feelings associated with "waiting" like frustration, indifference, and anxiety. Russell's waiting was unique in that it seemingly belonged to him but truly was not his own: his waiting was shared with his mother, and she rode the emotional roller-coaster that is "waiting" while Baker bore the weight of it all. Because of Baker's passivity while growing up, he spent most of his childhood stuck in a cycle of inaction – waiting for what was to come, and that became even clearer in the procession of events following Russell's finding out that his father was dead.

Or ask college collaborator **Wardah Malik**:

All you do when you are younger is wait. You wait to grow up and to have some sense of freedom. When you're younger, you wait for your favorite television shows to be on. You wait for school to start in the morning so that you can go home in the afternoon. In life, waiting is inevitable. People wait in lines for the candidate they think will change the course of life in America. I waited for a call for a job and now that I have one, I wait for my manager to tell me what to do when I am at work. You wait for someone to text you back and to give you the attention that you wanted. And, when I read a book – and it doesn't have to be about growing up – I wait for the climax because I want to know the best part of that book.

Or ask college collaborator **Nattapat Karmniyanont**:

Growing up is a kind of waiting for Russell Baker much the same as standing in line is an example of waiting for us. In both we are present in the moment, not out of a desire, in our case to be there on the line, but instead out of the desire for the thing that comes after the line. Waiting is thought of as something unpleasant, but I think a better way of classifying the feel of the wait would be doing something undesired in order to get something that we desire. And so Baker's childhood is filled with things he doesn't desire, like having to hand out newspapers while waiting for his life to unfold, which can be said to be something he desired or simply did to please his mother. Even when his father died, all he did was wait for the next thing to happen and to drag him along – all of it not desired by Baker.

We, too, wait to grow up or at least for our lives to progress. We wait for each morning with ideas in our heads as to what the day will hold or what you will do that day. This goes for even the most productive of people as well, although they are not as likely to feel that anything they did was an undesired step towards a far-off goal.

What is growing up, if we had to ask? Is it the process in which each birthday comes around signifying another year you spent alive and in the minds of others? Is it learning about the world and how it works so that we ourselves can integrate ourselves into it? All of it is a form of waiting to see what comes next if we really think about it. What we desired today and what we will desire later often don't align very neatly, but one thing is for sure, no matter what – you'll have to wait. Of course there are certain differences in how each person waits, and so here is what I believe Russell Baker missed in his wait to grow up:

- waiting for the new day. Patiently, anxiously, worriedly, quietly, no matter who or how, each one of us through our lives has stared out the window or lay on the bed thinking about the day that will come and wishing it to come sooner – or not at all, depending on the day;
- sitting in class as a form of waiting. Generally, many students find themselves losing their minds as they blankly stare into space, their interest lost to whatever Elvish language the subject at the time happened to be using (of course this did not happen in a class about waiting, ironically enough);
- waiting to be recognized. As a child, all of us have at least some time where we wait expectantly for a word of praise or some other form of recognition – whether that be trophies, top grades, a laugh – and that, I feel, makes up a large majority of the wait as we grow up.

Or listen to what **Shanya Hopkins** has to say in her original poem about all the "meantimes" in life before one has grown up.

GROWING UP IN THE MEANTIME

The night before the first day of 2nd grade,
I tried on your midnight black heels
clunking around your bedroom
while you slipped into our favorite dress.
The blue fringe beading
like tiny frosted icicles melting
into the soft of your thighs.
Slow down, you said, they would fit
someday.
But in the meantime,
you continued,
tonight was going to be the night you found me a dad.
The night before the first day of 6th grade,
I tried on your midnight black heels
tripping down the hallway
sprinkled with lust-dusted clothing
I closed my eyes and swayed
to the mixed vibratos from your laughter
dreaming of the day
when I would fill those shoes.
He opened the door and you drifted out
I clutched my dream.
Be patient, you said, they'll fit
one day.
But in the meantime,
you continued,
it was time for bed, you had to get back to my new daddy.
The night before the first day of 11th grade
I tried on your midnight black heels
stumbling around my bedroom
to the echoes of raised voices
while you made use of Rick's back for target practice.
Two slammed doors and
my new daddy was gone.
You sat on the edge of my bed,
a lone red face, frosted with tears,
coated with the sorrow of imminent waiting.
Hang in there, you said, the perfect fit is worth
the wait.

But in the meantime,
you continued,
we needed to find me a new dad, that couldn't wait.
The night before I said I do
I tried on your midnight black heels
prancing across your bedroom floor.
My heart grinned, and yours smiled faintly.
I sat on the edge of your bed,
they fit, I whispered, no more waiting
no more uncertainty
no more wondering,
they fit.
You still need a daddy, you said,
someone to help you take care of me.
I choked.
The delusions of widowed withered waiter.
But in the meantime,
you continued,
I need not worry,
you would wait, I needed to live.
For those who carry the burden of waiting cease to exist in the present.

CHAPTER 9

Are You on My Current Calendar –
And Am I on Your Past Ones?

So you think calendars are kept for the keeping of appointments. Date notes and responsibilities attended to. Bucket lists checked off. Although all of these uses might be true of calendars present and future, what about calendars past? Some people hold on to old calendars way beyond their shelf life, thinking that some day in the distant future – along a narrative arc of dusty details – they or their loved ones might just travel back in time to the past.

In her New York Times essay "My Mother's Calendars," Carol J, Adams looks back in 2019 on four decades of yearly appointment calendars that her mother kept from 1965 to 2003. Adams decides to take time to read them all (she sees them as one of the legacies left her by her mother, who died in 2009) – and she comes to realize that datebooks, appointment calendars, weekly planners "are about so much more than keeping track of time." She discovers that calendars are about relationships (for whom will I set aside time?) and responsibilities (what events matter most and what is my role in them?).

As Adams re-views her mother's calendars each morning one day at a time, persons past become present once again in a faded but vivid "this is us":

> My mother was relentless…in fighting for people's rights…advocating for birth control, taking women…for abortions…and advocating housing solutions for migrant

workers. On the earliest calendars these causes weave like counterpoint with her family obligations; at other times, the calendar takes its turn as a diary.... The stark capital letters across the date of April 4, 1968, shouting: "DR. KING ASSASSINATED!" reveal her shock and grief. They now appear as a scar.

My mother's calendars for 1969, 1978 and 1991 track her duties as a wedding planner for her daughters....Through that large house also traipsed 40 years of pets. Cyrano (a dog) "bit by a rat"; "take Cassie (the cat) to the vet – if you can find her."

Over time, the calendars began to reproach me...why wasn't I visiting her more?...In the 1990's she recorded so many health appointments for others that when she made an appointment for herself she wrote in parentheses "me" ... I knew the end, too: the empty calendar of 2004 as Alzheimer's lacerated her mind, and 2009, her death.

Each morning, my parents came to life as another year unspooled before me. At night, my dreaming self became an unmoored time traveler. Time is like that coiled spring binding each calendar.... The calendar's function in reverse now, not a record of what is to come but of what was. My mother's calendars remind me this is how life is lived: from commitment to commitment, with interruptions from injury or weather.

Keep notes for tax purposes, take care of your pets, see the dentist, vote, include culture in your life, use your privilege to be an advocate, laugh at yourself, keep learning, remember the birthdays of your loved ones.

College collaborators inspired by Adams' essay created a filled-in calendar month of their current self's appointments and responsibilities and then time-traveled into their 2030 futures so that they could peruse their now ten-year-old calendar and, after much self-reflection, write a letter to their past self about what it must have meant to be that younger self.

From 2030 Rabeya Rahman to 2020 Rabeya Rahman:

Dear Rabeya,

An overwhelming feeling of nostalgia had caused me to look back at memories, including the past dates on the Outlook email calendar that I've been using for years. The picture attached is a screenshot of the month of February and the first week of March. You're likely in senior year of college right now and before I say anything else, there is one thing I must say: BREATHE. It is mind blowing how busy I—you—have been keeping since such a young age. The entire calendar is full of deadlines, work dates, doctor's visits, and busy school schedules. Not to forget the green circled dates of when you're hoping to see Ferris, the thought of whom keeps you motivated throughout the entire week.

Oh, how lovely had the years gone by. Alhamdullilah mom and dad accepted him after some convincing. Ferris was my first guy best friend, my first boyfriend, and thank God my prayers were answered because he became my forever everything. Hang in there. It's hard not to worry with so many loose ends and an unstable mom. Having a large family can be problematic when the elders have an old mentality and a fear of the unknown. Know that they all come to accept things with minimal issues.

Keep up the determination and hard work because it all pays off in establishing yourself. Keep motivating him, too. Remember that none of this is useful or enjoyable if you don't look after yourself. Listen to the positive influences in your life, including yourself. Selfcare is highly important and mental health is key. Take time off to relax and look after your body. Love yourself because if you're not at your best, then no amount of success can make you as happy as you'd like to be.

Truly,

You <3

From 2030 Shanya Hopkins to 2020 Shanya Hopkins:

Dear Younger Shanya,

I was perusing the bookcases in mom's house and I found one of your calendars from ten years ago, would you believe she kept all of our stuff exactly how you left it? As I flipped through the months, pages soaked in ink, I reacquainted myself with you. You had a firm grasp of time, carefully planning out your days and leaving few moments of unscheduled peace, or chaos. Looking at February, I was reminded of the quote they plastered on our planners' senior spring, "A schedule defends from chaos and whim…It is a net for catching days." You avoided chaos by being a master of time. I counted four empty spaces in the entire month, four days in which you had nothing planned, four days with nothing but time to spend waiting for the next "caught" day.

At first glance your calendar gave me a glimpse of a girl happy to be busy, a girl satisfied by occupation. Yet, the deeper I think about your calendar and its connection to time, I see a girl who occupies herself not out of want, but rather out of necessity – to protect herself from a deep-rooted fear of waiting. By filling your days to capacity, you allowed them to bleed into one another, withholding yourself from feeling the anticipation and anxiety of waiting for the next moment to come. In your attempt to avoid waiting, you actually dove into it head first.

Your calendar reeks of waiting. You spent your days waiting for buses, subways, classes to begin and classes to end. You waited for special events, exams and even days off. You waited for birthdays, for dinners, for others, and even waited on people. While subconscious waiting was pleasant sometime, in most cases it was dreadful. You were selfless, and though you mastered your time, your time was never fully yours. Your waiting was never fully yours. Your calendar told the story of a girl whose time was consumed by waiting and equally by living. Your calendar showed me a girl who made living and waiting synonymous as opposed to two separate actions that fail to coexist.

Sincerely,

Shanya
(10 years older and hopefully wiser)

CHAPTER 10

On Hold for – and Holding On to – Dorothy Parker's 1928 Short Story "A Telephone Call"

Can a short story written almost a century ago, "A Telephone Call," still be timely despite its physically heavy and heavily symbolic black rotary phone? Yes, responded the students in "The Literature of Waiting" course, particularly when young people today appear "impatient" and increasingly "intolerant to waiting," and male and female date-role-playing hasn't changed enough.

Better still, this five-page story first published in 1928 is actually a telling example of what Andrea Kohler, in her 2011 book-length essay "Passing Time," called a "real manifestation of hope" as a form of waiting. Says Kohler:

> Biding our time in anxious expectation rather than jumping the gun also harbors the promise of happiness: it's the real manifestation of hope. When we're all excitement and expectation, it's as if we've momentarily lost consciousness. Like the dog that stubbornly anticipates the next bite with every bite withheld, expectation doesn't learn from the past. I can stubbornly expect something that reason tells me will definitely not happen, or I can know exactly when my waiting is supposed to be over and still wish to speed things along.

Easily found online, "A Telephone Call" features the excruciatingly anxious voice – and therefore the psychological viewpoint – of a nervous, fearful, and increasing tense young woman as she waits for the ring of her apartment's landline telephone as *the signal* that a young man of her acquaintance truly considers her his "darling."

Parker is today best known as the female wit from The New Yorker magazine who held her own around the otherwise all-male Algonquin Hotel's Round Table of raconteurs and is famous for her spot-on remark when informed of the death of the less-than-charismatic American president Calvin Coolidge: "How could you tell?"

But "A Telephone Call" – particularly when read out loud for its reasons, rhythms, and repetitions – shows Parker to be a master of other sensational sentences as well. Our college collaborators, when asked to choose their five favorite story lines of "dialogue" – with God, with the inanimate telephone, with her memories of the young man, with the young woman's own inner selves of fantasy and reality – had a hard time limiting their choices to a literal handful.

Listing as her "honorable mention number six" the line "Please don't let me hope, dear God. Please don't," collaborator **Shanya Hopkins** explained that "I just couldn't help but love it equally as much. I just find a certain complexity in the relationship between hope and waiting; while most people think that hope makes waiting tolerable, I would argue for the opposite."

Parker's opening sentences to "A Telephone Call" cry out with intense emotion: "Please, God," moans the young woman, "let him telephone me *now* (our vocal emphasis). Dear God, let him call me *now*. I won't ask anything else of You, truly I won't."

So, too, do the young woman's closing lines some five pages of angst later: "I don't even ask You to let him telephone me now (*that word again, but, oh, this time in contrast with a revealingly revised time frame*). God, only let him do it *in a little while*. I'll count five hundred by fives. I'll do it so slowly and so fairly. If he hasn't telephoned *then*, I'll call him. I will. Oh, please, dear God, dear kind God, my blessed Father in Heaven, let him call *before then*.

"Please, God. Please. Five, ten, fifteen, twenty, twenty-five, thirty, thirty-five...."

Our students in "The Literature of Waiting" course engaged in a spirited in-class (pre-distance learning) discussion (no, they didn't phone it in!) of the various verbal ways that Parker's young woman engages in her stream of consciousness monologue, "biding" her time "in anxious expectation." And they came up with multiple examples of such forms of waiting as:

- explaining logically and psychologically,
- supposing and rationalizing,
- fantasizing and speculating,
- agonizing and recriminating,
- superstitiously counting,
- cursing (at a transcendent and apparently unempathetic God, at the symbolic yet all-too-real-in-its-silence telephone, at the young man in question and out of the picture),
- game-playing with both mankind and the divine,
- bargaining with fate,
- praying and begging and pleading,
- wishing and hoping,
- expecting and dreading,
- enduring by ignoring reality and past history.

Later, several college collaborators imaginatively continued "A Telephone Call" a bit beyond Dorothy Parker's last words and Parker's "still waiting" ending. For example, **Nathalie Chazoule** extended "A Telephone Call" as follows (short and bitter): "500. I wait and then my telephone rings. Staring at it, I am back in *my* hell, but picking it up I might go to *yours*."

Paige Thorne had her young woman ask of God, after answering the ringing phone only to discover it's "a wrong number": "What is the lesson here, God? I bet you're up there laughing at me. How cruel of you to treat your child this way!"

Carolyn Reyes had Parker's young woman take herself to task for not picking up on her young man's use of the "darling" term of affection: "'Darling.' D-A-R-L-I-N-G. Who calls someone that unless they fancy them, right? I just wish I had said it back – Darling! Then he'd know. He'd really know how I feel about him and wouldn't keep me waiting like this. No."

While **Wardah Malik** had the young woman wonder: "What if I don't think about him for a while? Would that help? What if I watch a movie to ease my mind? Am I going crazy? I think so. Because it's crazy being next to the phone for this long. Waiting and waiting, hoping for it to ring. I probably shouldn't have told him I was going to wait for his call, maybe then he would've called earlier. What if I 'accidentally' call him and pretend I was going to call someone else?"

Lastly, **Maxine Lim** had the young woman go ahead and phone the young man and get a busy signal: "I just can't understand what's going on. Who's he even talking to? Could it be his boss? Maybe he's in trouble. Or maybe it's another woman."

Other college collaborators wrote a version of the story from the point of view of the young man *of* the story but not *in* the story (giving him both voice and a voice); or they wrote a "communications-themed" story modeled after the structure of "A Telephone Call" minus Parker's landline telephone and without any reference to romantic or realistic love.

A Young Woman Awaits a Telephone Call from a Young Man
By Ryan Langan

Forty, forty-five, fifty, fifty-five —

The telephone rang. I couldn't believe it. Oh, God, after all this time, you haven't forsaken me! Oh, I knew it. It knew it. I knew it! But…what if…it's a test? It isn't him on the other end of that line. I'll bet it's my mother. That woman never leaves me alone. Ah, it's still ringing! Oh, God, what do I do, God, please, tell me. I have to answer. This is what I've been waiting for. This call is all I've wanted, all I've needed. Oh, Lord, three rings. It's been a sufficient amount of time. He won't think I'm desperate. I'll answer coolly, easily. "Hey, baby," I'll say. He'll melt for me! Or is that too much? To combat his "darlings" with my "babys"? Oh, he'll go right back to hating me. I've never been enough for him. I shouldn't even answer. There's no need. It's all pointless, in truth. My fussing over his call, this telephone, this man. What do I need him for? I'll be free once this phone stops ringing…. Oh, God, it's stopped! Oh, my Good Lord, what have I done?! Oh, please let him call me back. Just one more time, God. I'll count to five hundred by fives. It worked the first time, didn't it? Five, ten, fifteen, twenty, twenty-five, thirty…

A Young Man Awaits a Telephone Call from a Young Woman
By Hester Milford

It sure was nice to hear from her today. Calling me up to say hello. Gee, she's so pretty. Such a nice young woman. I wouldn't want to appear over eager, now, would I? I called her "darling." Oh, gee. I think I called her "darling" twice. Is that overkill? I mustn't fret.

...

I'm fretting. Did she mention she would call me at five? I think she did. Well, as of now, it's 5:05. Has she forgotten? Does she hate me? She definitely hates me. Or, wait. Did I say I would call her? I was in such a tizzy when I heard her sweet voice drift over the line. I must've forgotten. How embarrassing. Ewell, I sure can't call her now. Mustn't come on too strong. Wait a day. Or two. I'm sure she has plenty other men interested. Does she call them up, too?

Ah. Now I'm very worried. I won't call. Must give the illusion of being busy. That's right. I'm a busy young man. Much business to attend to. Now it's 5:10. She hasn't called. I must go home. I have a phone at home. But does she have my home phone number? I should think not. Oh, what a predicament to be in. What trouble.

If only she was thinking of me...

A Young Man Gets a Telephone Call from a Young Woman
By Fawzi Saleh

"Hello, Charles?" Dorothy asked.
"What happened honey, why'd you call back?" Charles said.
"You said you would call me at five, Charlie, it's ten minutes past seven now," she explained.
"Oh I'm sorry darling, I lost track of time," he replied.

In the background of Charles's call, a toilet flushes. After that, Dorothy becomes more aware of the background and hears faint voices.

"Did I catch you at a bad time?" asked Dorothy.
Charles lets out a nervous chuckle.

"Well you see, uh... I had to work overtime because of the new play me and Sheldon were working on. I just finished, and I came up to the restroom to wash up."

Dorothy blushes out of embarrassment. She did not expect to call when he was in the middle of his business.

"Oh dear, I'm so sorry! I'll let you go now, but you're coming over tonight, right?" she asked hopefully.

There's a brief pause as Charles thinks of what to say.

"Well, hon, I'm sorry but I promised the guys I'd drink with them," explained Charles.

Dorothy's heart drops. She felt like crying.

"Oh Charlie! It's been days since we last saw each other. Just tell them you're busy, that you made plans with me and forgot to tell them, they'll understand, they really will," she said.

Charles sighed out of frustration. This is what really irritated him, her demanding and controlling nature. When they first met, she was fun and witty. But soon she became a burden, wanting to constantly be with him. Even when they weren't together, she would hound him with calls. Her insecure attachment to him made him feel more like a father than a lover, and he despised this.

"Baby I've had a long day, I'm exhausted, I'll come over some other time," he informed.

Dorothy sank back on her couch and her body went limp. All that waiting, and now she was being told he wouldn't meet with her. She felt defeated.

DING!
By Paige Thorne

Pick up
Put down

Pick up
Put down

Is anyone thinking of me?

DING!

Pick up

Ooh, a meme!
What's the best reply?
Think, think, THINK!

Meh,
That'll do

Put down

DING!

Pick up

A text!
Hmmmm
Let's see what everyone else says
Like Like LIKE

Put down

(Thirty minutes later)

Pick up
Put Down

Pick up
Put Down

Connecting With an Ice Cream Sundae? It's Your Call
By Gabriella Tuchman

I should not be pacing back and forth. Ooh, I should look at what number is currently on the big black screen. I hope my number does not come. I should leave just now. Okay, I'll look. I'll see what number is on the screen. If it's less than three, I'll stay, but if it's more, then I'll leave. Five is only two more than three, I should stay.

No, I want to leave. I mean what if I mess up? It's not worth it. I can just go home. Or I can go to the grocery store self-checkout. Yeah, that seems like a good plan. I can leave the store now. Hear the bell ring as I leave. They'll just skip my number.

But wait. I took a number – now they'll know I was here – so I should just stay. It's just as bad to leave now as it is to leave later. They'll know I was here. And then they'll talk and be like, "Why would someone take a number and then leave – that's so rude." And then the other guy behind the counter will add, "Yeah, I bet it was that weird girl pacing back and forth." Okay, so there's only one person working behind the counter so I guess that exact conversation can't happen. See, I should stay. There's nothing to be nervous about. I'm just ordering some food. I followed all the instructions. What if I misread the instructions? What if I actually was not supposed to take a number at all?

No, of course I was supposed to take a number. Why would the number be by the door? I should be here. But, really, can I be here? I'm freaking out about ice c ream. What a loser.

Something so simple. It's a maximum of two sentences. I can say, "Hello, I would like a small mint chocolate chip ice cream, please." It's so easy. I bet the guy at the counter won't even look me in the eyes. He'll just take my order by looking at the cashier screen.

But, still, this is so stressful. What if I forget the "please" or mix up the words? I really should just get going. Oh, what number are they on? I haven't even been keeping track. Oh, my gosh. There are only two people in front of me. I need to make a decision fast.

I can talk to the cashier.
I can't talk to the cashier.
I can talk to the cashier.
I can't talk to the cashier

I don't know what to do, and it's almost my turn. "Hello, may I please have a mint chocolate chip ice cream, please." Nope – I said "please" twice. What a weirdo. See, I should leave. No use. That's it. I can go to the grocery store and buy some Breyer's. I don't need some fancy ice cream sundae from an ice cream shop.

Yes, I do. I deserve this ice cream. I promised myself this ice cream. All I need to do is order and pay and then I can leave. Just like that. I want ice cream and I will get ice cream. I don't need to be nervous. In fact, stop being nervous., You got this. I don't got this – my number is next. I've been pacing back and forth the whole time. I learned that if fish don't continue moving, they sink. Get that, fish sink. But I'm not a fish. I can't compare my pacing to a fish swimming. I'm getting ice cream. This is not a moment of life and death. Wow, I should just walk myself out. But I'm sure they'll be calling my number any second and I've been here this long. Just talk to the cashier. Form words. And then I'll be good. He's not scary. Here I'm not scared.

Here's my number.

A Desperate Call for Inspiration
By Nattapat Karmniyanont

Inspiration, where are you? I kinda need you right now. Won't you answer the call? Please? For me? I'll keep writing until you come. You'll come, right? You have to. Please come. I don't have any plans. Won't you come to help? Will you come if I play a song? Which song? This one? This one? How about this one? Another? Not that one? WHICH is it! Must I serenade you like jesters to a king? Must I spread myself upon the altar to have you glance at me?

No, no wait. Yelling won't work. Clear my mind? That will work, right? But if I clear my mind, how can I write? Can I, write? Were all those other times luck? Did I just cobble words together? Was there ever anything as grand as an inspiration? No, there has to be something. Thinking about it wouldn't help. No, it would. Wouldn't it? Does it please you? Does it please you to plague my mind? Leaving behind prints but no body. Vestiges but no substance.

Maybe I need a break. Just sit back and wait. You'll come then, right? You will, won't you? I don't know. It's scary not knowing what to do. Without you, what will I do? How can I keep on going? You held my hands. You whispered to me sweet words that lit up the page. Promise me you'll come back. You said you would. I can't create without you. Please come back.

Can you even hear me? Do you even care? You smirk and turn your head elsewhere. You'll leave me behind. You'll leave me to languish in the agony of an empty page. The torture that is a blank mind. The hell that is a ... I've run out of analogies.

Please, inspiration, just come. I want to make this longer....

CHAPTER 11

Waiting for Love in Ha Jin's 1999 Novel "Waiting"

If you were, as I was back in 2018, starting to research a college literature study course that would look into "the literature of waiting," you would probably immediately put WAITING FOR GODOT down on your lined yellow legal paper and then stop to wonder whether there were many other literary titles with the word "waiting" in them. I remembered having seen a pretty good Broadway revival of a Noel Coward play called WAITING IN THE WINGS and I soon recalled the labor union setting of Clifford Odets' one-acter WAITING FOR LEFTY.

Was there a play or novel or short story with just the word "waiting" as its title? Turns out (actually I turned to the online books available from the Brooklyn Public Library), there was a 1999 novel by a Chinese-American author, Ha Jin, that I was not familiar with. The novel, set in Communist China over a twenty-year period beginning in 1963, was simply called WAITING and had even won a National Book Award. I decided to check it out (from the library and for consideration for my course that would come to be prosaically called "The Literature of Waiting").

It became the first novel my students would read as a whole class when the course got under way. After a brief class discussion by way of introduction and a similarly brief look at the novel's prologue, students were assigned to read each of the novel's three distinct parts one at a time so that we could talk about the nature of WAITING's "waiting" as it changed over the course of some twenty years. Here are the critical thinking prompts that the class was given governing its reading of and thinking about Ha Jin's novel, as well as the choices students had for demonstrating their insights into its three major characters through a piece of creative writing homework.

Prompts:

- *For each of the three main characters – Chinese army doctor Lin Kong; village woman Shuyu, Lin's wife by an arranged marriage; and army hospital nurse Manna Wu – what specifically does "waiting" look like, feel like, and actually consist of in the Prologue and Part One of the novel?*
- *Create a separate "timetable" of waiting for each of the novel's three major characters showing how their lives changed in the form waiting took within each of the novel's three parts.*
- *Would you say the "it" each character was waiting for is "love"? How would each of them define "love"? Whose definition do you most agree with – and why?*
- *For all three major characters was "it" (what they were waiting for) "worth the wait"? What, for each, were the effects of time on their love? Which characters in the novel, if any, would say "be careful what you wish for/wait for"?*
- *A reviewer of the novel WAITING in the New York newspaper "Newsday" said that the story of the novel was "so quietly and carefully told that…we read on <u>patiently</u>, pleasantly <u>distracted</u>, wondering <u>when</u> something will happen. Only when we've finished do we understand just how much has, and how much <u>waiting</u> can be its own painful reward." How do you feel about the specifics of this review – and why (the "waiting" words of the review have been underlined by Mr. Eidelberg)?*

Here is a far-from-complete timeline for character Lin Kong's "waiting" across some three hundred pages of the novel WAITING:

- waiting to get up the courage to ask his wife, Shuyu, for a divorce this year;
- waiting to understand why his daughter is seemingly upset with him;
- waiting to hear Shuyu's answer about agreeing to a divorce in front of the judge;
- waiting for next year to once again bring up the topic of divorce after Shuyu's brother comes to her defense in the judge's presence;

- waiting as a kind of longing (to be with Manna Wu);
- waiting for Manna Wu to maybe make the decision for him because Lin Kong feels as though he is unable to;
- waiting for a promotion, and then waiting to see if the promotion will be worth it;
- waiting for the right time to once again ask for a divorce;
- waiting to see whether Manna Wu will find Liang Meng to be a suitable replacement for him;
- waiting for the crowd in front of his house to cease upsetting and threatening him;
- waiting to find out about Manna Wu's date with the commissioner;
- waiting to recover from his sickness;
- waiting to do something, tell someone, about the rape he has just learned of;
- waiting year after year through eighteen years for the divorce from Shuyu;
- waiting to see whether the divorce will crystalize his feelings about Shuyu and Manna Wu;
- waiting to see whether his daughter, despite being upset with him all these years, will move from her village to be closer to him in the city;
- waiting for a few months before marrying Manna Wu so as not to start even more rumors;
- waiting for the wedding, and then waiting for the "boring" wedding to be over;
- waiting to satisfy Manna Wu's expectations of him in bed;
- waiting to find out the deeper truth about Mei's letter to Manna Wu;
- waiting to find out what gender their child is;
- waiting, again bored, to find out whether he actually made the right choice in marrying Manna Wu after all these years;
- waiting to see whether Manna Wu will make it through the difficult birth of their child;
- waiting to see whether his building paternal suffering will end;
- waiting to understand how Manna Wu's illness will take its course;
- waiting to reconcile his feelings about love toward Manna Wu, and waiting for her to die.

Similar timelines were created for the two adult women in Lin Kong's life – Shuyu and Manna Wu – and, ultimately, based on these comprehensive timelines, students went on to write imaginatively – in either prose, poetry, or drama – on one of the following choices:

Choice #1: Write a personal waiting journal entry as one of the novel's three major characters *from her or his emotional and intellectual perspective at the conclusion of the novel WAITING.*

Here is a Choice #1-type example of an entry about his wife Shuyu from Lin's personal waiting journal *early in the novel* (poetically created for him *by college collaborator* **Chyna Chung**):

A woman of no intellectuality.
A woman of no education.
That much of a peasant.
How can she experience such emotion when she doesn't properly understand it?
No love. No happiness. No joy between us.
She cleans. She cooks.
She raises our daughter.
She takes care of my ill father.
She maintains the house during my absence.
She always waits for my return and for my attempt at the inevitable divorce.
Oh.
Maybe that is it.
That is her representation of love
– and I am the one who doesn't understand her experience of it.

Choice #2: I know they don't celebrate Valentine's Day in communist China, but this is an imaginative piece of poetic writing you might like to do: create a Valentine's Day-type card (the ENTIRE CARD – its images and its "lovely" words) – from one of the three major characters to either of the other two.

Choice #3: Create the dialogue of a dramatic counseling session between a qualified marriage counselor and Lin Kong and either his first or second wife (Shuyu or Manna Wu); please resist any temptation you might have to be so dramatic as to have the two wives present in a thruples therapy session.

Shanya Hopkins creates the text of Manna Wu's "Happy Valentine's Day" card to, of all people, Shuyu:

To Shuyu,

For years you kept me from the love of my life – your husband. While you faintly knew of my existence, I resented you – and at the same time I wanted to know everything about you. Today marks Lin's and I's third valentine's day as a married couple and your 21st as a widow. Lin has been mine since my fingers etched hearts in his palm that night in the theater, and every year we spent together at the hospital, a piece of your marriage died and resurrected itself in the shape of our love. While our love blossomed like orchids signaling a sprung spring, your tiny feet bore foundation to a woman aged and withered. You see, Lin and I's love must be hard for you to understand because it is unbounded – boundless. But, it is not with malice that I write this card to you. It was your simpleness that allowed him to easily fall in love with the idea of my complexities, and your essence of the past that propelled him into my future. Thank you, Shuyu – your unwillingness to let go just made our love stronger and withstanding.

Happy Valentine's Day (with love),
Manna Wu

How silly an American holiday, by Nicole Sanchez

Comrade Manna Wu,

Yesterday marked Valentine's Day, an American holiday where love between two is celebrated. American men often buy their partners frivolous chocolates and bouquets of roses. Bouquets are so in demand that that they are often sold out and so the sellers who have remaining roses sell their product at a much higher price. How silly a holiday Americans have accepted into their calendars. How does one even celebrate love? What do you think? What do you think our leader would think?

While I am away, please don't think of Shuyu; the divorce will soon come. Like I told you, please, Manna, give me more time. I have not lost that thought in my head. I want to have you as my wife, Manna. I just need you to wait longer, allow me that time. I will be going to the countryside as I do every year and will try to convince Shuyu's brother to not overstep. I wish you'd understand – many people have been holding this divorce back. I am sorry to be away from you, as you know I am fulfilling my duties away from our hospital. My duties are important and I have to attend to them properly – I am hoping to go up in the ranks. We can both get promotions that will help occupy the time. I hope you receive this letter in good health and I find you well when I come back.

Sincerely,
Comrade Lin Kong

A love letter from Manna Wu to Lin Kong, by Anne-Lilja Rentof

Dearest Lin,

Ever since our hands embraced at the opera, I have known that you are my one true love. I long for the day when the Party allows us to be together as husband and wife so that we may at last experience the passionate love that I know awaits us.

Yours,
Manna

A love letter from Manna Wu to Lin Kong, by Patrick Diaz

To Lin,

I know this must be a troubling message to receive in secret. Although we are not supposed to have an abnormal relationship, I often find myself thinking of you in the night. How am I to meet another man who makes me feel this way at my age? You may want me to move on for the sake of ease, but I am prepared to wait for your divorce from your wife, however long that may take. I love you, and even though you do not show it, I know you love me, too.

From,
Manna

A love letter from Shuyu to Lin Kong, by Paige Thorne

Dear Lin,

I love you very much, and here are my reasons: I love how handsome you are, I love how rational you are, I love your courage to become an army doctor, I love how much you love our beautiful daughter, Hua, I love your laugh. You will always have a home with me in the country.

With love,
Your (ex)wife, Shuyu

The Waiting Journal of Shuyu
By Gabriella Tuchman

I wonder why he wants a divorce. Have I not been a good wife? No, I know I have been a good wife. I wait for him faithfully. I raise his daughter to be strong. I make sure he has enough to eat. I give him everything. I don't sleep in the same bed as him because it makes him uncomfortable. I give him everything! Why does he want a divorce?

Even more importantly, why did I say yes to the divorce? Why would I agree to something that I don't want to do? I want to make him happy, but I love him. I hoped that over time he would grow to love me just like I grew to love him.

Is the point of marriage really love, though? The point of marriage is to make your parents happy and make sure that you are able to take care of your parents. It is something beautiful. Your parents took care of you when you were young, so you must take care of your parents when they are old. It seems perfectly clear to me. He needed someone to take care of his mother and I did it with a full heart. Taking care of people is my job. I am here to nurture and support others.

He knows that marriage is supposed to be for life. He knows that we made a commitment to each other forever. It is not a monetary commitment. It is a commitment to a relationship that helps bring about another generation.

Does he think it does not hurt me that he never comes back? That when he does come back, he comes back for such a short time? I wait for him because that is what wives are supposed to do. Does he think he can change tradition and forget about me? I have been so good to him.

I should not have said yes to this divorce to make him happy. I will not say no because that is actively going against his wishes, but I will cry to show him how I really feel. Then he will realize that we should stay married. I will not tolerate him making a mess out of both of our lives. We deserve to stay together. I am deciding, we are not getting a divorce. It is my right to continue this marriage and I will.

The Waiting Journal of Lin Kong
By Ryan Langan

The way I see it, the heart is never to be fully satisfied. Perhaps that is what made all of this waiting happen – the inability to know, the futility in trying to know, the helpless surrender to time and its mysteries strewn out ahead of us. I've now got two wives, two families, and still I am no closer to an answer.

What do I want? What do I want? Shuyu, my first wife, who I rejected for so long, is not the idle and distant creature I had always thought her to be. No, she is beautiful in her own way: true, and patient; she has waited for me all these years as I have waited to know my own heart. And Manna, with whom I have suffered, with whom I have joyed, with whom I have waited.

How strange it is all this time waiting: waiting for Shuyu to divorce and waiting to come back to her, waiting to be with Manna and waiting to leave her, constantly in oscillation between these two poles like an astral body forever and only existing in time – it is time that wrought all this.

I know not yet what I intend to do. I do not know who I must be with, who I must leave...who may be waiting somewhere, sometime else. Waiting, waiting, this most common and tragic of human acts. It is all there is for us in our state of unknowing. And it is all there is for me and my lost soul, my waiting and wanting heart, for there is truly no way to satisfy one who is always waiting.

The Waiting Journal of Lin Kong
By Trever Polk

I must confess – although it makes me feel guilty, it's true – that at this point in my life I'm waiting for Manna to die. Perhaps I should feel guilty because, after all, she is too, whether she wants to or not.

Shuyu, I don't know. I can't say what I feel is love. I've never felt true love and I was married to her too long to just now feel it for the first time. Perhaps it is love, just a different kind, a familial kind. She always did look like she could be my aunt. Time will tell whether we live together again to raise the twins. We'll have to wait and see.

The Waiting Journal of Manna Wu
By Liala Ahmad

As I sit by my babies, watching them stare absent-mindedly at the ceiling, I wonder if they too are waiting for Lin to come home, if they think about him when he is gone, waiting for him to return so we can feel like a family. I wonder if they wait at all. I wish I didn't. I'm so weak these days. I know I need rest but my mind doesn't. When Lin leaves the house to do who knows what, I'm left reeling. It just can't be that after all of these agonizing years of waiting to marry my husband, my marriage is agonizing me. It seems as though my life fell apart when I fell in love with Lin. I was in denial but I know that he never truly fought for us, never truly tried to get a divorce. He was never proactive in being with me, even now.

Marriage did not solve anything. I remember how I used to dream of being intimate with Lin and after we finally wed, his sex drive no longer matched mine. Maybe it never did. Did he ever love me? Some way to show your wife your love! Working, working, working. What a shit excuse! I can't help but wonder…is this how Shuyu felt? He can't even dote on his dying wife. All of these years of sticking by Lin, I was sure that the wait would be worth it, if anything to guarantee that I would not be alone. I was wrong. With a bitter laugh, I realize I'm a widow and a spinster.

Take One: A Marriage Counseling Session for Lin and Shuyu – A Dramatic Scene by Jason Chetram

Therapist: So, Comrade Kong, what brings you and your wife here today?

Lin: Well, Doctor, me and Shuyu here are in an unloving marriage, and I believe that it's time we go our separate ways.

Therapist: Is that true, Shuyu?

Shuyu, who was not paying attention initially, becomes alert to the sound of her name.

Therapist: Shuyu, is it true that you do not love your husband anymore?

Shuyu: No, I love him very much. He is good to me.

Therapist: ...Right. Comrade Kong, how's about you just tell me why you feel there's no longer any love in your marriage.

Lin, immediately thinking about Shuyu's appearance and her bound feet that he finds repulsive, stops himself from speaking a word of either. Although he dislikes both a great deal, he can not find it in himself to say such things in front of Shuyu. This renders Lin silent, absorbed in his thoughts.

Therapist: Well, Comrade Kong? Is there a reason?

Lin: Yes, yes there is. You see Doctor, I work at a military hospital in Muji City. And I'm only given a few days a year to see Shuyu back in the village, and I'm afraid the distance has made my heart grow cold.

Therapist: You know, they say that distance makes the heart grow fonder, in fact. It would appear that distance hasn't affected Shuyu in the same way. Shuyu, do you believe that this distance and seeing your husband so little makes your heart grow further from him?

Shuyu: No, something to look forward to. Like a holiday.

Therapist: Well put, Shuyu. Comrade Kong, you mention you work at a hospital, are there nurses at this hospital?

Lin: Of course there are, we tend to many patients.

Therapist: Are these nurses youthful? Attractive? Perhaps you are blinded to the reason why you married your wife because you see the next best thing. Comrade Lin, is there someone at the hospital who you have your eyes on?

Lin, immediately thinking about Manna, and about the repercussions of even hinting at her very existence, breaks into a slight cold sweat.

Lin: No Doctor, there is no other woman. It is against military rules to have abnormal relations with other staff members.

Therapist: Comrade Kong, what do you mean by "abnormal"? Are you implying you have a "normal" relationship with another woman? Please explain yourse-

Shuyu: Stop. Enough. My husband is a good man. He would not take another woman.

Lin, a nauseating feeling in his stomach, can feel his sins crawling on his back.

Therapist: If you insist, Shuyu, I will not press the subject further. But Comrade Kong, I will say this, if you choose to be fickle now, you will be fickle again in the future. It would be best to lose this habit now.

Lin: Yes, Doctor, and perhaps we should reschedule for another time, I'm not feeling well.

Therapist: Yes, it might be for the best to end our session here.

Lin: Thank you for your time.

Lin and Shuyu nod their head at the therapist and leave his office. On the way out Lin wonders how it is Shuyu could think so highly of him despite his thoughts for Manna.

Lin: Let's go get something to eat before we head back home.

Shuyu: Hmm.

Shuyu follows Lin's lead cheerfully.

Take Two: A Marriage Counseling Session for Lin and Shuyu –
A Short Story by Fawzi Saleh

Lin stared up at the ceiling. He was at a loss, he didn't know how to dissuade her. The counselor was now furiously scribbling, trying to capture every word of their exchange. The awkward silence prompted Shuyu to glance at Lin, but he avoided eye contact.

"Lin? What do you think? Are you willing to change your mind?" the counselor asked.

Another child, Lin thought to himself. He could barely remember how he had made his first. Still, though, the idea wasn't unrealistic. They did have enough money to support another child, and there had been cases of healthy babies from older couples. He looked up at Shuyu and saw her hopeful face. This was the happiest he had ever seen her.

Lin turned to the counselor. "Yes, I suppose it's possible," he replied. The counselor nodded satisfactorily and Shuyu, excited as ever, jumped in her chain joyfully. Suddenly, the red plastic comb in her pocket fell and landed near her feet. She had received the comb as a token of friendship from one of the nurses. Shuyu treasured it, carrying it with her everywhere she went. As she reached down to pick it up, Lin saw her bound feet. His lungs ceased function for a few seconds.

"Well, I'm glad your issue has been resolved. If you ever need more help, don't hesitate to reach out to me," the counselor said.

As they walked down the hall, Lin couldn't help glancing at her feet. His goosebumps perked as he imagined the bound feet rubbing his skin. What if her feet unwrapped? He suddenly felt very sick. His stomach growled loudly and Shuyu turned around to look at him.

"Are you hungry? Don't worry, I'll make multigrain porridge, and then at night we'll...," she said and winked. The images of porridge and her bound feet mixed and swirled. Lin became dizzy and covered his mouth to avoid puking.

"Yes, of course, honey, now let's go home," he said weakly out of the corner of his mouth.

CHAPTER 12

When in the Course of Daily Pre-Pandemic Human Events: Making Time – and Marking Time – for a Personal Waiting Journal

"We live our lives waiting," Viviene Robinson, a wise student from my fall 2019 Hunter College course on "The Teacher and Student in Literature" wrote me soon after that course had ended. And where was Viviene when she wrote that? With time figuratively on her hands (but not literally because she wasn't wearing a wristwatch), she was waiting "on line" (residents of New York City would say "in line) to buy her favorite smoothie. Meanwhile, as a time-conscious multi-tasker, Viviene was also working her way through one of the assigned novels in that course she was taking with me (on "The Teacher and Student in Literature") and she suddenly realized that reading was one of the things she most often did when she found herself busy…waiting. Waiting for something or someone. In this instance, "waiting for" her smoothie to be brought to her by the guy who had been "waiting on" her.

Now, where had time gone? When would her smoothie be ready to quench her thirst and calm her nerves (I did say that she was a student of mine, right?)? And then the smoothie with the name "Viviene" appeared and her "then" had become "now." She couldn't wait to taste it!

Enter the Personal Waiting Journal for all students in "The Literature of Waiting" course for the spring 2020 semester: one of the ways students would write regularly about "living a life of waiting." Halfway into the course, after the Covid-19 virus had caused a national emergency and the closing of public and private colleges and universities in New York State, students kept their journals during their sheltered-alone days and came to write, in part, on what a waiting life was like when they were "busy" waiting for the coronavirus pandemic to end.

Some of the students' personal waiting journal or diary or notebook entries (in which they stopped to "take note and make note") also became the inspiration for extended pieces of creative writing on aspects of the waiting experience as well as on the physical, emotional, and psychological imposition of "waiting out the pandemic." But what made the original entries even possible was the instruction to "start by pointedly becoming aware of how your moment-to-moment existence can be seen as a 'now' that immediately becomes a 'then' that subsequently becomes its own 'now' only to be replaced by the next 'now' (another 'then') – time and time again. So just as we live our lives 'dying,' we live our lives 'waiting' – waiting to see what will come about in the next hour, the next minute, the next moment before it vanishes into the fog or disappears upon the echo. Waiting is an occasion that happens more than just occasionally. It is fixed in the process of the present, unlike expecting, which occurs in the present but is fixated, literally 'hopefully,' on the future – onto some future product, some future event, some future occurrence. For the human species there can often be 'great expectations,' but all too seldom is there 'great waiting.' Unless we seize the moment and make it so – as some of our college collaborators have. And so welcome to their world of worrisome but also wonderful waiting."

Personal Waiting Journal Entry of Patrick Diaz (That Later Inspires Patrick to Create the Piece of Imaginative Writing That Follows Right After It)

Waiting for my train to leave the station and it's taking insanely long. I am sitting here, having finished my reading, doing nothing. If I had some assignments to do I could do them, but I am too responsible a student for that. Or am I? Is it really responsible to not account for delays and to sit idly? Maybe the only reason I'm pondering this is because I'm not doing anything right now. What I wouldn't give for a menial task right about now. Instead of being here for fifteen minutes, I could have spent an extra fifteen minutes with Tracy. I could have made a nice French omelet and some herbal tea, sat at the table and enjoyed life for a few minutes. Instead, I am sitting in a beaten down train car that smells of urine.

Waiting to Wait: A Typical Start to a New York City Subway Commute
By Patrick Diaz

I made my way towards the train through a series of poorly planned Bronx crosswalks, the first of which leads to another crosswalk in between two busy multi-lane streets. This intersection was always a nightmare, but on this particular day, the street lights were sync-ed up for some reason, leading to traffic congestion in every direction. It also means that, when I missed my chance to cross safely, I had to wait even longer. When I was done waiting and finally crossed the busy street, the light changed so abruptly that I was forced to wait a second time. Then I hurried my way down towards the Westchester Square-East Tremont Avenue Number 6 train station. I heard the train coming even before getting to the station, so I ran full speed up the stairs, up the second flight of stairs, past the Metrocard machines, through the doors, and finally to the turnstiles. I took out my Metrocard and swiped. "Insufficient fare." I went back to the Metrocard machine and refilled my card.

Having missed the train, I was no longer in a hurry. I swiped once more and walked up the stairs toward the platform. "Delay," I read in bright green lettering. I waited on the platform for twenty minutes. I walked back and forth along the platform until I heard the rumbling and screeching of the train in the distance. I jogged quickly towards the end of the platform and, waiting, with a look of relief on my face, for the rushing wind of the train to pass by and the sound of the doors finally shuffling open. When the train arrived, I walked in, grabbed a seat, and waited. The train started going express, stations full of people rushing by the window. With each passing stop I grew more relieved. I pulled out an assignment I had neglected (not one for this class, Mr. Eidelberg!) and began working. Something about the rumbling of the train helps me focus. When the train got to Hunts Point Avenue, I heard a crackling of the loud speaker.

The booming voice of a conductor with his mouth too close to the microphone interrupted my focus: "Attention, passengers; we're being held in the station momentarily due to a sick passenger at 125th Street. Once again, we're being held momentarily by the train's dispatcher; we'll be moving along once we get a green signal. Thank you." I looked down at my phone to check the time: 9:37. There was no way I was going to be on time.

The Indulgent Adversaries
Imaginative Writing Inspired by an Entry in My Personal Waiting Journal
By Anne-Lilja Rentof

Anxiety is a lurker. I'm never truly without it. It's always just…there. Waiting for something to gripe over. It lingers at the corners of my self-conscious, waiting for me to come across something on the sidewalk that I'll "have" to step around – no matter how seemingly insignificant to the occasional onlooker – for fear of getting myself or someone else sick. It waits with anticipation for one of the endless thoughts that plague my mind to pique its interest, so that it can latch on and shove it in my face for the next few days to prove to me how horrible a human being I am for having had that thought. It waits expectantly for me to say something stupid, so that it can spend the rest of the week berating me for my ridiculous lack of social skills. It hovers in the background until I find a new hobby, so that it can add it to the list of activities it has spoiled for me on account of the pressure I feel over needing it to be perfect. It eagerly waits for assignments to be given – oh, how it loves the uncertainty of not knowing if what I've done is what my instructor is looking for; and waiting for a grade is like I've given it a cookie. It throws a wild party the night before a test; and the unsettling calm and building anticipation I feel during the week before the test is just anxiety setting up for the big bash it's getting ready to throw.

It waits for the moments when I'm alone, when I'm at my most vulnerable. It waits for those moments late at night, when it and my racing thoughts – which it orchestrates – are my only companions.

It waits – it dares me – to fight back, sits and leans back, chuckling, as I dig my heels in and try desperately to maintain a sense of basic equilibrium in my own mind. I wait, at once optimistic and dubious, for a reprieve.

I wait for a solution to appear, to make itself known, to come riding in at long last. Then I realize, with mounting confidence and renewed resolve: I am the solution.

My Remarkable Talent
Imaginative Writing Inspired by an Entry in My Personal Waiting Journal
By Ryan Langan

I've got a remarkable talent for missing trains, buses, ferries, you name it. I miss them by seconds. By fractions of seconds. I get doors closed in my face more often than anyone alive. Take today, for example. I woke up at 10:50. Typically I have to leave by 10:52 to make the 10:57 at Jefferson. I left at 10:53, missed the train by one second.

"Hey, hold it! Hold that door!" I shouted, not at anyone in particular but at anyone who would listen. The old man within the doors literally smiled at me as they closed. What have I done to deserve this?

Needless to say, I spend a lot of time waiting around. And, usually, while I'm stewing in the common frustration of the commuter, interesting things happen. In the same way I have a proclivity to missing trains, I have a proclivity to draw strange individuals to me. Last night I missed my ferry to Staten Island. (By one minute, of course.). While I waited, a disturbed man approached me, talking to himself, maybe singing. We looked each other up and down a few times, wordlessly. Finally, he said, "Good to see you, Shake."

"What?" I asked. "I'm not Shake."

At this he laughed heartily. "Ah, Shake, you kill me. Knock it off."

"I am not Shake, man. My name's Ryan."

"Dude, I've been waiting for you for like forty minutes. I don't have time for this. Just give me the bag."

"I don't know what you're talking about."

At this point, he threw his arms up. He started screaming and yelling about how he's been waiting around all day. He pushed me and I pushed him back, and before I knew it, the ferry terminal security was pulling us off each other. We were taken into their office, questioned, and forced to fill out incident reports. The whole process took about twenty-five minutes. Now, the ferry only runs every half hour. I ran out of the office as the boarding doors were closing. Right as I got up to them, the terminal employee shut them and I missed it, by one second, yet again.

Hippity-Hoppity
Imaginative Writing Inspired by an Entry in My Personal Waiting Journal
By Gamal Amin

"Hippity hoppity...this is now my property," said some British guy probably in New York in the 1600s as they stole the land from the Native Americans and the Dutch. Fast forward 400 years, and here I am standing in the same place where the British guy probably hippity hoppitied. The only difference is that I am not stealing anything from the Natives and Dutch. Instead, the bank is stealing my soul because of all the student loans I have. I'm waiting for the day I finally pay off all those student loans, because then I can finally get myself a home and also say "hippity hoppity... this is now my property." Instead, that dream so far does not seem to be a reality given the present-day economic situation and housing bubble. As a result, I try my best to think in the present. But, when I say I can't wait for something, it is not because I am excited, rather it is because I literally can't wait for it, as I do not want to.

Family Feud
Imaginative Writing Inspired by an Entry in My Personal Waiting Journal
By Liala Ahamd

Fighting with someone you live with can be painful, toxic (yet cathartic), and all around intense. But after the dust is settled and the hurtful words exchanged linger in the anger-infested air, what do you do? I don't know about you, but in my family, pride prevents you from apologizing. Especially not immediately after a fight. No, usually fights end in door slams, adrenaline-driven-I-hate-yous and other dramatic ends.

But with family, there's never really an end, is there? Living under the same roof with someone means you're bound to run into them. And whether or not you're the type of person to let things go easily or if you carry every fight in your heart, you eventually have to make amends. However, instead of asking them if they paid the bill, cleaned the bathroom, have plans for the night..., you wait for them to do the asking. After the first few times of bumping into each other without exchanging a word, you convince yourself to disregard the mutual ignorance and come up with reasons as to why they should apologize first. You are content to pretend like having them in your life is optional and let your petulance prevent you from giving them even a perfunctory apology. You wait for them to break the ice, minding the fact that they are likely waiting for you to do the same. Instead of putting your pride aside, you, of course, continue your walking-on-eggs routine, as if both of you aren't waiting to get back to normal. You wait and wait and wait until you are desperate to disperse the tense air. Your stomach rumbles, your heart is heavy, and you realize you can't go another day like this. So you decide to prompt them with the only trivial subject that matters and hope that they respond. After letting out a deep breath, you step into the kitchen and when their back is turned, you ask, "What's for dinner?"

The Evolving Waiting Prayer
Imaginative Writing Inspired by an Entry in My Personal Waiting Journal
By Shanya Hopkins

I preyed on me and I prayed for you.
For 18 years, I wondered,
what were you like? Would life be better with you in it? Would
you love me?
And because I loved the idea of you,
I hated the idea of me.
I preyed on me and I prayed for you.
Yearned for you. A man that belonged to me,
whose arms bore home to solace and fingers served as sponges,
wiping and absorbing the tears and pain after hard days.
My ears pined to hear the soft whispers of I-love-you's roll from the lips
that my heart longed to see smile for the first time.
I opened the door and there stood a stranger,
you were the only recognizable one.
You knew who I was, you'd watched from afar until we were both ready.
Now was the time. You sold me that story on wanting to spend time
together and even said you had lined up a job interview for me.
An interview for me? You believed in me?
Throw on something nice,
you said,
something airy and easy.
A dress?
The job interviewer was going to be late, of course we could wait at your
girlfriend's apartment in the meantime.
I hoped it'd take hours.

This was the moment I waited for.
Let me look at you,
you said. I'd really grown into a beautiful young lady.
WOW. You finally noticed me, admired me even?
Who could've imagined that 18 years of praying would've finally paid
Off.

You said:
Take that dress off, I want to really see you.
I wanted you to see me for who I really was,
and be proud to finally know me.
I ached for you to want me. And you did.
You preyed on me and I prayed for death.
That soft whisper turned to forced haste
The hands that I wanted to hold me,
protect me,
now scared me.
The right cupped my breast and the left,
served as a sponge, penetrating my vulnerability
and soaking,
soaking up my fear.
Your tongue skated on my cheek,
figure eights on my frosted tears.
Did this mean you loved me?
There were two strangers on that couch,
and I recognized you, dad.

The Fire That Time?
Imaginative Writing Inspired by an Entry in My Personal Waiting Journal
By Trever Polk

It was a chilly day in late February, early evening. Class had just let out and I'd high-tailed it to the subway in three minutes so I could get home as soon as possible. Inside the building it had been warm – that uncomfortable warm you only feel in public buildings with centrally-controlled heat – but now, down on the uptown platform, it was cold from the air emanating from the street through the grates. I stood cross-armed, then tried putting my hands in my pockets, and started to adjust to the chill, until I detected a familiar scent. It smelled like someone had lit a fireplace.

At first I thought that sounded nice and was wishing I could have one. Then I realized there was little chance it was actually a fireplace, given that all the buildings above were stores with luxury condos on top, which as far as I know don't have a chimney. So then it occurred to me that a building could be on fire. But that would be nonsense: those condos were not made out of wood. The sort of people who would dwell in a place like that have no need for even wood paneling: make it nice and clean, sanitized. The train pulled up and I boarded into a crowd, which would probably make me warm. Still, I thought of the smell on the platform. I knew I'd never find out what it was or where it was coming from. Still, I wished for a nice fire on a cold day.

The Corpse Flower
Imaginative Metaphorical Writing Inspired by an Entry in My Personal Waiting Journal
By Michael McClenahan

Recently I found myself waiting for a meal that I was particularly excited to eat. When it came, it was just as delicious as I had anticipated. I was especially hungry and ate it ravenously. Nevertheless, when it was over, I felt disappointed. Despite having waited for the meal for over an hour and it having been cooked perfectly, I felt an emptiness and dissatisfaction as soon as I was done eating it. I wanted to go back to the moment just before the meal came when the anticipation for it was at its peak.

It reminded me of a time, several years ago, when New York City was preparing for an exceptional sight, *Amorphophallus titanum*, also known as the "corpse flower," which was getting ready to bloom for a brief 24-to-36-hour period. The blooming was something of an event. It can take a decade or more for the temperamental flower, one of the largest and most putrid-smelling in the world, to open.

The corpse flower popped on the evening of July 28. In order to capture the opening, the New York Botanical Gardens mounted a camera to live-broadcast the development of the bloom. After several media features, thousands of New Yorkers eagerly watched the live video feed on YouTube, waiting for the corpse to open.

I, on the other hand, waited in line along with crowds of other people for a glimpse of the flower during the public unveiling. When we were finally herded into the viewing room, the smell was utterly bizarre. The flower itself was alien and theatrical as it rose out of the tropical foliage. It looked like its name – *amorphos* meaning "misshapen" and *phallus* referring to the shape of the large cluster of flowers in its center. Part dead fish, part rotting trash, the smell made it difficult to stay in the room for long.

The event made for a strange contradiction. To wit, the flower swelled majestically with the budding of life only to rapidly expire and leave behind the smell of a corpse which designates its name. It felt like a more physical manifestation of the act of waiting itself. Waiting is always a waiting for – a desire for something that moves metonymically from object to object. Each time we acquire the thing we had been waiting for, it dies; that is, it becomes unimportant to us as soon as we inevitably find ourselves waiting for something else, something better.

CHAPTER 13

Paging Playwright Clifford Odets: What Is It We Are Left Waiting for in 1935 When We Are Left "Waiting for Lefty"?

Well, to put it in one word as college collaborator **Jason Chetram** did, "What people are waiting for is in one word, 'Lefty.'" Jason adds: "They are waiting for and relying on the union leader, Lefty Costello, to be able to champion change, and it is only when Lefty is found dead at the end of Clifford Odets' play WAITING FOR LEFTY are they able to take action on their own." Jason's answer was in response to the single prompt for Hunter College students' focused thinking as they read straight through Odets' seven vignettes of a one-act play written and set in New York City in 1935 in the midst of the Great Depression.

Other students offered such end products for the play's taxicab drivers' waiting as: waiting for hope, waiting for an improved economy for service workers, waiting for a living wage, waiting for the end of poverty, waiting for the elimination of union corruption, waiting for true workers' solidarity, waiting for the taming of the abuses of capitalism, waiting for courageous workers to stand up to exploiting bosses, waiting for the demise of prejudice and discrimination, waiting for improved social status and eventual social equality, waiting, fearfully, for the promise of theoretical communism, waiting for the end of backroom politics by political machines, waiting for the diminishment of human vulnerability, waiting for real change in workers' lives, waiting for a savior, waiting for action in any form, waiting for nothing because the taxicab drivers stop their waiting and take action by standing up for their rights and going on strike.

Writes college collaborator **Shanya Hopkins**:

> Playwright Clifford Odets was very methodical in the structuring of his political, philosophical, social, and economic commentary into the narrative of his play WAITING FOR LEFTY. Rather than simply using one storyline – that being the story of the union meeting – Odets makes use of seven related episodes or vignettes to allow the reader to understand the broader implications of such issues such as low wages, union corruption, the political machines, poverty, social status and the threat/fear of communism. This methodology more heavily highlights these issues and allows us to see how they affect the most vulnerable in American society. This is very different from Harold Pinter's way of addressing his ideas in THE DUMB WAITER because while Odets chooses to highlight key issues solely through narrative and plot, Pinter uses stage settings and the environment and scenery of the stage, as well as brief dialogue, to critique society's faults in terms of social class and economic power.

Note: Clifford Odets' original seven vignettes featured such archetypal characters as:

- *union boss Harry Fatt and wounded world war veteran Joe during a union meeting in which Fatt tries to dissuade the men from striking;*
- *Joe and his wife, Edna, in an argument about whether driver Joe should strike;*
- *the Lab Assistant Episode in which the industrialist Fayette tries to persuade chemical lab assistant Miller to spy on a project's leader;*
- *The Young Hack and His Girl episode, in which Florence and her brother Irv argue over Florence's continued dating of boyfriend Sid because Sid earns little money as a cabdriver;*
- *the Labor Spy Episode, in which a company spy is fingered as someone who has been breaking up strikes for years; and*
- *the Interne Episode, in which, Dr. Benjamin, a senior hospital intern, is fired because he is Jewish;*
- *a final episode in which a man named Agate Keller incites the drivers "to unite and fight," and not wait for Lefty, who may never arrive.*

Considering the question of whether any of these seven episodes should be edited or even eliminated from a 2020 production of WAITING FOR LEFTY, **Shanya Hopkins** writes:

> While I wouldn't edit anything out of Odets' play, I would add more vignettes; I believe this would allow the audience to further develop deeper understandings of the play's characters and more profoundly explore the complexities of the play's universal and still prevalent social and cultural issues. And, if I were to be cast in a 2020 production, of all of the play's fifteen characters I would want to play Edna, simply because she is the play's fiercest and strongest character; her story is one of the most important in WAITING FOR LEFTY because it is one that most often gets lost in history. Edna breaks many stereotypes – and she holds her own.

An Alternate Version of a Clifford Odets WAITING FOR LEFTY Vignette: Not With Florence and Sid But With Edna and Joe and a note from college collaborator Rabeya Rahman:

I chose to do an alternative version of the vignette in WAITING FOR LEFTY in which Florence and Sid decide to go their separate ways, after realizing that despite their love, their lack of financial stability is enough for them to abandon the idea of a future together. In the Clifford Odets vignette, Florence tries to reassure Sid that she doesn't care about money and that she'd rather they stay together. Sadly, Sid replies that he's seen it happen in the past how those who decide to stick together despite financial concerns end up not working out – that the female will end up hating it all and be dissatisfied. This reminded me of the earlier vignette featuring Joe and Edna. In a way, Sid and Florence are THAT couple: they have kids, they struggle with financial instability, they're evidently unhappy with things. With that in mind, I wrote an alternative to the later vignette, replacing Florence and Sid with Edna and Joe.

Opens with a girl and brother. Edna waiting for Joe to take her to a dance.

EDNA: I gotta right to have something out of life. I don't smoke or drink. So if Joe wants to take me to a dance, Ill go. Maybe if you were in love, you wouldn't talk so hard.
IRV: I'm just saying it for your own good.

EDNA: I know what's good for me and Joe is good.

IRV: What about mom? She's worried sick and you'll worry her to the grave. That boy is bad idea, Edna.

EDNA: Why are you all so set against him?

IRV: Mom told you plenty—it ain't him. It's that he ain't got nothing. Sure, we know he's serious, that he's stuck on you. But that don't cut no ice.

EDNA: He makes enough. And I work too. It's not just you running the house, you know. I stand there behind the counter the whole day. I think about him all the time! I love him!

IRV: Love ain't gonna pay the bills, Edna. You got to think long term! Dammit! I remember when you were a baby with curls down your back. Now I gotta stand here yellin' at you like this.

EDNA: MONEY MONEY MONEY! It's always about money and never about the simplest pleasure in life. Love. That's never enough! MONEY!! MY GOD, IRV! *A tear drop starts to trickle down her face.*

IRV: Don't yell, Edna. You gonna stop seeing him?

EDNA: *Silence...* I'll talk to him tonight. *Doorbell rings. Irv walks over to the door and opens it.*

IRV: Hello, Joe.

JOE: Hey, back atcha Irv. Nice seeing ya. *Irv looks at him with an almost perfect poker face, aside from the glimmer of sadness that washes over in his eyes right before he walks away.*

EDNA: *Still standing in the same spot, she begins to rock back and forth, fiddling with her hands behind her back.* Hello, Joey.

JOE: Hello, Honey. You look beautiful as ever.

EDNA: And you look tired.

JOE: I just need a shave.

EDNA: Well, draw up a chair up to the fair and I'll ring for a brandy and soda... like in the movies.

JOE: Well, if it were a movie, I'd bring a big bunch of roses.

EDNA: How big?

JOE: Fifty or sixty dozen—the kind with long, long stems—big as that... What's wrong Edna? You been fiddling with them gorgeous hands of yours behind your back like how you do when something's wrong. What's bothering you, darling?

EDNA: Naw, I just need a shave. *She smirks and breaks out into a laughter that is ever so short-lived.*

JOE: What's on your mind?

EDNA: Poverty. War.

JOE: What's on your mind?

EDNA: I got us on my mind, Joe. Night and day!

JOE: I smacked a beer truck today. Did I get hell! I was driving along thinking of US too. You don't have to say it—I know what's on your mind. I'm rat poison around here.

EDNA: Not to me...

JOE: My brother joined the navy and that uneducated basketball player gonna get paid a whole lot for defending this damn country that leaves us with little ways to make a good living. I'm tired of being a dog, Baby. We want to have kids, but that sort of life ain't for the dogs which is us. Baby! I get like thunder in my chest when we're together. If we went off together, I could maybe look the world straight in the face, spit in his eye like a man should. But this world and the darn system it's made of is constantly against us... Maybe we better stay apart?

EDNA: *Rushes towards Joe and hugs him around the neck.* Baby stop. Baby, listen. Oh, baby. I swear I wouldn't care. Irv was trying to tell me this just a short time ago. How money and living is hard and a relationship built on all love and no finance cannot happen. But I know it can! It must! I love you, baby! We can work together! Let's get married! Three years engaged. Let's get married soon! I swear it. I wouldn't care...

JOE: You would, you would—in a year, two years, a bunch of years, you'd curse the day. I seen it happen. I love you too, Edna. But... *He starts to cry. He tries to maintain composure as much as he can as he quickly wipes away the tears again and again, but the tears keep falling. He sits down on the nearest wooden chair and buries his head in his hands.*

EDNA: *Comes down on her knees, also crying. She lifts up his head and stares into his eyes.* I don't care, baby. I love you. Forget the world. Forget Irv. Forgot my mother. Stupid girl I am. I'll work more behind the counter. We'll have kids one day. I wouldn't care. I wouldn't care! *She hugs Joe around the neck as they both embrace and wet each other's shoulder with their tears.*

JOE: I seen it happen... I seen it happen... I seen it happen... *Joe mumbles over and over again. The lights darken around them and then the one spot light on the two characters begins to dim until there's nothing left but darkness.*

A Prequel to the Joe and Edna Vignette in Clifford Odets' WAITING FOR LEFTY and a dramatic note from college collaborator Shanya Hopkins:

I created a whole new scene for the play, envisioning it as a prequel to the "Joe and Edna" scene in WAITING FOR LEFTY – either as an opening additional part to the original scene or as an entirely separate scene.

The lights fade out and a white spot picks out the playing space within the space of seated men. The seated men are very dimly visible in the outer dark, but more prominent is Fatt, the industrialist, smoking his cigar and often blowing the smoke in the lighted circle.

A tired but attractive woman of thirty (Edna) rushes into the room towards the door, fastening the tie on her apron. Behind the door stand two men, of brutish build, in blue overalls – one of which has a pocket stuffed with bright yellow paper.

Childish squeals echo in the background.

Edna: Emmy, take your brother out of the bath and get him dressed for bed please.

Emmy (*screams from out of view*): Okay mommy!

The sound of knocks at the door.

Edna: I heard you the first ten knocks. I'm coming!

Edna looks through the small spheroid peephole. She hangs her head solemnly, as she unlocks the door, coming face to face with the two men.

Edna: Good Afternoon Fellas.
Both Men (*in unison*): Good Afternoon Ma'am.
Man One: We're here for Mr. and Mrs. Joe Collins.
Edna: I am Mrs. Collins.

Man One: Mrs. Collins, we're from Sir's Home and Furniture and we've come to repossess the items from your lapsed contract.
Edna: Lapsed contract? But we've made the last three payments in full and on time. I was going to pay it by the end of the week, honest.

Man Two: Mayb—

Man One firmly bumps Man Two with his shoulder. As Man Two drops his head, Man One and Edna exchange forced glances.

Man One: I'm afraid that's not an option ma'am. The document clearly states that it is at Sir's will to begin the process of repossession up to eight hours after the first missed payment.

Edna: I understand, but—

Man One: No buts Mrs. Collins. A contract is a contract and this one is binding. According to the contract your payment was due by 8 pm yestereve. It's now a quarter to two in the afternoon so we're here to collect. If you'll excuse us...

Edna steps to the side (back against the door) and the two men enter the apartment. As Man Two walks in, he takes off his hat, holds it tight to his chest.

As the men begin prepping the furniture to be moved, Edna watches helplessly as she sips her tea from the kitchen.

Edna: Those fucking pricks. One full day – We couldn't even get one full day to try and get the money together. Maybe Joe could've gotten another two-dollar advance from his supervisor, even though he didn't seem too happy giving it to Joe the last time. Maybe if he promised to work two days straight?? Probably not. I wouldn't even have to worry about these things if my husband wasn't such a coward. I planted all my hopes and dreams in Joe, and he left his to wither under the weight of the union. Ha! The union – what a joke. Paying union dues is about the only thing that Joe does faithfully and what does the union do for him? Abuse and blind him. The man's got no fight in 'im, he just takes it. My daddy warned me about this, Joe's lack of a backbone and all, and I stood up for him – and for what?! For this? When is he going to stand up for Emmy and little Joey? Hell, when is he going to stand up for me? We're barely getting by...

Edna opens and closes the cupboards.

Edna: Nothing, absolutely nothing. While Joe's out there playing choir boy
    in the union, what am I to do? What are my kids to eat? A few cans
    of salmon and a big cup of water to divert their young minds from
    the hunger pains? That was yesterday's dinner. Emmy is already
    growing out of her clothes and it's getting harder to hide, but does
    Joe care? No. Instead of taking action, striking and demanding
    better wages, he'd rather wait; wait for someone else to take action,
    wait for instruction from the bosses, wait, wait, wait. Well I can't wait
    any longer. You know, maybe running into Bud Haas last Sunday
    in church was truly God's Plan. He has a great job and he looked
    good – well, at least he looked well fed. I hope I didn't throw his
    number—
Emmy: Mommy, Joey is being a bad boy!

*Edna puts the mug down and storms out of view (presumably to the room
with her children).*

*Meanwhile the lights brighten back to the two men who are now down to
their last piece of furniture.*

Man Two: Saul, do we have to take the couch? Look around, she clearly
    has kids. If we take the couch, where will they sit?
Saul: They could sit on the floor for all I care Bob. We're here to do a job,
    a debt is a debt.
Bob: I know Saul. I'm just saying. Is there no other way to work this out?
    Maybe they're just going through a hard time. The contract said he's
    a taxi driver and I heard some buzz down at the pub last night that
    the cab drivers are barely getting paid enough to survive.
Saul: That's tough Bob, but again it's not our concern. They had two
    weeks from the last payment to get the money. There is nothing we
    can do. Sir paid us to repossess all of this furniture and that is what
    we are doing, that is our concern.
Bob: But Saul—
Saul: Enough. There's nothing else to discuss. What's done is done. Now
    grab that end and lift.

*As Saul and Bob carry the couch out the door, Edna reenters the room
and stands alone in the center.*

Edna: Is this what my life has come to? Has my physical reality finally
    caught up to the emotional emptiness that I've been feeling for

some time now? The pictures on the wall show a happy family, a family unburdened by financial distress and a family willing to do anything to keep afloat. What happened to us?! What happened to him?! Screw the boss. Screw the union. Actually, screw the whole goddamned system.

Edna begins to tear up.

Edna: I've got to pull it together. Someone has to be the man of the house, and if Joe won't do it then I will. Not just for me, but for the kids too. I bet Bud would never put me through this, he's a real man. A real man that makes a living. But I love Joe, I do. Maybe I'll give him one last chance. One more chance to grow a pair. Let me go clean up before he gets home.

Edna looks around the room one more time before heading to the kitchen to toss some water on her face and freshen up.

...

The tired but attractive woman of thirty (Edna) returns to the living room, drying her hands on an apron. She stands there sullenly as Joe comes in from the other side, home from work. For a moment they stand and look at each other in silence. Proceed with Odets' original "Joe and Edna" scene.

A 2020 Modified Version of the Intern Episode Between Dr. Barnes and Dr. Benjamin in Clifford Odets' 1935 Play WAITING FOR LEFTY By Trever Polk

DR. BARNES, an elderly distinguished man, is speaking on the telephone. He wears a white coat.

DR. BARNES. No, I gave you my opinion twice. You out-voted me. You did this to Dr. Benjamin yourself. That is why you can tell him yourself.

(Hangs up phone, angrily. As he is about to pour himself a drink from a bottle on the table, a knock is heard.)

BARNES. Who is it?

BENJAMIN. (without) Can I see you a minute, please?

BARNES. (hiding the bottle) Come in, Dr. Benjamin, come in.

BENJ. It's important–excuse me–they've got Leeds up there in my place–He's operating on Mrs. Lewis–the hysterectomy–it's my job. I washed up, prepared . . . they told me at the last minute. I don't mind being replaced, Doctor, but Leeds is a damn fool! He shouldn't be permitted —

BARNES. (dryly) Leeds is the nephew of Senator Leeds.

BENJ. He's incompetent as hell.

BARNES. (obviously changing subject, picks up jar) They're doing splendid work in brain surgery these days. This is a very fine specimen. . . .

BENJ. I'm sorry, I thought you might be interested.

BARNES. (still examining jar) Well, I am, young man, I am! Only remember it's a charity case!

BENJ. Of course. They wouldn't allow it for a second, otherwise.

BARNES. Her life is in danger?

BENJ. Of course! You know how serious the case is!

BARNES. Turn your gimlet eyes elsewhere, Doctor. Jigging around like a cricket on a hot grill won't help. Doctors don't run these hospitals. He's the Senator's nephew and there he stays.

BENJ. It's too bad.

BARNES. I'm not calling you down either. (Plopping down a lab jar suddenly) Goddammit, do you think it my fault?

BENJ. (about to leave) I know . . . I'm sorry.

BARNES. Just a minute. Sit down.

BENJ. Sorry, I can't sit.

BARNES. Stand then!

BENJ. (sits) Understand, Dr. Barnes, I don't mind being replaced at the last minute this way, but . . . well, this flagrant bit of class distinction– because she's poor —

BARNES. Be careful of words like "class distinction." Don't belong here. Lots of energy, you brilliant young men, but idiots. Discretion! Ever hear that word?

BENJ. Too radical?

BARNES. Precisely. And some day like in North Korea, it might cost you your head.

BENJ. Not to mention my job.

BARNES. So they told you?

BENJ. Told me what?

BARNES. They're closing Ward C next month. I don't have to tell you the hospital isn't self-supporting. Until last year that board of trustees met deficits. . . . You can guess the rest. At a board meeting Tuesday, our fine-feathered friends discovered they couldn't meet the last quarter's deficit — a neat little sum well over $100,00,000. If the hospital is to continue at all, it's damn —

BENJ. Necessary to close another charity ward!
BARNES. So they say. . . .

(A wait.)

BENJ. But that's not all?
BARNES. (ashamed) Have to cut down on staff too. . . .
BENJ. That's too bad. Does it touch me?
BARNES. Afraid it does.
BENJ. But after all I'm top man here. I don't mean I'm better than others, but I've worked harder.
BARNES. And shown more promise. . . .
BENJ. I always supposed they'd cut from the bottom first.
BARNES. Usually.
BENJ. But in this case?

BARNES. Complications.

BENJ. For instance?

(BARNES hesitant.)

BARNES. I like you, Benjamin. It's one ripping shame.

BENJ. I'm no sensitive plant–what's the answer?

BARNES. An old disease, malignant, tumescent. We need an anti-toxin for it.

BENJ. I see.

BARNES. What?

BENJ. I met that disease before–at Harvard first.

BARNES. You have seniority here, Benjamin.

BENJ. But I'm a Jew! (BARNES nods his head in agreement.)

(BENJ. stands there a moment and blows his nose.)

BARNES. (blows his nose) Microbes!

BENJ. Pressure from above?

BARNES. Don't think Kennedy and I didn't fight for you!

BENJ. Such discrimination, with all those wealthy brother Jews on the board?

BARNES. I've remarked before–don't seem to be much difference between wealthy Jews and rich Gentiles. Cut from the same piece!

BENJ. For myself I don't feel sorry. My parents gave up an awful lot to get me this far. They ran a little dry goods shop in the Bronx until their pitiful savings went in the crash last year. Poppa's peddling neckties. . . . Saul Ezra Benjamin– a man who's read Spinoza all his life.

BARNES. Doctors don't run medicine in this country. The men who know their jobs don't run anything here, except the conductors on the subway. I've seen medicine change–plenty–fancy implants, novel cancer treatments–but not because of rich men–in spite of them! In a rich man's country your true self's buried deep. Microbes! Less. . . . Vermin! See this ankle, this delicate sensitive hand? Four hundred years to breed that. Out of a revolutionary background! Spirit of '76! Ancestors froze at Valley Forge! What's it all mean! Slops! The honest workers were sold out then, in '76. The Constitution's for rich men then and now. Slops! (The phone rings.)

BARNES. (angrily) Dr. Barnes. (Listens a moment, looks at BENJAMIN) I see. (Hangs up, turns slowly to the younger Doctor) They lost your patient.

BENJ. (stands solid with the shock of this news but finally hurls his operation gloves to the floor.)

BARNES. That's right . . . that's right. Young, hot, go and do it! I'm very ancient, fossil, but life's ahead of you, Dr. Benjamin, and when you fire the first shot say, "This one's for old Doc Barnes!" Too much dignity–bullets. Don't shoot vermin! Step on them! If I didn't have an invalid daughter —

BARNES. (goes back to his seat, blows his nose in silence) I have said my piece, Benjamin.

BENJ. Lots of things I wasn't certain of. Many things these radicals say . . . you don't believe theories until they happen to you.

BARNES. You lost a lot today, but you won a great point.

BENJ. Yes, to know I'm right? To really begin believing in something? Not to say, "What a world!" but to say, "Change the world!" I wanted to go to Scandinavia. Last week I was thinking about it–the wonderful opportunity to do good work in their socialized medicine —

BARNES. Beautiful, beautiful!

BENJ. To be able to work —

BARNES. Why don't you go? I might be able —

BENJ. Nothing's nearer what I'd like to do!

BARNES. Do it!

BENJ. No! Our work's here– America! I'm scared. . . . What future's ahead, I don't know. Get some job to keep alive –maybe drive a cab–and study and work and learn my place —

BARNES. And step down hard!

BENJ. Fight! Maybe get killed, but goddam! We'll go ahead!

(BENJAMIN stands with clenched fist raised high.)

"Gesundheit": A Waiting-Game Episode During the 2020 Coronavirus Pandemic Following the Killing of Lefty Costello in Clifford Odets' 1935 Play WAITING FOR LEFTY

A note from dramatist Jason Chetram:

My short play GESUNDHEIT contains the following reference to Clifford Odets' play WAITING FOR LEFTY: at the end of the sixth vignette, entitled "Interne Episode," we find out in the concluding episode that after waiting the entirety of the play for Lefty to arrive and organize the strike properly, Lefty Costello has been found dead with a bullet in his head. The news of Lefty's death is what sparks the labor strike to begin as the curtain falls on the stage.

In my own vignette, the curtain rises since I want to highlight what would happen if someone who is in a financially desperate position becomes inspired by the story of Lefty and takes proactive action to set things in motion. My point is to highlight the power of sensationalism and its power in society – what lengths people are willing to go to try and manipulate this sensationalism to suit their desires.

It is March 2020. Once-bustling metropolises grind to a halt, resembling ghost towns devoid of human life as depicted in post-apocalyptic science fiction stories. The coronavirus has effectively strong-armed Italy, Japan, and many other countries into a quarantine state. The United States, next to be grappled into submission, is facing a growing number of contagious patients flowing steadily into ICUs. Asian-Americans, as well as Asians around the globe, feel the growing animosity and racial tension as the people blinded by fear and ignorance seek a scapegoat to direct their anxiety and frustrations. However, this contagion, known as COVID-19, without a trace of mercy, has taken yet another victim. Investors around the globe watch helplessly as the savings they slaved day after day to amass nosedive in the stock market.

Life-savings diminishing at astonishing rates, with years of holding evaporating day by day, hour by hour. What was once an avenue for wealth has widened the gap with reckless abandon.

Now, in this scenario, it is common advice by all investors, amateur to gray alike, to hold your investments in the market. If you are taking your money out now you'll be at a loss, so you should just wait until the market rebounds, it always does, doesn't it? This means you're now playing the waiting game. A waiting game full of anxiety and self-doubt, hope dwindles but yet you have no choice but to keep playing because the choice to quit the game will prove to be yet another regret. But what if someone who has run out of time gets dragged into the misery of having to partake in this awful game of suffering?

Curtain rises on a one-bedroom motel.

Enter two men, Len and Russ, who are meticulously gathering their belongings. A neatly packed suitcase lies on the room's bed with an inconspicuous duffle bag lying next to it.

Len: You remember the story, right, Russ? That's why we're doing this, we're going to be heroes just like Lefty when all this is over.

Russ: Yeah, but remember how granddad ended that story? Lefty gets shot in the head! I don't wanna get shot in the head, Len! No way!

Len: Listen, Russ, we're not getting shot in the head, you know why?

Russ: Why's that?

Len: It's 'cause we've got each other to watch one another's backs, see. Lefty worked alone, he didn't have no brother like you and I.

Russ: Oohh, I get ya bro. Oh! We can be Righty and Lefty!

Len (sighing): Sure, we can be Righty and Lefty, now hurry up we gotta get started on the duffle bag. If anything is out of place, there ain't no going back.

Russ: Hey bro, I get why we're doing this, I really do, but ain't there any other way?

Len: No there ain't. We got too much debt. We're drowning in it. And just our luck that the fine gentlemen we owe are in cahoots with the black market and God knows what else.

Russ: What's the black market have to do it with it? It's Berg we owe the money to.

Len: Black market means we're gonna get opened up like frogs and get our organs shipped express across the world like Amazon Prime.

Russ: Ain't so bad, huh, Len? Always wanted to travel the world, right?

Russ (laughing to himself, stops abruptly): Oi, Len, listen to this, "drowning in debt," so that's why they call 'em loan sharks!

(Rus laughing uproariously now.)

Len: (kissing his teeth): The hell's wrong with you, now's not the time to be a comedian, and keep it down.

Russ: Oh, loosen up a little, get too stiff and you'll make mistakes.

Len: Hmpf, yeah, yeah, whatever, give me a hand will ya.

Len picks up the duffle bag and turns it upside down, emptying out the contents on to the bed.

(Both men start working on the assembly of the bag's contents.)

Russ: It's kinda like a jigsaw puzzle, ain't it?

Len: Kind of, just start assembling it, make sure everything's right, we ain't getting no test runs.

Russ: I know I know. So, just for old time's sake, what's the plan again?

Len: The hell you mean "old times sake." How'd you forget the plan already?

Russ: It's just a refresher, come on, and even if I did completely forget, it ain't like you would just not tell me anyhow.

Len: Alright, alright, so remember in that video game we played a couple of years ago, the guys in the game wanted to raise their stock value, so they went around taking care of the competition. That's what we'll be doing, taking out the trash, hopefully, it'll be enough to kick the market back into gear. If you want more details, the nitty-gritty, I'll tell you later, but for now, just focus on your hands. What we're about to do might not fix the market right away, but we just gotta nudge it in the right direction, the media will take care of the rest.

Russ: Crazy to think, huh? How it all happened so fast. It took years to get as far we did and then it's all gone, like it never even effin' happened. What the hell did we go to college for? Spent four years studying economics and 10 years penny-pinching and investing in the market, doing everything the right way, by the book. And all for what?! For some bat soup virus to shit on everything we worked for?!

Len: Cool it, Russ. I know.

Russ: And Berg. Oh God, Berg. He believed in us, that's why he lent us so much money to use. He knew we were good for it. But now he's got his own people to answer to, twisted people, I tell ya. And now we can't pay it back and neither can he. He's got his wife and kids, we've just got each other. If those men get to his family before we make this right no doubt they'll-

Len: Enough! Enough, rambling! Listen, Berg's a good man, and he's also a smart man. He'll figure something out to deal with his problems, we just gotta deal with our own. That man believed in us, so we're going do right by him.

(Russ sharply exhales.)

Russ: You're right, Len. You're right. I'll go make us some tea, let me go light the gas. Besides, we're done with the assembly now, aren't we? We've gotten pretty good at this.

Len: Yeah, a cup of tea and then we'll head out.

(Russ is now fixing two cups with teabags after setting some water to boil.)

Russ: Good thing about this virus though is that it's got everyone wearing masks, no questions asked.

Len: You dope, it was the virus that got us into this mess in the first place.

Russ: At least we don't got it ourselves.

Len: That is one saving grace. If we'd had it, no way we would be able to go through with the plan, not a chance. After the tea let's head out before we give the virus a chance, I really don't like the looks of this motel anywa-

(A buzzing is heard from Russ's pocket. To Russ's surprise, his phone gets a text message; Len stares at him, appalled.)

Len: Who the hell are you texting? I told you to get a burner -

(A buzzing is heard from Len's pocket. The men look at each other in shock.)

Russ: Did they figure us out?

Len: No, no, there's no way, there's just no way that's possible. Let's just check the message, go on.

(Russ looks at his phone, his eyes widened, a look of defeat washes over his face.)

Len: Well who's it from? What's the bastard want from us?

(Russ, broken, speaks with a shaky voice.)

Russ: It says "State of Emergency: The United States is now in a quarantined state. Only military and authorized personnel are allowed to go outside."

Len: No...what the... no, not now...

Russ: What about the plan? What about Berg?! What about us-s-s? Wh-wh-wha-

(Russ's eyes begin to tear up, his mouth quivering as it opens and closes, as if he's about to start hyperventilating; Len walks up in front of his younger brother, face to face, and right as he put his hand on Russ's shoulder to comfort and console him in their moment of utter defeat by the hands of the virus...)

Russ: Wha-AACHHOOO!!

Curtain.

CHAPTER 14

Who Are the Barbarians Whose Arrival We Await in J. M. Coetzee's 1980 Novel "Waiting for the Barbarians"?

Our "waiting course" reading of 2003 Nobel-Prize winning author J.M. Coetzee's novel WAITING FOR THE BARBARIANS coincided in March of 2020 with the worldwide coronavirus pandemic and, consequently, with the substitution of student "distance learning" (and, frankly, a kind of "distancing teaching") of the novel over the course of a total of four online sessions.

Naturally, this was something the instructor of "The Literature of Waiting" had neither expected nor anticipated, so several of the "prompts," all of which had been created to stimulate on-campus class discussions, wound up becoming questions to be "answered" in writing for "homework," and the instructor never did get to do one of his favorite in-class activities – namely, have students compare and contrast the various front covers of different editions of the work of literature under study.

However, college collaborator **Shanya Hopkins**, who, the previous semester, had seen the instructor "do his thing with covers" a number of times in his other Hunter College course ("The Teacher and Student in Literature"), took it upon herself to seek out online three different covers for the 1980 novel WAITING FOR THE BARBARIANS. Her analysis of these "cover stories" follows my prompts.

Prompts

- *How does "waiting" figure in the content of the story, the lives of any and all of the characters, and the themes (points of view) that Coetzee, as author, might be exploring? Where does the "waiting" appear, what does it look like, what does it feel like, what constitutes it?*
- *What are all the various functions of "the border" throughout the story's plot? Would you agree – or not – that "waiting" is, in one way or another, architecturally the foundation of Coetzee's novel, and the bricks of his story, and the mortar of his authorial transitions, and the thematic steeple atop his finished structure? (Be prepared to argue persuasively for your position.)*
- *Who is the narrator of the story and how does that fact affect your understanding of such questions as: who are the "barbarians," what exactly makes them "barbaric," and how do they constitute a threat to freedom (why are they considered the enemy of the Empire – and what, exactly, is meant by the term "enemy")? As you read the novel, how does your understanding of the term "barbarian" coincide with or differ from the novel's? Where was there a change in any of this for you?*
- *In the original language of the ancient Greeks, the word "barbarian" literally meant "the other." How does this linguistic fact connect with one of the functions of "the border" in the novel's story?*
- *How does "love" (romantic or realistic) play a part in the lives of the novel's characters?*
- *In your reading of the novel, what is the nature, function, and importance of "communication" within the Empire and between the Empire and beyond?*
- *Differentiate the various non-physical ways any of the novel's characters experience "torture"?*
- *In Pogo, a famous Walt Kelly comic strip of several decades ago, the strip's main animal character – and that would be "Pogo" – coins (for cartoonist Kelly) the line "We have met the enemy and he is us." How apt would it be to talk about this still-quoted line at the end of Coetzee's novel?*
- *How does this novel compare (and contrast) with such "waiting" literary works as the play THE DUMB WAITER by Harold Pinter and the novel WAITING by Ha Jin?*
- *A two-act opera based on the novel (composed by Philip Glass with a faithful libretto by Christopher Hampton) premiered in*

2005, and a stage adaptation of Coetzee's novel opened in his hometown of Cape Town, South Africa, in 2012. How does Coetzee's novel lend itself (or not) to being dramatized for the stage as live theater? Also, based on your knowledge of African history, how fitting was premiering in South Africa the play version of WAITING FOR THE BARBARIANS?

- *A motion picture version of Coetzee's novel was completed late in 2019 and is likely to be released for worldwide distribution later this year. Based on your knowledge of American history, what might be the appeal of such a film to an American audience? Also, what might be the film's worldwide or universal appeal?*

- *Coetzee's novel's title comes from a 1898 poem of the same name by the Greek poet Constantine P. Cavafy. After you receive a copy of Cavafy's poem and read it at least twice, you should be prepared to talk about what specifically is in Cavafy's poem that might have appealed to Coetzee.*

- *Also, what would you say is the poet Cavafy's answer to the question he opens his poem with – "What are we waiting for assembled in the forum?" And one more thing: do you think that the novelist Coetzee would agree with the last line of Cavafy's poem (which says that "those people were a kind of solution")? Of course, be prepared to give your reasons why or why not.*

From College Collaborator **Shanya Hopkins**: "One More Thing" Concerning the Front Covers of Various Editions of the Novel WAITING FOR THE BARBARIANS

One of the things we often looked at when starting a work of literature in our previous course on "The Teacher and Student in Literature" was the cover of the book or, most often, the various covers for different editions of the same novel. With our distance learning, I felt like we got robbed of that experience, so I did a little research of my own and found three covers online for Coetzee's WAITNG FOR THE BARBARIANS and wanted to share some of my ideas and see what you thought.

The first cover is the cover of the edition that I own. The girl shown has stringy black hair with a bang across her forehead, a white fur-like coat, and "pretty" features. When I first looked at the cover, when I got the book in the mail, I believed her to belong to the group that was "non-barbarian" – she seemed innocent and pure, especially since she was surrounded by flowers. I believed her to be one of the ones doing the waiting for the barbarians. As I read the novel it became clear that she fit the description of the blind "barbarian" girl, who the Magistrate grew to have an affinity for. However, with the progression of the novel my opinion on which side she was on did not change. It became clear that she was in fact "waiting for the barbarians," with the barbarians being the members of the Empire, the Magistrate included.

On the next cover, we see a small child-like figure hiding behind straw figures that were made to look like soldiers guarding a border wall. For me, this symbolized the deceptive nature of the Empire because while it had no true evidence of a threat from the so-called "barbarians," the Empire evoked fear and support from the people by bringing in soldiers and sending them out to search for prisoners. In all actuality the soldiers were immature with a child-like naivete that fueled an unwavering obedience and a lack of questioning of authority, even when their morality was called into question. The hiding child also serves to symbolize the townspeople and how they willingly remained in ignorance, shielding themselves behind the military and violence to avoid actually looking over the border themselves (had they given themselves the opportunity to see, they would've realized that there was no "barbarian" threat and that they were hiding behind the real barbarians).

The last cover was particularly interesting to me because I felt that it heavily contrasted with the image of the girl on the first cover. It is more masculine-looking, with harsher features and a troubled expression – void of happiness. The girl's body is marked, seemingly representing the scars from her torture in the novel. These scars provide a physical representation of the girl's history, which is a major recurring theme with the Magistrate in the novel and could've contributed to his slight obsession with the blind "barbarian" girl.

Many, many thanks, Shanya – that more than covers it!

Students in "The Literature of Waiting" course came up with the following fairly comprehensive but far-from-complete list of examples of "waiting" carried out by the characters in J. M. Coetzee's WAITNG FOR THE BARBARIANS:

- waiting for the defeated aboriginal enemy (the barbarians according to the Empire) to return and take back their land;
- waiting to lose their freedom to a conquering enemy;

- waiting anxiously with the frontier town's Magistrate for the representative of the Empire (Colonel Joll) to leave (and to leave the Magistrate alone and in the stillness of his almost-"retiring" life);
- Colonel Joll's waiting to get "the truth" from "the enemy" before he quits the frontier town;
- waiting for understanding and resolution as the Magistrate acts out the roles of half-hearted seducer, confused father, and perverted interrogator ("The joy has gone from my life. I spend all day with lists and numbers, stretching petty tasks to fill the hours");
- waiting it out as the Magistrate, the girl, and the contingent of Empire soldiers travel in treacherous weather well into the lands of the "barbarians" to return the girl to her people;
- waiting for the Magistrate's tortured time in the local jail to be over and for him to have his day (and say) in court;
- waiting for Joll's return;
- waiting for suffering and pain to finally be over;
- waiting for the night to pass and for things to calm down during the panic caused by the soldiers' destroying of the villagers' homes;
- waiting to see whether the soldiers would abandon the town or stay through the winter;
- waiting for death;
- waiting to be forgotten by history (only time will tell).

For an imaginative piece of writing, students were asked to create a poem that would have as its title "Waiting for the Barbarians." The poem could have any content, look, diction choices, sound, tone, poetic techniques, length, structure, and rhythm; the only requirement was that this original poem could legitimately be entitled "Waiting for the Barbarians" (and that any reader of the poem would see that to be the case).

Almost a dozen of these "waiting for the barbarians" poems follow, beginning with one by college collaborator **Nattapat Karmniyanont** whose three columns of poetic lines get read, for maximum meaning and effect, in the following manner and sequence:

✓ first the line of words in the left-hand column, immediately followed by (and down to) the single word in the middle column (with particular vocal attention to the three different punctuation marks that follow the word "barbarians");

✓ then, up to the line of words in the right-hand column, immediately followed by (and again down to) the single word in the middle column (with particular vocal attention to the three different punctuation marks that follow the word "barbarians");

✓ and then, back to the next line to be spoken in the left-hand column (and so on until you reach the questioning tone of the final three lines of the poem).

Waiting for the Barbarians?
By Nattapat Karmniyanont

They rape, they kill!		They burn, they steal!
	Barbarians!	
Our families, our friends!		Our land, our home!
	Barbarians!	
They cut, they cleave!		They stab, they gore!
	Barbarians!	
We're starved, we're hurt!		We're tired, we're dying!
	Barbarians!	
They'll die, they'll regret!		They'll bleed, they'll beg!
	Barbarians!	
Spirits help us against		Lord aid us against
	Barbarians!	
We fall, we perish!		We drop, we succumb!
	Barbarians!	
The land weeps blood		The rivers dyed crimson
	Barbarians.	
They shout, they cry...		They weep, they pray...
	Barbarians.	
We killed, we maimed		We stole, we raped
	Barbarians.	
We ran, we fought		We hid, we blamed
	Barbarians.	
They're hurt		They're dying
	Barbarians	
We're bloodied, we're		We're monsters. We're
	Barbarians?	

Waiting for the Barbarians
By Trever Polk

They'll come from the streets,
they'll come from the parks,
not from the wilderness,
but from the countryside farms.

Somewhere in a house is a man or
a woman, thinking how nice it'd be
if their spouse was gone.
One is in the right and one in the wrong,
one is the bad guy and the other is good,
but if they're the thinker or the thought of
I can't tell at all.

On someone's street in front of some house some night
there is a man in a car, or not, just standing
with a machete or a gun, waiting for the time
when the target can be seen.
The target doesn't know, yet they too are waiting.

Not five miles away, maybe at the same time
five men in suits sit at a boardroom table
discussing how to handle the crisis:
not the one their drugs cause others
but the one the others are causing them.

And a few hours south, a building old and white,
like the nearby house's past residents,
sits and waits for tomorrow, when
men and women will come inside,
dwell in the bowels of it,
argue what changes should or should not be made.

Who is waiting and who are they waiting for?
Everyone waits for the other;
someone sometime will always be the barbarian,
someone else will always be waiting.
Are they, too, barbaric?
It depends who you ask:
even the Greeks did some horrible things.

Waiting for the Barbarians
By Bianca Correa

As I prepare myself for the long day ahead of me, I peer out my bedroom window and as expected there are many citizens marching towards the town square.

I sigh and feel my chest tighten as I walk out my front door and onto the streets, joining my fellow citizens in the march towards the great town square.

As we arrive at the town square, we are met with the emperor's court jester and he begins to announce the news that we have all dreaded as we marched in unity.

"We have been notified that the barbarians have entered our land and are heading in this direction," he exclaims as the women and children start to whimper.

He pauses and states, "It is safe to assume that their objective is to destroy our empire and claim this land as their own" – but is interrupted by the sudden arrival of our grand Emperor Baron.

"My people. My beautiful people. We must protect our land at any cost against the evil barbarians.

We must defend the lives of not only our family and friends but our neighbors, our people," he firmly states as silence fills the crowd.

Silence so profound that you can hear the person next to you take a breath.

"We will take the war to them and destroy their people just like they were planning to do to us," Emperor Baron passionately exclaims.

Emperor Baron continues with his speech but I can no longer hear him as I'm filled with dread and anxiety.
Why can't we stay our ground and protect the empire?
Why must we stoop down to the level of the Barbarians?
I watch him walk towards his steed with his knights and I can't help but wonder.

As the crowds disperse, I stay in the shadows and observe the emperor's court jester.

He's speaking with consuls and I can't help but notice the change in his facial expression.

From a face filled with sorrow to an evil smirk.

Who are we waiting for?

Are we truly waiting for the evil barbarians that seek to take our land?

Or is Emperor Baron and his court the barbarians, led by a thirst for power and land?

Who are the barbarians?

Waiting, for the Barbarians
By Patrick Diaz

I used to see
The Beauty,
In the sand,
Blowing in the wind
In the smile
On my father's face
I used to see
The beauty
In fire
Now I don't see,
And the fire reminds me
Of charred flesh,
And my father's death
At the hands
Of Barbarians,
The memories
Of beauty
In still moments
Through the night
A breeze
Through sand
A smile on
My father's face
My life before,
the Barbarians came.

Waiting for the Barbarians
By Fawzi Saleh

They are the enemies.
They are the cause of problems; all chaos stems from them.
And so the colors of yin yang battle eternally, light and dark each pointing the finger at the other.
But just like light is the absence of darkness and vice versa, there really is no such enemy.
Or at least, it begins with ourselves.
The mirror shows the origin of all problems, the real enemy.
Yet pride does not allow us to admit this.
And so we wait.
We wait by looking for people who seem like good candidates.
And once we've identified them, we label them and attack.

Waiting for the Barbarians
By Gabriella Tuchman

They will not find me
For I am hidden quite well
I will stay silent

I hear them coming
I await their arrival
They do not scare me

They will ransack town
Yelling, smashing, destroying
Time to run away

I am all alone
Waiting for Barbarians
How should I respond?

Waiting for the Barbarians
By Carolyn Reyes

These men are clearly superior, stronger, better
They play tricks on the mind more than anything
They may flood our fields but then they leave.
It's a never-ending cycle of fear
What if one day they decided to stay?

How can we defend ourselves?
Do we even try?
They've been watching us.

They've been watching the whole empire
They can probably run the show better than us
Does that mean we surrender?

The agony is in waiting to see what they will do
The agony is all the years and seasons spent fearing instead of living...
Well, we do live a life, but one that is only surrounded by them.

Waiting for the Barbarians
By Gamal Amin

Tell me why...
I cannot wait for you.

Tell me why...
I must conquer you.

Tell me why...
It is something that I must do.

Tell me why...
Is it true?

Tell me why...
Have you witnessed the slew?

Tell me why...
The barbarian is within you.

Waiting for the Barbarians
By Jason Chetram

Idiots, every single one of them
From their idiot ideas to their idiot voices
Idiots, born without a brain stem
When another idiot joins, another rejoices

What makes an idiot, an idiot?
Someone who is not me, myself or I
Even those who are born unfortunate?
They shall be idiots till the day they die

Outsiders get labeled barbarians
As such I am the same
Outside of me are all barbarians
But this loneliness brings much pain

Idiots, as far as the eye can see
Idiots, without them there is no "me"
A sense of self comes from a sense of other
My fellow idiot, oh brother, my brother.

Waiting for the Barbarians
By Rabeya Rahman

Psst. Did you hear? The Barbarians are coming!
The Barbarians are coming?
The Barbarians are coming!
Oh dear. The Barbarians are coming!
…
…
…
The Barbarians are coming!
The Barbarians are coming!
The Barbarians are coming!
…
…
…
The Barbarians are coming!
The Barbarians are coming!

The Barbarians are coming!

...

...

...

The sun's setting.
Maybe not today then.

...

...

...

The Barbarians will come.

Waiting for the Barbarians
By Shanya Hopkins

Know thy enemy and expect the worst.
They are coming.

Soothe the anxieties that plague the feeble minds,
Galvanize the men to begin preparations,
Prepare the animals for slaughter.

Draw up the plans,
Dig the trenches,
Succumb to impatience,
Prepare the men for war.

Know the enemy and fear the worst.
They are coming.

Take preliminary action,
Clear the fields,
Set fire to the square,
Prepare the children for slaughter.

Allow the lingering fears to sketch
the images of the barbarians,
know thy enemy, know thy self,
They are coming.

Wait in relief.
Wait with joy.

For the Barbarians cannot destroy what ceases to exist.

Know they enemy, know they doom, and should they not arrive,
Know thy gloom.

Waiting for the Barbarians
By Christina Louie

We sit in shiny castles
with our chests puffed out,
noses turned up

Because we are the ruling.

We tell all the townspeople to
brace themselves for

The Outsiders.

Big, mean, savages:

They will burn your land,
Rape your daughters,
And eat your flesh.

They will overthrow our
Rational Legislation
for their savage ways –
They will make you all slaves.

Because they do not speak our language,
Because they do not look like us,
Because they are not the same people as us.

They are not meant to be
Liked,
Bargained with,
Or spoken to
They are only to be
Hated.

And what can we say,
We will continue to protect our Nation;
We will get rid of these pests;
We will stomp them right out of existence;
We will name them the

Barbarians.

Waiting for the Barbarians
By Valeria Diaz-Huertas

Waiting for the barbarians
When will they arrive? You ask
Nobody knows
Are they already here?
Perhaps

Is it you?
Is it I?
What do they look like?
Who exactly are the barbarians?
Do they know they are barbarians?
Do they know what we call them?
What it means?
Would they agree?

When they arrive will they announce themselves?
Will they say: we are the barbarians?
Or will they say that we are the barbarians?
Will they look at us?
At our faces, our houses, our customs?
The same way we look at them
At their faces, houses, and customs

CHAPTER 15

Can't Wait to Read Charles Dickens' 1861 Novel "Great Expectations" And Five Other Works of "Waiting" Literature?

Well, Then, Expect to Meet (1) Pip and Estella and Mrs. Havisham, (2) Robinson Crusoe and His Man Friday, (3) Completely Fine Eleanor Oliphant and Her Mother, (4) Eleanor Vance and Her Haunted House, (5) Rosencrantz and Guildenstern (But Not Really Prince Hamlet) and (6) Newland Archer and Madame Olenska in an Age of Innocence

"My father's family name being Pirrip, and my Christian name Phillip, my infant tongue could make of both names nothing longer or more explicit than Pip. So, I called myself Pip, and came to be called Pip" – the opening sentences to Charles Dickens' 1861 novel GREAT EXPECTATIONS.

Reader-as-Waiter Shanya Hopkins on
Waiting for, Expecting, and Manifesting "Great Expectations"

Waiting and expecting are active participants in a symbiotic relationship, married together by characteristics of their nature. When one "waits," actively or inactively, one remains in a state of repose until something happens. This act of waiting is often unwanted, and a state not entered into by choice. One "expects" that said person to hold the belief that something will happen (definitively, of course) or that they will in time become the bearer of an anticipated moment, action, or thing. Upon carrying said expectation, one "parks" it mentally and in the interim, temporarily moves on in an occupied waiting. In the 1861 novel "Great Expectations" by Charles Dickens, Pip develops "great expectations" and in turn participates in an active "waiting," whose nature evolves and takes different faces over the course of his life.

In the first stage of his life, Pip develops an unyielding appetite for a higher-class society lifestyle and a world in which he was uncommon – a *gentleman*. This appetite, developed after a brief encounter with the wealthy Miss Havisham, fostered the "great expectations" that would change the course of his life. From the development of these expectations, Pip begins his waiting; in hoping and waiting to one day become a gentleman and get closer to Estella, Pip's "waiting" takes the form of manifestation. He takes a truly determined approach to waiting – through lessons, by pursuing knowledge from anyone he could obtain it from, and by becoming hypercritical of the "common" world in which he resides. He grows a dull impatience with waiting for his expectations to come to fruition and even attempts to change his environment to conform to the one he expects, as seen in his attempted educating of Joe.

In the next stages of his life, his teenage years and adulthood, Pip continues to wait for the manifestation of his "great expectations." In waiting to obtain social status, wealth and honor, he expects that his social advancement will ensure romantic advancement with Estella; and it is this expectation that fuels the essence of his waiting. In the process, Pip deluded himself in order to make "waiting" for his expectations more bearable.

Ultimately, it becomes clear that his expectations clouded his waiting and thus clouded his humanity in terms of his relationships with those who cared for him despite his social class fortune. He feels disappointment and embarrassment when he realizes that his life was truly not how he expected it to be, and that happiness and loyalty were not tied to wealth, but rather existed more predominately in the "common" world which he ran from with his "waiting." The ultimate betrayal of his expectations comes with the discovery that his benefactor is not of the status he so lusted after, and furthermore neither is the girl he loved but never obtained (if we err on the side of Dickens' original ending to this classic).

In my fourth reading of the novel, this time with the "waiting," I once again found myself entranced with Dickens' use of language and imagery. "Great Expectations" is a multidimensional novel that continues to give to its readers all the way through to the end. Without question it should be studied, in its entirety, as a novel in the course "The Literature of Waiting." Rather than replacing one of the other novels, "Waiting" or "Waiting for the Barbarians," "Great Expectations" would fit perfectly as the third novel of the course. Dickens' novel explores the individual themes of "waiting" tackled by the other two novels. In the novel "Waiting" by Ha Jin, Lin, Manna, and Shuyu take part in a "romantic waiting" that in multiple ways leads to disappointment upon the conclusion of their waiting. Furthermore, Lin's waiting leads to internal realizations regarding his motives for waiting and the role of "waiting" in desire.

Similarly, in the novel "Waiting for The Barbarians," the Magistrate, in "his waiting," self-reflects on the idea of romantic love and desire. In "Waiting for the Barbarians," we also gain perspective into the intertwined relationship between "waiting" and the consequential effects on social order in response to action or inaction. In this characteristic "waiting," the Magistrate also realizes that in the course of this waiting his personal moral compass has come into question and, in turn, his "waiting" takes him on a journey through the relationship between morality, humanity, and justice. "Great Expectations" encompasses many of the experiences with "waiting" as exhibited in the other two novels primarily through the eyes of Pip, but also in minute ways through the other equally important characters. The novel provides an uncommon foray into the relationships "waiting" has with romance, society, class structure, and morality. Pip, Lin, and the Magistrate all experience an emotional evolution (even though very small in Lin's case) and learn about themselves through their "waiting." Thus, all three novels provide insights into the psychoactive aspect of waiting.

Despite my love for Dickens, I would not recommend the incorporation of director David Lean's 1946 film adaptation of the novel into the course "The Literature of Waiting." While the film is cast quite well and captures the essence of the novel's locations through masterful cinematography, the condensed version of the story leaves much to be desired. A few scenes into the movie I noticed many key characters were missing and, as such, their dialogue was missed in the early character developments. Pip's relationship with Joe was not addressed in the slightest, in Pip's younger years, and as a viewer I felt robbed of "Joe" moments that were pivotal in Pip's development.

The film also bounces from scene to scene, missing meaningful connections between Pip and his environment as well as between the characters and events. The rearranging of events in Pip's life, such as the premature passing of Mrs. Joe, the complete absence of Orlick, and Pip's student-teacher relationship with Biddy completely took away the essence of the novel I've come to love so deeply. With so many key elements missing, it would serve no value in any consideration of "waiting" in "Great Expectations."

Reader-as-Waiter Nattapat Karmniyanont on the 1861 novel GREAT EXPECTATIONS by Charles Dickens

Is waiting a momentary act done while the object of your desire draws closer to your grasp? asks **Nattapat Karmniyanont**. Or Is it a life-long journey that you realize was filled with activities that constitute little more than a momentary pause to distract you from the absolute totality of human mortality?

It's both, and so much more. What about those moments where you achieved your present goal, but then, after a brief sense of accomplishment, you wait again. To me, these ideas are expressed best in Charles Dickens' novel "Great Expectations" for the simple fact that we get to witness the entire life of another person.

Pip waited through his life in a combination of complaints, resignation, and distractions. We see his wait for Estella, his wait to be a gentleman, his wait for money, but what about his writing lessons? His brief apprenticeship? His dinners with Herbert? Well, certainly many would half-heartedly list them as scenes of waiting, much the same way we would sigh with exasperation "of course the train is late" without much thought, but that's just it. Life isn't all "waitings" that reveal some big theme at the end or "waitings" that lead to some big pay-off at the end; most of our waiting is those pointless waits that we can't explain away and don't think much of.

Now comes the hard part: which novels do I feel should be replaced with "Great Expectations." Both "Waiting" by Ha Jin and "Waiting for the Barbarians" by J. M. Coetzee are amazing novels about waiting. One a vivid depiction of life for Lin Kong as he navigates through the legal and moral system of Communist China to try and achieve happiness. The other a powerful piece shedding light on the hypocrisy associated with labeling and the dark side of any government shown through writing that will leave the haunting scenes stitched into your mind.

Coetzee's piece is crafted with a careful hand, assembling the numerous intricate parts in such a way that they all come together into a great machine to shine a light on all who read it. This piece is like a lighthouse, giant structures used to shed light on the truth behind the situation – in this case, the truth about the barbaric nature of civilization out for its own gain.

However, if "Waiting for the Barbarians" is like a lighthouse, then the topic of waiting would be like the sun. A lighthouse is constructed for a purpose, and so every part from the shining beacon to the sturdy base must work together to bring that purpose to view. In this sense, waiting in the story is a cog in the machinery, it is a means to an end, a way to further develop the story. While this practice is all well and good, use all the tools you have to craft your work, as they say, but this artificial wait is too forceful, too filled with meaning. It undermines the meaninglessness that most real waiting represents. Those meaningless moments that accumulate into who you are. Simply, waiting is not the point of the novel, the barbarian is.

On the other hand, if "Waiting for the Barbarians" was a lighthouse, then "Waiting" by Ha Jin is a bonfire. The main theme of this piece is very straight forward. Lin wants to be happy, and this leads him down the path to divorce Shuyu to marry Manna, but also a trail of regret. The quiet, uneventful waiting of each character intermixing with the stressful and chaotic waiting of life, in general, creates a very relatable atmosphere. And while Coetzee's waits are always drowning with hidden meanings and insightful commentaries, many of Jin's "waitings" are just that – waiting. Lin's agitated escape to the park, showing his anger and disillusionment. Manna's ecstatic impatience for Mai Dong's letters, showing her love-struck heart. Shuyu's patience, showing her single-minded reality. These simple acts of waiting add to the more human aspect of waiting, not as a catalyst for change or time for societal reflections but as a fact of life. Turning the work as a whole to a piece about intrapersonal struggles that will come up as we progress through our life of waiting.

So, now that we have reached this point, which piece should it be? For this course entitled "The Literature of Waiting" with the aim to explore "the existential relationship between human life and time," what kind of waiting are we actually looking for? I'm waiting to figure that out myself.

But, would it not be a great benefit to us, rather than taking a glimpse at a moment spent waiting, to experience the "waitings" of a whole life? I believe there is more to waiting than just waiting for A and B or for a moment that will lead to some great revelation. So, with a heavy heart, I say that "Great Expectations" should replace "Waiting for the Barbarians."

On a side note, if the 1946 movie version directed by David Lean was to be considered, then I would say that all three works can be included. However, the movie version does not include certain waiting scenes that I thought would be great if added, like the scene where Joe tries to compare bread with the worried Pip and the letter Pip wrote for Joe – but other than that I think it would be an adequate substitution.

Readers-as-Waiters Nattapat Karmniyanont and Shanya Hopkins Exchange Distance-Learning Emails on Their Respective Reactions to Charles Dickens' Waiting Novel GREAT EXPECTATIONS

From Nattapat to Shanya:

What can I say about such a great piece of work to do it justice? I don't know, but I can say that your "waiting" essay on "Great Expectations" was excellent. From the beginning to the end I can feel your love for this book emanating from your awe-inspiring writing. I absolutely agree that Dickens' take on the intricacies of "waiting" is a must for a course on "The Literature of Waiting," although my heart goes out to our future colleagues in that course if they are required to read all three "waiting" novels in their entirety. As for the movie version of the novel, I know, right? Those Joe moments – Joments – were my favorite parts of the story and I was very disappointed in the exclusion of these Joments.

From Shanya to Nattapat:

Good evening (or very early morning), Nattapat,

I appreciate your feedback on my work and your picking up on my love for this classic. From the moment I read (and reread) your piece it resonated. Your writing was insightful and a masterful exploratory foray into "waiting." Your first paragraph tackled one of the "study of waiting"'s biggest questions and, in the same token, spoke volumes about what can be "expected" from "Great Expectations."

When I knew I would be reading the novel for this course on "The Literature of Waiting," I resolved to approach it differently. Through fresh lenses I sought to pay closer attention to the finer details, including the smaller moments of waiting (already knowing the big moments, of course), so that I could see if there is a pattern to the ways in which people wait and if life's moments of waiting are interconnected. Your analysis of Pip's waiting hit at the core of my focused reading. While I don't fully agree that most of our waits (or Pip's) are pointless – nor do I claim to have all the "waiting" answers – your deconstruction of Pip's life was attentive, calculated, and thorough. I was thrilled to see someone else also consider the small moments of waiting in the novel.

Now on the hard part – your decision on how the book should be added to the course. Your use of the lighthouse metaphor regarding "Waiting for the Barbarians" by J.M. Coetzee was so amazingly creative and much appreciated. It allowed me to look at the novel from a "brighter" point of view, a view less foggy and clouded than my personal bias stemming from my strong liking of the novel. I am intrigued by your analysis of the novel's relationship with waiting. I don't see "waiting" as the means to an end in the novel; rather, I believe the concept of the "barbarian" is the means. The idea of the "barbarians" was a catalyst to jumpstart the Magistrate's consciousness of his waiting. I found "waiting" to be the most prevalent theme in the novel, and I believe that the novel masterfully approaches and displays the multiple and varied types of "waiting" in nature.

While I agree that the plot line and central theme of the novel "Waiting" by Ha Jin are more straightforward, I believe that "Waiting for the Barbarians" is genius in that it provokes thinking about "waiting" by making the reader wait. It would break my heart if "Waiting for the Barbarians" was removed from the course, but I definitely agree that "Great Expectations" should be added.

Future students of "The Literature of Waiting" would appreciate your concern for their reading load, but I believe in their capabilities. Professor E's courses are in no way for the faint-hearted, and anyone who stays with a course of his after reading his syllabus and calendar of assignments on Day One of the class has the will and capacity to succeed. I definitely think it is doable (we did it! And did it well, might I add!). Maybe this could be a spring break reading assignment?

I have enjoyed every experience that I've had with your writing this semester (in class, in print, and digitally), and I hope that we have this opportunity again.

Thank you,

Shanya Hopkins

P.S. Glad you agree about the movie; they left out a lot of key moments in Pip's relationships and it definitely did no justice for the novel.

P.P.S. Sorry for the long email – I have a bad habit of long emails and long titles for my writing pieces.

Reader-as-Waiter Massiel Sanchez on the 1861 Novel GREAT EXPECTATIONS by Charles Dickens

In "Great Expectations," Charles Dickens illustrates the precarious nature of expecting and waiting.

Becoming a gentleman didn't grant him what he wanted. In order to realize this, though, he had to wait, wait to see the validity of his expectations. Here Dickens highlights a troubling reality: we tend to figure everything out when it's already too late. There is no way around it, in order to obtain wisdom, we have to wait…, make some bad decisions, wait some more and only then do we begin to truly understand ourselves and our desires.

As a Shipwrecked Robinson Crusoe Might Have Uttered When He Saved an Escaping Prisoner from Being Eaten by Cannibals: "Thank God, It's Friday."

Reader-as-Waiter Gamal Amin on the 1719 Novel ROBINSON CRUSOE by Daniel Defoe

Ask yourself this: why is it that Daniel Defoe's "Robinson Crusoe," a book written in the 1700's, is still an iconic text today? If there is any book to substitute for one of the other "waiting" novels in our course on "The Literature of Waiting," it is "Robinson Crusoe." The reason is because this novel is innovative, and "Robinson Crusoe" is emblematic of "waiting." It tells the tale of a human being, a soul, trapped on a deserted island.

The book was so captivating that the readers back then thought it was real, and for good reason. Because it is related to the human experience of waiting, "Robinson Crusoe" is the tale of a shipwrecked sailor who is without human companionship until the unexpected arrival of another man whom he names "Friday" because of the day of the week he appeared. (Crusoe teaches "Friday" English and converts him to Christianity.)

Humans are social animals, and nothing makes you long more (and that's a type of "waiting") for human contact than social isolation. Such lack of hope and desperation (another type of "waiting") does not necessarily capture the reader's imagination because the reader does not have to imagine it. The reader experiences it. The novel "Robinson Crusoe" should be considered a requirement for the course on "The Literature of Waiting" not for its physical realism – a shipwreck, deserted island, and so on – but for its emotional realism which, at its core, is more "real" than anything else to represent the acts and emotions of "waiting."

Reader-as-Waiter Wardah Malik on Spiritual Awakening as a Kind of Waiting in the 1719 Novel ROBINSON CRUSOE by Daniel Defoe

I think the 1719 novel "Robinson Crusoe" by Daniel Defoe should become a required reading in the course "The Literature of Waiting" because I believe the themes of the book – survival, spiritual growth, and self-sufficiency – are a part of everyone's everyday life, and to understand these themes is very important. Overcoming fears and obstacles in your life takes a lot of hard work, and reading a book that has those certain themes can help a person figure out what they have to do. The theme of survival and spiritual growth leads Crusoe to realize that wants and needs are different parts of life, and not the same. Just because you want something doesn't mean you need it in your life. Being away from civilization and distancing himself from negative aspects of his life made him stronger.

A spiritual awakening is a type of "waiting." On the island, Crusoe had to look inward and make goals that he would like to achieve. Having spiritual growth sometimes means you have to "rebel" against your family and do your own thing, so your perspective on life changes. Learning to become a better person in your life is important for spiritual growth. This book can help many others.

Reader-as-Waiter Fawzi Saleh Gives a Decided "No" to the 1719 Novel ROBINSON CRUSOE by Daniel Defoe

"Robinson Crusoe" is an interesting read, but I don't think it is of the caliber of the other "waiting" novels we have read in "The Literature of Waiting" course. It has many flaws. First, while there is a lot of waiting (waiting to go out to sea, waiting to escape from slavery, waiting to leave the island), I don't think the waiting theme is realistic. The most obvious waiting period is while Robinson Crusoe is stranded on the island and I think close to zero people reading this book will ever be stranded on an island. Not very relatable. Ironically, how Robinson Crusoe waits (gathering food, building the canoe) can be summarized as "keeping yourself busy," and I don't think anyone needs to read this book to learn that fundamental truth. Even the other themes Defoe touches on, such as religion, are not relatable by everyone. For instance, I don't consider myself very religious, so I find it hard to relate to Crusoe's interaction with God, and I know many atheists would consider it laughable. Most important of all, the novel is too long and dull. The text is dense, and I sometimes found it difficult to follow Defoe's monotonous descriptions; I actually skimmed several sections of the book to avoid falling asleep.

Meet Eleanor Oliphant, an Out-of-the-Ordinary Heroine, Who Says She Believes She's "Completely Fine"

Reader-as-Waiter Trever Polk on the Nested Waiting in the 2017 novel ELEANOR OLIPHANT IS COMPLETELY FINE by Gail Honeyman

To make a decision for what I'm supposed to argue for this essay is actually more difficult that I'd like it to be. From a subjective perspective, I enjoyed "Eleanor Oliphant Is Completely Fine" by Gail Honeyman much more than the other two novels we've read. I especially didn't enjoy "Waiting for the Barbarians," so from my personal perspective I would rather have read just this book instead of both of them. However, it's pretty difficult to make a convincing case based solely on my own preferences.

If I look at it from an objective perspective, judging based on how each book fits into the course theme, I'm tempted to say it would be difficult to include "Eleanor Oliphant Is Completely Fine" in the course. This isn't because it can't be viewed as "waiting literature" – it certainly can – but rather that it doesn't fit that category as easily as "Waiting" and "Waiting for the Barbarians." In my opinion, it would make sense to include all three, with those two books coming first and Eleanor Oliphant later, because it allows the class to develop an idea of the different forms waiting can take in literature. "Waiting" is about everyday waiting, the obvious kind, while "Waiting for the Barbarians" is about a lurking sense of waiting, a sort of cultural waiting that's part of the group consciousness rather than the individual one.

If the class weren't introduced to these different types of waiting, I don't think the waiting of Eleanor Oliphant would even be apparent. The waiting in it is a peculiar form, in which the waiting – Eleanor waiting to meet the musician – ends up not being what she wanted, but she nonetheless finds what she really did want – in a certain sense what she, subconsciously, was waiting for – in the process. This is a sort of nested waiting, and I think it would be difficult to analyze it without the experience the class would gain through the other two novels we've read.

This being said, I'm not sure that it would be possible to fit all three novels in the course without having to cut other, non-novel readings that were just as, or more, valuable. So, if the class could go on for more sessions than it does in reality, I would include all three. However, since it can't, I have to say that, while I personally would prefer to have read "Eleanor Oliphant Is Completely Fine" instead of "Waiting for the Barbarians," the latter book may be more useful for honing students' idea of waiting, and thus is probably a better inclusion.

Why Eleanor Oliphant Is Completely Fine for The Literature of Waiting Course, According to Maxine Lim

The 2017 novel "Eleanor Oliphant is Completely Fine" by Gail Honeyman is one the best books I've read in the last year, not only because of its linguistic merit but because of the complex characters Honeyman carefully constructed and wove into this tragic but surprisingly light and witty story. I strongly believe, for multiple reasons, that this book should be put into the curriculum instead of such other novels as "Waiting for the Barbarians" and "Waiting." This story portrays a strong independent female character who doesn't compromise her independence for a man, unlike Manna Wu, Shuyu, and the barbarian girl. Although love is intertwined in all of the stories, Eleanor is the only character that focuses more on personal growth than prospective romance. This book also addresses mental health in an empowering way as opposed to the other stories we have read.

Eleanor Oliphant is an isolated woman with a tragic past who suffers from PTSD and substance abuse, but the book is so much more than just that. As readers we are waiting to find out how exactly Eleanor got to be the way she is, both physically and mentally, while also waiting to find out what her mother did all those years ago. This part of the story unfolds like a page-turning mystery novel where I couldn't stop reading.

Eleanor is a strong female character, unlike other female characters we've read about. Supporting herself from a very young age and having to overcome such adversity, Eleanor is relatively well adjusted and well liked (by the reader at least), considering the circumstances. She doesn't allow workplace bullying and ridicule from almost everyone she encounters to affect her, and although it becomes very clear that her independence is a crutch, the reader is still left impressed with how she brushes off comments I certainly wouldn't be able to take silently.

Eleanor embodies the resilient liberated woman who doesn't care what anyone thinks about her and eats frozen pizza and drinks vodka unapologetically. In the beginning we take note of the excessive solo drinking but also reflect fondly on college days with friends where we had one too many shots and ended up eating delivered pizza on the kitchen floor at 3:00 am. You relate to the universal struggles Eleanor encounters and identify with her common experiences like idealizing some stranger in a bar or feeling a little too great about how a new outfit makes you feel. Unlike many other characters we've met throughout the course, you root for her because you see yourself in her and you want this underdog story to have a happy ending. You also hope this ending entails a disheveled white knight, but you don't rely on that to make it a happy one.

Romance is a theme seen in all three novels we have read so far but I believe this story is the only one that portrays it positively towards women. Eleanor isn't wasting her life and career on a passive inept man the way Manna Wu and Shuyu did. She isn't written to satiate some erotic pleasure the author receives by writing (as in "Waiting for the Barbarians") smut about a primitive young woman being kept as a "dirty simple pet" to sit by his feet and be fondled with oils to help him sleep at night. She is the main character and the men are supporting characters, which was a refreshing change of pace given there haven't been any notable female protagonists in the course so far.

Although Eleanor has an infatuation with the unlikeable musician that makes her act irrationally and at times pretty pathetic, we see how this fixation has more to do with her needing a distraction and her disillusionment about her own life. She wants to believe that when she gets him everything will fall into place because he's exactly the kind of man her mother would approve of. It isn't about him, it's about her life crumbling around her and her not wanting to see that. Raymond is one of the few male characters I would enjoy having a conversation with. Although he's a little odd at times, he respects Eleanor and her boundaries. He takes a huge part in her sobriety and basically saved her life when she was on the brink. Even then, he didn't expect anything from her even though it's clear they have feelings for each other. Given all of this and the butterfly-inducing final scene potential that author Honeyman had at her fingertips, she still didn't allow this to be a romantic ending.

This story has romantic themes like many others but it is mainly about the journey of one woman to accepting herself and becoming whole again. She does this not only through human interaction but personal reflection and intense therapy where she uncovers repressed horrors. This is the most interesting part of the story, and that should be the focus, not whether Raymond and Eleanor will end up together.

Eleanor Oliphant is a very moving character who I identify with in certain ways. Her journey towards mental wellness was inspirational and, at times, emotional. This author tells the story of a survivor of abuse who learns to rely on other people and utilizes mental health resources to cope with her situation instead of drowning in vodka. It is the ending many hope for but don't reach after going through the foster care system and struggling with poverty and no family. This story is a beacon of hope among all of these tragic stories of mental illness, one that should shine in our class. Not to mention, the language is modern, and its personable yet broad vocabulary would captivate college students far more than the other two books. For these reasons, I believe firmly that the next "Literature of Waiting" class should read "Eleanor Oliphant is Completely Fine."

Reader-as-Waiter Bianca Correa on the Discreet Waiting in the 2017 Novel ELEANOR OLIPHANT IS COMPLETELY FINE by Gail Honeyman

I think the novel "Eleanor Oliphant Is Completely Fine" by Gail Honeyman should be a part of the course "The Literature of Waiting" and follow the two "waiting" novels that we have studied so far.

In "Eleanor Oliphant Is Completely Fine," Eleanor is not seemingly awaiting anything and is living her purposeless life while feeling immensely lonely, without a glimpse of hope. Her life begins to change when she slowly but surely starts to build social bonds in her community, but we have yet to come across an act of "waiting." However, this all changes when she begins to develop a crush on a local singer that she found through social media and begins to anticipate meeting him, believing he will notice her if she goes to his concert and fall in love with her, ultimately curing her loneliness, as well as giving her a sense of purpose in her life. Alas, her unrealistic expectations are struck down when she meets the singer after she attends one of his gigs, realizing that her hope for a brighter future was based on a misplaced crush and, in reality, she was subconsciously avoiding the cause of her sadness and loneliness.

At the end of the novel, we realize that Eleanor was indeed awaiting something throughout the novel but this form of "waiting" was discreet. Her anticipation to meet the singer solely served as a distraction from what she was truly waiting for, to be forced to come face to face with her childhood trauma in order for her to truly heal and build a meaningful life in which she feels like she has a purpose. I believe this book is important in improving our understanding of "waiting" and illustrating how acts of "waiting" may not be obvious at first glance.

Reader-as-Waiter Anne-Lilja Rentof Feels Strongly That the 2017 Novel ELEANOR OLIPHANT IS COMPLETELY FINE by Gail Honeyman Should Some Day Be on The Literature of Waiting Syllabus Because It Sends Positive Messages About Mental Health Awareness and Self-Care

Gail Honeyman's "Eleanor Oliphant Is Completely Fine" is not only a wonderful novel but also an excellent exercise in waiting that should be included in the Spring 2021 curriculum. It is a clever, poignant work that is relatable on several levels. It imitates life and day-to-day social interactions and the ever-present struggle of the socially awkward. More than once, especially at the beginning of the novel, I had to remind myself to be patient with Eleanor because I did not know what she had been through to make her think and act the way she does. Many of us have had similar social experiences from both points of view. On the one hand, many of us may have come across someone whom we did not understand and who may even, at first, have seemed crass and unfeeling. We might have failed to consider the things that that person might have gone through. On the other hand, many, if not most of us, have also been the ones who have been misunderstood. It is this that endears us to both Eleanor and Raymond—each of whom represents a different side of the fence.

We learn to be patient with Eleanor, and as we watch and wait, Eleanor's character blossoms into someone about whom we come to care deeply. The story development feels natural from a clinical standpoint. Gradually, as Eleanor becomes more comfortable with other people and with herself, we learn more about her past. As she waits for the moment when she finally feels ready to face what has happened to her, so too do we wait to have it revealed to us. It is as if the reader is taken along on a therapy session, even long before Eleanor agrees to see a therapist. Waiting is, in essence, a large part of a therapist's job: they wait for the client to feel comfortable enough to open up to them. Most importantly, it sends positive messages about mental health awareness and self-care, which I think is very important. I am not sure which I would replace, but I feel as though "Eleanor Oliphant Is Completely Fine" should definitely be on the syllabus for "The Literature of Waiting."

"Silence lay steadily against the wood and stone of Hill House, and whatever walked there, walked alone" (this sentence appears in both the opening and closing paragraphs of Shirley Jackson's 1959 novel THE HAUNTING OF HILL HOUSE)

And now, here are four all-uppercased words that appear – UNPUNCTUATED – on an inside wall of Hill House. But what do these words mean when you read them aloud?

HELP ELEANOR COME HOME

Which punctuation – below – do you feel accurately represents the connection between this Eleanor, who is not "completely fine," and Hill House?

> *HELP ELEANOR COME HOME.*
> *(In other words, somebody should provide Eleanor with all the practical help she needs in order to be able to return home to the family she fled from.)*

> *HELP, ELEANOR, COME HOME.*
> *(The character Hill House asks Eleanor for the help it needs from her, which, for Hill House, means that Eleanor should realize that she really belongs to Hill House; it is her only true home: she is meant to be one with Hill House itself.)*

> *HELP ELEANOR; COME HOME.*
> *(Somebody – Theodora? – first needs to help troubled Eleanor at Hill House; and then that person should leave Hill House and return to the home they had before the experiment at Hill House was conducted.)*

Reader-as-Waiter Carolyn Reyes
on Female Waiters in the 1959 Novel THE HAUNTING OF HILL HOUSE by Shirley Jackson

"The Haunting of Hill House" by Shirley Jackson is a well-written book about an experiment into paranormal activity gone wrong. I believe the book should be added to the required reading list in place of "Waiting for the Barbarians" because of the themes it presents, writing style, characters and mystery. The book, personally, was a much better read than "Waiting for the Barbarians" because the characters are more fun and relatable to a certain extent. The characters come more to life in the Jackson piece versus Coetzee and we are more aware of their backgrounds, which makes the reader more engaged and actually want to read and indulged to see what happens next; reading the book was like watching a movie because the author makes it so easy to visualize everything and feel like you're there with these people.

Each character waits for different things at different times. Throughout the book Eleanor, the narrator, seems to be waiting to be accepted and wanted by someone. Her waiting came to an end in a horrific way when she finally felt accepted by the house like they had an understanding of each other so deep that she never wanted to part from where she felt she belonged, costing her life. She mentions often that "journeys end in lovers meeting," showing clearly that she will feel satisfied after she is done waiting for a lover.

The house in a way is another character that also has its own background story, although dark. Each character is joined in waiting to see what the house will do each night. They all came together initially with the common goal of waiting to see what happens at Hill House and if it is haunted or not. Even when discovering the house was indeed haunted past a scientific explanation, the characters continued to wait to see what would happen next as the house did its waiting, each night knocking on bedroom doors waiting to be let inside.

Theodora is the opposite of Eleanor, more vibrant, open and alive; the progression of their relationship and figuring out why makes the book more alluring. They seem to have a love-hate relationship with one another and it seems like a lot of Theodora's waiting is to see how she can upset Eleanor only to make up with her. Additionally, while the characters each do their own individual waiting the readers also wait in suspense, which makes it more enjoyable.

Reader-as-Waiter Paige Thorne Anticipates the Paranormal in the 1959 Novel THE HAUNTING OF HILL HOUSE by Shirley Jackson

"The Haunting of Hill House" by Shirley Jackson is a book about four strangers brought closer together and eventually torn apart by the oddities of Hill House, a house whose angles are all off, causing unfamiliarity and uneasiness among its visitors, along with the uninvited visitors within its walls. "The Haunting of Hill House" should be incorporated within "The Literature of Waiting" course curriculum because with this book the reader joins the characters in waiting, and waiting is apparent through all of the book, as the characters all wait throughout their stay in Hill House.

During most of my time reading "The Haunting of Hill House," especially before the first paranormal encounter, I found myself waiting for it to happen and eagerly reading out of anticipation. The theme of mystery in the book also shows how the author makes readers wait effectively. For example, in between scenes we learn information about the characters and see them develop, which I think maintains a reader's interest as they wait for the paranormal scenes. This process helped me connect to the characters within the book, as they had taken breaks from their personal lives to take this "vacation." Having these moments within the book heightens the waiting that both the characters and the reader experience.

An important feature of this book is that the characters are always waiting for obvious and less obvious reasons. Most of the paranormal encounters happen at night, causing the characters to be free during the day. Their waiting behaviors consist of eating, playing games, getting to know each other, and exploring Hill House. I think that this is an important feature of the book, as the characters occupy themselves as a form of waiting.

Another reason why this would be a great book to feature is because of the open-ended ending. I think this work will produce wonderful creative writing, in which a student extends the lives of any of the characters after having lived in Hill House. After the book ended, I was left with many questions and scenarios in my mind about the characters and the future of Hill House. Another creative work that could come from this is noting the repeated phrases within the text, which caught my eye.

Reader-as-Waiter Chyna Chung on Eleanor's Finding the Home That Wants Her Back in the 1959 Novel THE HAUNTING OF HILL HOUSE by Shirley Jackson

Shirley Jackson's "The Haunting of Hill House" novel displays a combination of thriller acts that included differentiating what is real from what is not real right before your eyes.... Sooner than later paranormal experiences occur throughout the house that specifically affect the character Eleanor Vance. She hears voices of her dead mother, she experiences cold spots, and comes upon bloody messages. The technical protagonist of "The Haunting of Hill House" is Eleanor, but the main difference about the novel is the house itself, which slowly manifests itself into the minds of the people living there by making them question themselves and others.

In Eleanor's case she is the one waiting to find a home that wants her back, which causes her to find a home in Hill House. It is possibly the reason as to why the house attached itself to her – she was the one who felt she needed to belong to a home to fulfill the needs her mother and sister never gave. Eleanor gains an inhuman connection to the house as she feels she has become part of the house and can sense everything that happens inside of it. For safety's sake, Dr. Montague demands that she leave the house and go home. But on her way there, Eleanor thinks of a way to stay at Hill House forever – she begins to drive full speed and steer into a tree, killing herself. This results in the ending of Dr. Montague's experiment; the characters go their separate ways, and Hill House stands alone.

Reader-as-Waiter Patrick Diaz on the 1959 Novel THE HAUNTING OF HILL HOUSE by Shirley Jackson as a Story of Active – Not Passive – Waiting

"The Haunting of Hill House" by Shirley Jackson is a story told in moments of waiting. What differentiates "The Haunting of Hill House" from some the other novels, though, is that all the characters' individual acts of waiting shine through brilliantly and clearly. While the waiting that is happening is often uneventful, it is never dull and always seems to be building to something.

No character's waiting is better exemplified than Eleanor Vance's waiting throughout the novel, and none of her waiting is exemplified better than on her drive to Hill House. Throughout her drive we are met with many images that take us along with her on her drive, but without any context it's just an ordinary drive. Because it's told from the lens of Eleanor's feelings about the drive, her life up to that point, and what she hopes to achieve by accepting the invitation to stay at Hill House, we are given enough context to remain interested and alert about her drive. Through her lens, a dull drive is transformed into an exploration of the unknown and fantastical parts of her route to the house. It's adorned with poisonous plants, decrepit road signs, and a house with two white lions in front. What we see through her lens, however, are omens, fairy tale journeys through forgotten wildernesses, and an alternate life where someone has been waiting for Eleanor to arrive. This draws the reader in, gives a sense of Eleanor as a character, and helps us pass the time along with Eleanor.

Playwright Tom Stoppard and the Structure and Themes of His HAMLET-Flipped Play ROSENCRANTZ AND GUILDENSTERN ARE DEAD (Where every exit is an entrance somewhere else, and no person is a minor character in the story of their own life)

Reader-as-Waiter Ryan Langan on Tom Stoppard's 1967 Play
ROSENCRANTZ AND GUILDENSTERN ARE DEAD

"Rosencrantz and Guildenstern Are Dead" by Tom Stoppard is a play that's a play on a play – how's that for wordplay? – and in this structure, it exhibits more than just the typical elements of a work of literature. In essence, it is the other side of the coin of "Hamlet" and gives the audience the chance to look at what happens to the characters situated outside the main storyline. What happens to them, of course, is mostly being made to wait. What's more, it serves to illustrate the way in which the actors who play the minor characters in a play are likewise situated outside the play, waiting. Because of this, the study of this play in a course on "waiting" shows waiting in a literary sense as well as waiting in a literal sense. There is a strong commentary on the relation between the creative work and the real world. Although this takes place in a fictional world, the thematic implications bleed into reality.

Rosencrantz and Guildenstern are much more relatable characters to the modern reader than, say, Hamlet. Common human experience looks a lot more like the waiting, debating, and humor of a Rosencrantz and a Guildenstern than the dramatic arc of a Prince Hamlet. What Stoppard is doing in his play is elevating the mundane, the actual, and the normal to a level of lore such as Hamlet is considered. He is making a title of a sidebar. He is bringing the everyday subject (characters that readers can see themselves in) and the concept of waiting to our attention and showing that there is a story to the small characters as well, and that story, often overlooked, is one filled with an abundance of time.

Reader-as-Waiter Rabeya Rahman on Why Tom Stoppard's 1967 Play ROSENCRANTZ AND GUILDENSTERN ARE DEAD Should NOT Be a Part of the Literature of Waiting Course (Particularly If Students Don't Remember William Shakespeare's 1600 Play HAMLET All That Well)

The play "Rosencrantz and Guildenstern Are Dead" by Tom Stoppard is an interesting read that follows the role of two characters in Shakespeare's play "Hamlet." In "Hamlet," the play ends with the death of the leading character Hamlet, and Claudius, Laertes, and Gertrude, as well as the announcement that Rosencrantz and Guildenstern are dead. Little backstory has ever been given with regards to the identity of these two characters until Tom Stoppard wrote his play "Rosencrantz and Guildenstern Are Dead."

Stoppard's work is a confusing yet attention-grabbing tale about the inevitable death that looms over everyone, but especially Rosencrantz and Guildenstern. Death is the overarching theme of the play, and the entire work of literature is essentially the wait for it – which is one hundred percent appropriate and related to this class on "The Literature of Waiting." Yet, I would not recommend this play to be used in future classes as a replacement for either of the novels that we have studied: "Waiting for the Barbarians" by J.M. Coetzee or "Waiting" by Ha Jin.

"Rosencrantz and Guildenstern Are Dead" consists of three obvious forms of waiting: waiting for the play's coin-flip outcomes, waiting for death, and waiting for what happens next in the sporadic transitions from one scene in the play to the other. The play begins with a lengthy coin-flipping session between Rosencrantz and Guildenstern as they the pass time wandering around. They each choose a side of either "heads" or "tails" and flip to see what the coin lands on, only for it to result in the same outcome of "heads" each turn. Based on probability, one would predict that the coin would land at least once on the "tails" side, but each attempt seems to prove otherwise. Readers of the play are left somewhat on a cliffhanger to see if the coin eventually lands on the tails side. The coin flip is brought up throughout the play and in every instance there is suspense in waiting to see the outcome of which side it lands on.

In addition, the topic of death is brought up early in the play as inevitable and poorly understood. The play begins with Rosencrantz and Guildenstern discussing what happens after death and this topic follows them throughout the rest of the storyline. The group of actors known as the Tragedians and the Player make ominous comments about how those that are meant to die in a play will die. This hints to the readers that despite the fact that this play is only inspired by Shakespeare's work, Rosencrantz and Guildenstern are meant to die in this one too as it is also a play. At the king's castle, in Elsinore, Denmark, the Tragedians rehearse their play in which they have two characters who eerily resemble Rosencrantz and Guildenstern and end up dying after a series of events – all of which foreshadows their demise in real life. It is a matter of waiting to see how it all unfolds.

Throughout the entire play, the readers are almost as confused as Rosencrantz and Guildenstern in the sudden changes of scenes. These two characters are generally confused in their role as they simply go along with the storyline and do whatever is expected of them. The plotline of the play is parallel to the story of Hamlet, with numerous overlaps. The characters of Shakespeare's play are going in and out of the scenes inside the royal castle at Elsinore, and every now and then, they give instructions to Guildenstern and Rosencrantz to do certain tasks, including assisting in the killing of Hamlet. These two men just do it – without asking as if it's their purpose. As for the readers, we can make some decent sense of the play with the help of pre-existing knowledge of Shakespeare's "Hamlet." Otherwise, reading this play would be a great lost cause because a majority of the events and the significance of things are rooted in the original work. We wouldn't know who Hamlet and the others are, or why Rosencrantz and Guildenstern are at the castle in the first place.

Overall, Tom Stoppard's play is a good read about two rather insignificant characters from Shakespeare's Hamlet; however, I would not recommend it to be used to replace the two novels that we read in this English course: "Waiting for the Barbarians" by J.M. Coetzee or "Waiting" by Ha Jin. This play contains different forms of waiting, which is the main focus of this class, but because it requires knowledge and understanding of Shakespeare, it can be confusing or distasteful to some readers. I, myself, have forgotten a lot of information about what happened in "Hamlet" and generally would not willingly want to read Shakespearean literature or anything related to it.

Reader-as-Waiter Jason Chetram on Why Tom Stoppard's 1967 Play ROSENCRANTZ AND GUILDENSTERN ARE DEAD Should Be a Part of the Literature of Waiting Course (Whether Students Are Familiar With William Shakespeare's Play HAMLET Or Not)

If we, the collective human species, were all a part of some elaborate grandiose play, according to the Player, we would all die simply because we were scripted to die. As characters in this play of life, we would act out our lives all the while waiting for our looming finale. In the play "Rosencrantz and Guildenstern Are Dead" by Tom Stoppard, our heroes Rosencrantz and Guildenstern attempt to find some sort of semblance of meaning and logic in their bizarre adventure, but due to some rather unfortunate character limitation, it is to no avail. However, one saving grace from their fruitless journey of finding meaning in their existence is how we the audience can observe the act of waiting through this duo. "Rosencrantz and Guildenstern Are Dead" should be taught alongside the likes of "Waiting for the Barbarians" and "Waiting" for its similarity to these other works as well as the extra dimension of existentialism it brings to the table.

Rosencrantz and Guildenstern, from their perspective, are alive and well and have done nothing deserving of the fate of death. However, in "Hamlet," they were killed off by Shakespeare and even as Stoppard says in the title, "Rosencrantz and Guildenstern Are Dead." The two characters are fated to die, and there is nothing they can do to prevent it. Dealing with the idea of death is one you can not avoid when it comes to existentialism and "Rosencrantz and Guildenstern Are Dead" begs the question "What if we all die because we are fated to?" At first glance, the question seems pointless, as it can be simply answered as yes, or rather it doesn't necessarily matter. If you die, regardless of the cause and the circumstance, it could easily be claimed that it was fated to be that way. However, when we focus on what the word "fated" means and what fate really is, the answer to the question becomes increasingly muddled. "Rosencrantz and Guildenstern Are Dead" may not provide any answers when it comes to the idea of waiting, existence, or death, but it is definitely thought-provoking enough to have its readers come to their own conclusions, if not, approach their conclusions.

THE AGE OF INNOCENCE, a 1920 Novel by Edith Wharton, Makes the Reader Want to Unread the Whole 1980 Novel WAITING, So I Would Highly Recommend That It Replace It

The Novel THE AGE OF INNOCENCE vs. the Novel WAITING
By Liala Ahmad

Waiting is a concept we humans are all too familiar with. A lot of people in my generation are in school / at the beginning of careers or relationships, waiting for their lives to start. For the characters in "The Age of Innocence," the 1920 novel by Edith Wharton and "Waiting" by Ha Jin this is no exception. What is exceptional, however, is that the characters in these works are in similar situations but wait rather differently.

After reading "The Age of Innocence" I am not surprised Wharton is a Pulitzer-Prize-winning author. This novel is filled with so much depth, emotion, and insight so eloquently told that it was a joy to read. Although the novel is primarily based on waiting, the reader cannot only bear it along with the characters but also remain present throughout it, unlike the experience I had while reading "Waiting." In this essay, I will outline the reasons why I believe "The Age of Innocence" should replace Ha Jin's novel "Waiting" as mandatory course reading.

Although this novel cannot strictly be in the "coming of age" category because none of its main characters are transitioning from childhood to adulthood, the protagonist, Newland Archer, shows such character growth that it is reminiscent of the concept. In the beginning of the story, he is presented as a typical New York elitist whose head is steeped in the roles set by the restrictive society he grew up in. Enter Madame Ellen Olenska. Once Newland learns of the details of her controversial divorce from her husband, he surprises himself when he defends her decision.

Throughout their interactions and even when Ellen is not around, he is left to think about the freedoms of women, or rather the lack of freedoms that women possess. He realizes that next to no one in his tight circle shares that same belief. This is initially what draws him to Ellen, the fact that she was a feminist, a stand alone in their generation, unyielding in her beliefs of equality. As the novel goes on, he realizes (with despair) that he too, is a feminist. He wants her to be liberated from her cheating husband and he wants society to accept that. However, he finds that his friends and his family are not as progressive as he is, including his then-fiancee. It is this undertone of the novel that really makes Newland a protagonist one wants to root for. As Newland's character adopts more progressive views, his relationship with conservative New York society starts to fissure. This sense of isolation allows him to empathize with Ellen and respect her, ultimately deepening their relationship. This makes for an interesting plot that keeps the reader engaged and cheering for the main characters.

This experience was a stark contrast to the one I had while reading "Waiting." As a reader, I found it hard to root for the protagonist, Lin Kong. His character was so stagnant throughout the novel; he only became self-aware towards the end, where he realizes that he never loved either of his wives and essentially wasted his life (and theirs) on empty dreams. We feel sorry for his first wife, Shuyu, but only distantly since we do not become all that acquainted with her character. The only other character that evokes emotion is Lin's second wife, Manna, and that emotion is sympathy. Manna first expressed her feelings for Lin and pursued him; she tried to consummate their relationship early on and cement that they were a couple by urging Lin to divorce Shuyu. However, Lin was much too complacent and fearful of the societal repercussions to do anything.

One could argue that since he went to court to divorce Shuyu, that was an action on Lin's part. But it was not his failure that made him unlikable; it was his lack of drive, his defeated attitude, his negative outlook. These aspects of his personality made him unable or rather unwilling to truly fight to be with Manna. The reader has to sit through the deterioration of their relationship and instead of it blooming into love, it becomes monotonous and passionless; to witness it is disheartening, frustrating and frankly, annoying. In Newland Archer's case, he at least tried to instill some change; he defended Ellen to all his family, knowing what it would do to his reputation; he boldly kissed Ellen in her house; he traveled to Boston just to hear from her; he suggested and planned to consummate their relationship; he even planned to run away with her.

What the two main characters have in common is that they both had relationships without really being in relationships. The difference, however, is two things: passion and time. Lin and Manna were in each other's lives, trapped in their cycle of waiting for nearly two decades, while Newland and Ellen, in reality, were only in each other's lives for a short period of time.

It was these short spurts of time together that perhaps inspired the characters to yearn so deeply for the other. They had not spent enough time with each other in their oppressive society for their feelings to easily fizzle out; instead it had the opposite effect: whenever they reunited they were filled with unbridled passion. Whereas Lin and Manna had spent so long under watchful eyes and uninspired hearts that their feelings were bound to also be oppressed and, in Lin's case, never even fully develop.

The frustrating part of waiting is a major plot point in both novels, and both do a good job of portraying the perils of wanting something you simply cannot have without becoming a leper in the eyes of society. It just so happens that "The Age of Innocence" does a better job of not dragging the storyline. Even though Ellen and Newland go on to live separate lives in separate countries – never crossing paths for decades – I would prefer this lack of closure then the ending of "Waiting." To witness Lin and Manna finally be together after decades of waiting but not be happy was somehow more depressing. Add to that the fact that Lin implies he would be with Shuyu after Manna dies is so utterly disappointing it makes the reader want to unread the whole novel. To the benefit of future students, I would highly recommend replacing the novel "Waiting" by Ha Jin with "The Age of Innocence" by Edith Wharton.

Andrea Pinzon Gets Anxious Over Edith Wharton's novel "The Age of Innocence"

As most readers and literary colleagues have seen, waiting is demonstrated in many different ways: through letters, lies, stories, singing and, perhaps, any way of measuring how time moves on. In movies we see aging, wrinkles and baskets and baskets of love letters that one partner never receives, as in "The Notebook." In Edith Wharton's novel "The Age of Innocence," we have the story of Newland Archer, a man engaged to (and, later, married to) May while in love with May's cousin, Countess Ellen Olenska. Although the novel "Waiting" by Ha Jin and "The Age of Innocence" share the common theme of a love triangle and the quiet and secret love of two people, "Waiting" shows to be a fairly predictable novel – there isn't much suspense, while "The Age of Innocence" has a better share of what one would call an ending worth waiting for.

Ha Jin's "waiting" revolves around the military doctor Lin Kong and his various attempts to divorce his wife Shuyu. During this time, he meets a military nurse, Manna Wu, whom he falls madly in love with. As their love grows, his wish to divorce his wife rises and leads him to insist every year until she agrees to finally let go. During this time that Lin is attempting divorcing Shuyu, he and Manna Wu cannot show their affection for each other, so their wait grows and their love intensifies because of this great expectation of divorce. However, Manna Wu's waiting gets cyclical in the story; hence it wasn't letting the readers do the waiting, which, ideally, is how I believe the concept of waiting should be taught in a course like ours. This constant cycle made the prediction of the ending of the book quite simple, where eventually Shuyu would bend and finally let go of someone that wasn't hers anymore.

In "The Age of Innocence," Edith Wharton shows the act of waiting in many different ways that are intriguing to a reader such as myself. For example, the established relationship between May and Newland Archer is one that the reader is waiting to see – in one way or another – be destroyed. Countess Ellen comes into the picture and her immediate attraction to Archer makes us see, and be in suspense about, the impending troubles to come. Because this novel involves love triangles between as many as four different characters, the suspense is pretty high. The reader is in constant expectation of the split between May and Archer and of the evolving of Archer's relationship with Ellen – hence, constant suspense.

Also, the theme of innocence is huge in the concept of waiting. At some point, whether we like it or not, and whether we are aware of it or not, our innocence goes away. In May's case, her innocence is one that is waiting to go away, and then she goes on to tell Ellen about the pregnancy she is not sure of, she does it on purpose and her innocence is no more. Her innocence wilts and enhances the waiting of the readers as to what she might do next.

Of course, with each character in the novel, there is "waiting" – and each of them experiences it differently. In contrast to Lin Kong in "Waiting," Newland Archer takes waiting into his own hands; in other words, waiting for the one he loves was for him to decide – and not either woman. In Ha Jin's novel, it was Shuyu who had the power to manipulate Lin Kong's life and his waiting to be with Manna Wu, but waiting was a more detailed experience for the reader of "The Age of Innocence" because we were more expectant of actions within the New York society rather than in a more predictable communist China. "The Age of Innocence" keeps its readers in constant suspense, such that one could not bear waiting to flip to the next page. For being highly engaged with the feeling of waiting, Edith Wharton's novel is the right one for our course on "The Literature of Waiting" to dive into.

CHAPTER 16

Fearful Waiting in the 1967 Hollywood Movie "Wait Until Dark" and in Noel Coward's 1960 Play "Waiting in the Wings"

When it came to making her choice of independent reading from among six classic and contemporary "waiting" works in our "The Literature of Waiting" course, college collaborator **Gabriella Tuchman** chose the fairly lengthy classic novel GREAT EXPECTATIONS by Charles Dickens because, as she relates, "I was so excited to have the chance to read a classic like GREAT EXPECTATIONS because I had never read it or any other Dickens in school. GREAT EXPECTATTIONS was beautifully written, and the scenes were evocative. I felt myself in the room with Miss Havisham ... and I sneezed from all the dust that accumulated on her belongings."

In her analytical piece on GREAT EXPECTATIONS, Gabriella goes on to point out that the Dickens novel is "full of waiting" – it has a "pervasive element of fear" – and fear is one of the kinds of waiting that prevents action. "Fear," says Gabriella, "is an important type of waiting because a person believes that he is in imminent danger and therefore acts based on the fight or flight principle. The fear, and the waiting, is the moment of inaction, waiting to see whether the fear is justified and how best to react." In GREAT EXPECTATIONS, she continues, Pip always waits for someone to find out that he helped the convict and provided him with stolen food – and this fear of Pip's, this one decision, influences his actions for the rest of the novel.

In her essay, Gabriella goes on to recommend another long novel that exemplifies fear as a form of waiting – the contemporary novel THE GOLDFINCH by Donna Tartt – in which the main character, a young boy by the name of Theodore Decker, steals a painting from off a wall of the Metropolitan Museum of Art in New York after a bomb has blown up the museum room the painting is hung in. Once Theodore realizes what he has done, he feels that he cannot return the painting and "this moment of inaction because of his fear determines his actions for the rest of that novel."

Fear as a form of waiting is both context and content for two very different works of "waiting literature" briefly examined in "The Literature of Waiting" course: Noel Coward's 1960 play (his fiftieth!) WAITING IN THE WINGS and the 1967 Hollywood thriller film starring Audrey Hepburn, WAIT UNTIL DARK.

WAITING IN THE WINGS examines a community of retired London stage actresses – two of them feuding rival divas who once both loved the same man – living together (sort of) in a charity retirement home specifically for aging and no-longer-employable actresses. Although the phrase "waiting in the wings" optimistically refers to what performers about to go on the stage are literally doing as they await their cue to go on (hanging back in the not-visible-to-the-audience left and right wings off to the sides of the playing stage), figuratively speaking the term suggests a start to things, a beginning, a birth.

In Coward's play, what is realistically waiting for these reluctantly retired actresses in these same figurative wings is the feared figure of Death. In a defense of his play, which did not get great reviews and was not a financial success – Coward wrote that he "considers that the play as a whole contains, beneath the froth of some of its lighter moments, the basic truth that old age needn't be so dreary and sad as it is supposed to be, provided you greet it with humour and live it with courage."

In director Terence Young's WAIT UNTIL DARK, Hepburn plays a young blind woman, Susy, afraid for her life as she tries to outwit two criminals who are searching in her apartment for hidden drugs. Susy defends herself by putting the criminals in the dark along with her, breaking almost all the bulbs in the apartment. (To immerse 1967 movie viewers in the suspense during the climactic scene of WAIT UNTIL DARK, some movie theaters dimmed their lights to the legal limits, and then turned them off, one by one, until the audience was in complete darkness.) One New York movie critic praised Audrey Hepburn's performance, liking in particular the final scenes of the film in which the actress "manifests terror" and attracts "sympathy and anxiety."

Another critic agreed that "there are some nice, juicy passages of terror (including the famous moment when every adolescent girl in the theater screams)." Fear fact: that climactic moment is ranked tenth on Bravo's "100 Scariest Movie Moments."

Students in "The Literature of Waiting" course interested in earning extra credit (while sheltered at home from March 12, 2020, to the end of the course on May 7) were asked to detail in writing how "fear is a form of waiting" as depicted in *either* excerpted scenes from WAITING IN THE WINGS *or* from selected YouTube clips from WAIT UNTIL DARK.

I'm afraid (an expression, not an expression of actual fear) that no one opted for this particular extra credit with respect to the Noel Coward play about retirement as a waiting for death; however, college collaborator Anne-Lilja Rentof had no qualms about taking on the waiting fear of watching the film WAIT UNTIL DARK.

Watching "Wait Until Dark"
By Anne-Lilja Rentof

Fear is very much present in the life of Susy Hendrix. Having only relatively recently become blind, she is still learning to adjust to a life without her sight. As a result, she often relies on the help of the people around her. The three criminals in the movie take advantage of this, attempting to trick her into trusting one of them and then conning her into believing her husband is in trouble.

She is fearful to be left alone by her husband, Sam, but recognizes that she must become more independent, and so resigns herself to wait until he returns. She fears not having anyone to rely on in case she needs help. She lives in fear of this for a great deal of the movie, as she must otherwise rely on her other senses, particularly her hearing, in order to be able to tell what is going on. If someone means her harm, or an accident such as a small fire in a cigarette ashtray starts, she must either wait for that person or use her other senses—hearing, smell, or touch, to help herself and resolve the situation on her own. The fear of having to remain helpless for an uncertain amount of time is overwhelming and elevates her panic.

During the scene in which her young neighbor Gloria throws a tantrum and begins throwing things around the kitchen, Susy becomes fearful because not only is it dangerous for her to have unknown and possibly sharp objects lying around the house, but it hinders her in that she no longer knows where things are. Susy becomes fearful that Gloria has simply left, and Susy must choose to either break down and wait for help or try and clean up on her own.

The scene after Susy sends Gloria to find Sam, when Susy discovers that her phone line has been cut, is the first time she well and truly breaks down, because she realizes that she is at the mercy of these criminals, and that she must wait for help, knowing there is not much else she can do to bring someone to her aid, and not knowing whether she will be able to stall the criminals long enough for help to arrive. The fear of not knowing what will happen to her is compounded by having to wait for the inevitable confrontation.

In the climactic scene in which Roat traps Susy in the apartment, he takes full advantage of her lack of sight and the fact that she uses her other senses to compensate. He confuses her by throwing objects to different areas of the room and brushing her face and hands with cloth. This disorients her almost completely and she must wait until either she can even the playing field by smashing the last remaining lightbulb in the apartment or Roat slips up. The waiting and uncertainty compounds an already terrifying situation, as she knows that given the chance this man will kill her. She is able to stab and fend him off until she can plunge the apartment into total darkness, but remains hidden behind the refrigerator door until Gloria and Sam return with the police, unable to be completely sure that Roat is, in fact, dead. The relief she feels when Gloria and Sam return is palpable, having had to wait in uncertain fear, unable to see and virtually out of options if her previous efforts to protect herself have been unsuccessful.

CHAPTER 17

Waiting Out (Enduring!) the 2020 Coronavirus Pandemic While Sheltered Off-Campus and At-Home with Giovanni Boccaccio's Waiting Work on the Black Plague of 1348 – "The Decameron"

"Once upon a time…."

The time is 1348, the place is a secluded and abandoned villa on the outskirts of Florence, and Giovanni Boccaccio is framing his masterpiece – THE DECAMERON – an assortment of exactly one hundred stories that he will publish in 1353. These ten-by-ten tales are told by two handfuls of individuals (seven young women and three young men) who have fled a once-flourishing but now plague-ridden urban center to come together – perhaps contagiously – to "wait out" the Black Plague by making up, by recalling, and by telling stories to one another. (A tall order, but there is nothing like a good story to keep your mind off your troubles!)

The time is 2020, the place is an almost empty New York City, and Hunter College students are, as one of them pessimistically put it, "under house arrest." As undergraduates in Robert Eidelberg's "The Literature of Waiting" English class, some twenty-seven of them are, of course, still keeping their required Personal Waiting Journal, and in early April, they are also reading, in English translation, the first four of Boccaccio's "Decameron" tales (tall tales, but short ones).

Students' focus for reading and analysis was simple and sweet: after thinking about, and enjoying, and comparing these first four tales of what would be a total of ten tales per day over a span of ten days, select the one tale (just one!) that you would read out loud to a family member you are currently "sheltered alone" together with because of the coronavirus public health emergency (or that you would speak aloud over the phone to an isolated relative, neighbor, friend, or classmate).

Listen, now, to college collaborator **Gabriella Tuchman** as she tells in an email to her "Waiting" classmates why she would choose the third story.

> While I enjoyed all four of the stories from THE DECAMERON that we read, my favorite story was the third (narrated by Filomena), in which a Jewish man, Abraham, who is known for his avarice, outwits the Sultan of Babylon. When the Sultan asks Abraham a leading question with no correct answer – which of the three religions (Judaism, Christianity, Islam) is the truest? – Abraham answers that all three are equally true. I would read this story aloud for a number of reasons. Firstly, because it starts out in an anti-Semitic manner of describing the Jew as a miser only to prove the stereotype wrong, and, secondly, because Abraham answers in a very Jewish way, which is through a parable. There are many instances in Jewish tradition in which a parable is used to explain an answer, and since my family is Jewish, we are very familiar with these tropes; it would be like reading a bedtime story.
>
> A third reason I would read this story out loud is that it really spoke to me when Abraham explained his view on religion. Abraham says that each religion "believes itself to be the true heir, to possess the true law, and to follow the true commandments, but whoever is right ... is still undecided." Abraham shows that religion is not about proving who is right but about following a set of beliefs that you believe in regardless of what other religions believe. It is about following in the tradition of your forefathers because you believe that the tradition is important to you. Being right about the religion is not the most important part of religion. The most important

part of religion is believing in a God and following those commandments with others who believe the same.

I know that throughout history many wars were caused because one religion believed they were more important than another religion. For example, during the Crusades, Christian mercenaries killed many people of the Jewish faith, and during the Protestant Reformation, Protestants were killed for their beliefs. This shows that not only is there strife between religions but also between different sects within the same religion. Abraham's response is that the differences should not separate the religions but, instead, the differences should only strengthen your own belief because at the end of the day no one knows which religion is the most right.

College collaborator **Carolyn Reyes** also selected the third of the four stories because she felt that people in general should be open to educating themselves about other religions "rather than believing that yours – I'm Catholic – is almighty.... I feel this story is especially important with the religious persecution and hate crimes that occur. If you look at all religions, we all worship God in the end, and I don't feel it should be a competition for who does it correctly. I also like the story within the story about the sons and giving them all identical rings (so who is the *true* heir?); it fits in a larger way for society, like race with black and brown and white people.... At the core, we are all just people, and being different shouldn't allow you to pass judgment on others.... This story may be a lesson that people could learn in the time that they are waiting for the pandemic to end; it might allow us to come out better rather than go 'back to normal.'"

College collaborator **Wardah Malik** preferred the second of the four stories (told by Neifile) because "as our lives and the world as we know it have been put on pause indefinitely, we find ourselves with a unique opportunity to inspect old habits.... Both men in the story, while knowing of the 'foul and wicked lives the clergy lead' still decide to overlook these immoral actions and uphold the church's power in the world. But in our world, normal isn't good enough. There is so much unnecessary suffering, too much avoidable death. This fact often gets ignored or, worse, accepted. As we wait out the pandemic, we should reflect on the way things were corrupt before the pandemic and, given the chance, unlike Abraham and Jehannot de Chevilly, do something about it."

College collaborator **Paige Thorne** also selected the second story as her favorite "because it shows a lot about independence, decision-making and open-mindedness. I also enjoyed that Abraham did not succumb to the peer pressure of his friend; he was mature enough to be open to his friend's ideas but also to make the decision to go to Rome to experience the clergy there for himself. Despite seeing the endeavors of the clergymen, he was not afraid to join Christianity – and he joined solely because of the religion rather than not join that faith because of those who practiced it – that the actions of a group do not invalidate the entire practice of religion."

College collaborator **Fawzi Saleh** likewise chose the second story, for among other reasons, "because it is relatively short and readable, and its twist ending is unexpected...." Another reason "for picking this story is because it relates to the theme of religion. During a pandemic such as the Black Plague in which so many people are dying, people are naturally going to discuss God and religion. Some would invoke God for the purposes of protection, while others would take the pandemic as a sign to denounce God, citing that a just God would not inflict such a virus on His creation.... So overall I chose the second story for its controversial and religious nature."

College collaborators **Jason Chetram and Rabeya Rahman** both preferred the first day's first story about the life of sinner Ciappelletto.

As **Jason Chetram** relates, "Up to his very last breath, Ciappelletto had led a sinful life, and this story, stands out to me for its humor and wittiness, making it worth sharing – especially in these trying times. Whilst on his death bed, at an inn run by two brothers, after overhearing a conversation about how his death could spell ruin for their lives, he decides to uncharacteristically do a good deed for them. This deed was to lie to a friar and to get absolved so that he would be able to receive a proper burial and, thus, not bring a bad name to the brothers' inn. The motive for this act of kindness on the part of Ciappelletto could have been brought about by the kindness and respect the brothers showed him for the duration of the stay despite knowing the type of man he was. The friar believes all of Ciappelletto's manipulative lies and goes to great lengths to convince the other members of the church that Ciappelletto had lived a righteous life and had, consequently, earned a reputation as a saint despite actually being the furthest from it.

"I believe that joy could be derived from many points of this story. One facet in which joy is derived is in waiting to see just how Ciappelletto can one-up his previous lie and the fashion in which it is told. Another way joy can be derived is in how thought-provoking this story is. In the same way that Ciappelletto's words were empty, it could be said that the friar's words were no better. Whether being absolved could send Ciappelletto to heaven or not is something that cannot be proven, just as how Ciappelletto's lies cannot be proven false. In a sense, both men are con-men as they deceive others; however, the friar is seen to be just. We also see that Ciapelletto's lies were told for the betterment of the two brothers, a selfless act, when characteristically his death would have brought misfortune to the brothers and would have been something he would have taken delight in."

"The friar's lies are told to ease the minds of people and to instill righteous values; however, at the same time, they instill fear and stress in people. It is discussed in the story between these two that the friar tells Ciapelletto that he should not worry so vehemently over sins that the friar perceived to be small; however, under normal circumstances that small sin would bother anyone until they confessed to the friar and got the "okay" from him. This puts the friar in a position of power as he can influence the hearts and minds of the people who fear God. The debate over who was the better man in this story, the friar or Ciappelletto, is something to keep your brain occupied as we wait out our very own quarantine like this very peculiar group of storytellers."

And **Rabeya Rahman**? Well, Rabeya's reasons for choosing this same story as her favorite were a bit different and somewhat more personal: "I would read this story to Mom because it is such a messed-up story but still has a glimmer of hope.... I am Muslim and I am not fully aware of Christianity's belief in terms of the significance behind a sinner being buried with those who are considered pure. He'd end up in hell for his sins, no? While to all the people, he'd be thought of as someone who probably ended up in heaven? Whatever the case, a reader can take away that looks can be deceiving. Mom has told me plenty of times about the importance of leading an honest and pure life and to repent because we often can commit sins – big and small – without even knowing. Mom talks with a ton of fear for the afterlife and how she fears whether she's done enough to end up in heaven, and she compares herself to people who seem to be super innocent. This story kind of shows that even those who appear innocent can secretly be sinners (whether large or small). This doesn't relate directly to the coronavirus pandemic, but it does deal with the topic of death because it's something we've heard plenty of over the past however many months."

Finally, **Nattapat Karmniyanont** has the last word on the last story assigned – the fourth: "I have to say that my favorite is the fourth story. I love the way that Dioneo just began telling his story without the queen having to ask, as though she had this story excitedly in her mind.... Also, I felt the story was particularly insightful concerning the emphasis on the "men" part of holy men, and no matter how devoted someone says they are, at the end of the day Adam and Eve still ate the apple – and in this case both of the men partake of the fruit themselves. Additionally, I found the funniest part in all four stories to be the part in this last story where the younger monks outsmarted the Master Abbot with the line 'I shall behave as I have seen you behave.'"

As these latter-day Hunter College "Florentines" continued, off campus, to make entries in their Personal Waiting Journals, not surprisingly they found that they were fairly regularly observing and writing about a new and worrisome world. Almost everyone seemed to be waiting out the coronavirus pandemic through a glass darkly. Never before had "endurance" seemed the true definition of "time."

Some of these entries (at least ten were required, a contemporary "decameron") follow, as do entry-inspired pieces of imaginative writing that helped to keep both the students who wrote them and their collegial audience safe, calm, kind, and sane. Like the tales told out loud in Boccaccio's THE DECAMERON, these creative pieces speak to and document the temper of the times – times more of "hanging in" than of "hanging out" – but particularly of "hanging in there."

Enduring the 2020 Coronavirus Pandemic: Entries from the Personal Waiting Journal of Rabeya Rahman

March 17
I feel sad today. I can't take this stay at home idea. I need to go out. I must. It's so depressing at home. There are three other people in the house, but everyone's doing their own thing in their own bubble and more often than not, the house is dead quiet. I need human contact. I want to see my friends.... How much longer do we have to wait for all this to be over?

March 19
I found out that one of my uncles (mom's cousin in London) has coronavirus. He is fighting it and seems to be okay so far, so that's good.... Let the waiting continue.

March 20
All my science professors are still trying to figure out how to administer tests. I have one coming up next week for Microbiology. Meanwhile....

March 30
The most relevant waiting I did today was waiting for the group facetime call with my friends. We text every day and keep each other posted but haven't hung out in person in forever.... We're stuck in the house. The call was at 6:00 so it was a gruesome boring wait till then.

April 1
It has been a month since I have gone outside. Both dad and I haven't been working at all. Food is running out and we have to figure out groceries. Mom gets upset at the thought of dad going outside because dad smokes – he needs to be cautious during this period of health crisis. We have all been waiting for the pandemic to end or at least start getting better, but it hasn't happened yet. All day we've been looking on different online websites for home delivery of food but they either don't do it or it is currently unavailable. At last, after tons of patience and waiting, we found a website called DOWISK on which mom and I have decided to take a leap of faith and make an order. We had never heard of that website and prayed it isn't a scam.

April 8
I'm so bored. I have tried my best to keep up with the five prayers because this evening till tomorrow evening is known as Shab-e-barat, also known as "The Night of Forgiveness." Muslims around the world pray and repent extra on this day because Allah makes his decisions on who gets to live another extra day. I waited for each of the prayer times and stayed awake the entire night. I was just about done and satisfied with the stuff I did by 3:40 but then realized the morning prayer at dawn was about an hour and twenty minutes away so I went on my phone and wasted time on TIKTOK until then.

Imaginative Writing Inspired by My Personal Waiting Journal Entries
COVID-19 B.E.F.O.R.E. AND A.F.T.E.R.
By Rabeya Rahman

Being able to go outside
Everyday tasks to keep myself busy outdoors
Food, friends, fun, my forever
Overwhelmingly annoying commute to school and to work
Really stressed but super blessed
Everyone happy and healthy

Annoying brother playing on his PS4 all day
Forbidden from going outside
Teardrops and sadness
Everyone praying for relief and good days
Rained, it has, on our parade – GO AWAY COVID-19

Nattapat Karmniyanont asks: Is There Something to Wait for?

Have I been waiting? That was what I thought throughout the week trying to give myself an answer that I am satisfied with. Without having to travel outside, my daily schedule is in shambles, tossed aside like used latex gloves. The days merge with each other, morphing into a kind of amalgamation of time – of bright sky and dark nights – interrupted by the occasional online class or assignment. This might sound devastating to most, but I find it pleasant enough. I am not stressed, nor am I doing anything I am particularly opposed to. This, then, made me think about how my friends are handling the quarantine. Some are much like me and enjoy the extra free time and solitude; others, however, seem to crave interaction, thirst for active spending. It's quite strange. But this made me wonder. The reason I've been so calm so far is due to the fact that I still have many things that I would like to do, that I can do – I can read, play games, draw, write, work out, pick up a new coin trick, and so much more. And if all of those fail me, then I can retreat into my inner sanctum and construct a new world to occupy my time – it wouldn't be the first nor the last time I would stroll in, after all. In thinking that, now I'm curious. Until how long can my serenity last in this near isolation? How long will it take my inner world to evolve from a sanctuary into a dead zone? Well, now I'm getting interested. There is something to wait for, indeed.

***An Entry from Nattapat Karmniyanont's Personal Waiting Journal:
In Perplexed Anticipation***

4/9/2020

I am standing here, paper towel in hand, in perplexed anticipation. My mother, dutifully scrubbing all of the snack bags with the vigor of soldiers sweeping for mines, lathers once, twice, checks the crevices, checks the seals, checks the creases – safe! I stand back stunned, cradling the items with confusion and deep contemplation. Am I holding a defused bomb or bags of Flaming Hot Cheetos?

***Entries from Wardah Malik's Personal Waiting Journal:
An Apartment With a View of One World Trade Center***

3/24/2020

I woke up at 11:00 am to feed the cat. I had promised my friend to cat-sit/house sit for him for a few months while he was in Singapore so I've been staying in his apartment in the city even if I can't go outside. I drank a smoothie in the morning and called my friend to see how his day in Singapore was going. After a while I would just sit on the balcony and look at the view. The cat would relax outside on the balcony with me. The view was of One World Trade Center, which was nice! I had to stock up before I came here so I wouldn't have to leave the apartment as much. So, at around 4:00 pm I listened to music and painted some random things. My friend was growing some tomatoes on his balcony, so I picked some out and made something with them. For some reason, the internet stopped working so I had to wait for it to start working again so that I could play some music. For dinner I made myself some soup and almost finished it all in one day.

4/1/2020

I watched a documentary about animals. Around 12:00 am I started to draw random things that came to mind like mountains and other things. My brother told me he would call me so I had to wait for his call; we talked for three hours! I had to wait for the cat to eat the food so I could give her medicine at night.

4/5/2020

I made pasta today and I listened to some songs while waiting for the pasta to be done. I finished my painting of a friend. So I finished all my

Lays chips and I was waiting for myself to realize I shouldn't have finished all my chips. The cat kept me company outside again, which was nice. I called my nephews to make sure they are okay and safe. While waiting for them to pick up, I cleaned the kitchen a little bit.

Hopefully the World Doesn't Go Back to Normal, by Carolyn Reyes

Waiting for the pandemic to end. This pandemic made me realize how fragile reality is, everything that makes up reality can just be broken worldwide. I wake up and it's like time doesn't really exist anymore, neither do days of the week. Just tomorrow, yesterday, or today. All I do now is wait. It's not that bad, it's just crazy to really sit and conceptualize how the world stopped.

In my waiting, I use the phone a little bit toooooooo much now, it can't be healthy and I'm tired of it. I have tried to stick to my workout routine to keep me sane but that's about it. I just eat and sleep and work out all day. I go to sleep, wake up, and repeat. Going outside feels illegal now and I regret all my canceled plans because I wanted to stay home and do nothing. Doing nothing would be funner without having to attend these fake classes but then I'd really be doing nothing, so I guess it is what it is.

Waiting for this pandemic to end is scary because so many people all ill and dying and we never know when it's going to end or if we'll catch it. Life just seems very fragile. Waiting some days seems like an eternity or boring, and other days it goes by so fast. My sleep schedule is so messed up that day is night and night is day. But it's not too bad. In no way am I complaining about this waiting I'm doing because I know a lot of people's waiting is far worse – it's sad to think about the homeless, or those without food and essentials or who are home with an abuser now. But hopefully, the world doesn't go back to normal. Hopefully, this will make everyone want to be better instead.

Two Waiting Haikus and One Something Else, by Gamal Amin

You know what's scary?
Not ambulances wailing
But the birds' chirping.

Hiding and masking.
We are living in a cave.
Secluded. Waiting.

I yearn. I yearn for the life I had before the pandemic. I yearn for my commute – the Staten Island Ferry – with its breeze and calm rocking, the subway with its loudness, and the night bus home with its peace and quiet. I even yearn for the stale smell of piss that is always emanating from the distance somewhere. I wait. I must wait. I wait for the government to start taking it seriously. Then I wait for people to start taking it seriously. And I wait more. I wait for the cases to finally plateau. Not decrease, but plateau. I wait for the bodies to stop piling up every day. "200 dead today … 300 the next." "Did you know that so-and-so died?" "Wow, I can't believe it…." Can't believe it? I can't process it. I am lost and confused – in a daze. When will I wake up from this sleep?

A Coronavirus Pandemic State of Emergency, as Dramatized by Patrick Diaz

Waiting. At home. For anything.

I woke up on the fourth day of self-isolation to the sound of people outside my window. My first thought was "Are they not taking this virus seriously?" So, I looked outside, and sure enough there was a group of five elderly people gathered in a circle, talking about their week while smoking. I was in my apartment for the good of the ones standing five feet from my window, while they ignored the rules and continued to congregate and laugh it up. I felt like I hadn't seen the sun in weeks, and there they were leaning against the scaffolding outside my first-floor window having a blast. It's bad enough that I had no sunlight coming into my apartment because of this immense metal monster outside my window, but they had to go and ruin the quiet too.

I began to imagine If the virus had been a more tangible, seeable threat, would they still be ignoring it? The first image that came to my mind was out of a horror movie, a zombie movie to be exact. It made me think of the expository scenes of these movies where people are trying to go about their days like normal before they realize an apocalyptic event is taking place. Would old Fran, my neighbor (that's not her name but she looks like a Fran), see a man with his skin falling off of his face and think that everything is a-ok? Would she grab her morning cup of coffee and stand outside my window chatting without a care in the world, as a member of the living dead approached her slowly but surely? This is how the scene plays in my head.

The noise from an old flat-screen TV buzzes in the background of Fran's apartment. Fox news plays. Fran, a 76-year-old retiree, enjoys a sip from

179

her morning cup of joe. It's black, with eight sugars. The viscous syrupy coffee is just how she likes it. She talks aloud to herself as the TV news broadcast continues.

Fran: That's good.

Anchorman: President Trump said in his address yesterday evening that a state of emergency has been declared, almost two weeks after calling the outbreak a hoax. Today I am joined by Fox news correspondent Julie Band—

The TV cuts off. Fran takes one last long sip of syrupy coffee. She puts the cup down on her M.A.G.A campaign coaster. She stands up and looks around her one-bedroom apartment. Across her dining room is a small bookshelf populated by magazines. On top of it is a small blue ceramic bowl with a set of keys and a green box of menthols. She grabs a cigarette and her keys and walks out her front door, and closes her door behind her. She walks through the lobby, out the front door. She's greeted by John, a wideset man in his early 50's who shares her passion for Donald Trump. His white hair is messy, but his dark, pitch-black handlebar moustache sticks out from his face.

John: Mornin'. You catch the news this mornin'? Gosh darn, gov'ner says we have to stay home. Some of us got work to do.

Fran: You said it. If the situation was really as bad as they say, Trump would've announced a state of emergency sooner. Meanwhile the media won't give him a break.

John: You got that right, sister.

They continue to talk but unbeknownst to them, a figure approaches. The tall figure, hair ruffled and limping, is wearing a black suit. The figure spots the two chatty cathys and turns to walk in their direction. The figure grunts and begins to walk towards them.

Figure: uuuuuughhhnng.

From across the street the two see him, hear him, look over, and continue talking.

John: Looks like someone had one too many last night.

He chuckles to himself. The two continue talking. The slow-moving figure encroaches and extends his arms out to grab John.

John: Watch where you're going, bozo!

He pushes the figure away, the figure falls forward onto the pavement, exposing his uncovered rear, with an X-shaped scar across his back.

John: What the hell? Buddy, are you all right?

He leans forward to help the man up. He extends his arm and the man turns his head towards him. His face, now bloody and beaten from the fall on concrete, does not emote.

Figure: uuuuuughhhnng!!! UUauhhhagghh!!

It lurches its neck forward and grabs John's arm and takes a giant bite.

John: AHHHHHHHHHHHHHHH!!!!! Son of a bitch bit me!

He kicks the figure in his face and runs inside, leaving Fran to fend for herself. Fran, frozen in disbelief, stands there staring at the puddle of fresh blood that sprayed from John's arm. She looks at the figure, black congealed blood slowly drips down his face. Her mind moves to her morning coffee, syrupy and black.

Fran: What the hell!? What the hell!?

She turns to run, but the figure grabs her shoulder. Panicking, she falls backwards. The figure collapses on top of her. She closes her eyes, giving into her fate. WHAM, a broom stick goes flying into the back of the figure's head. Standing over Fran is none other than Patrick Diaz, the Puerto Rican fella that lives in the apartment next to hers.

Patrick: Shouldn't you be social distancing??!!

He extends his hand, and helps her up. They run inside and shelter themselves in their respective apartments.

End.

Waiting (Poetically) During the Coronavirus Pandemic, by Fawzi Saleh

The sun's rays penetrate the black blinds
Awaking, I go to my laptop, beginning my homework
Within seconds, darkness approaches, and I go to bed
This is the Pandemic, when day and night are glued together
The TV is turned on and there is the governor
"It will get worse," he says
Hours later, the president replaces him
"It will be over soon," he informs
This is the Pandemic, when confusion is rife
Down the street, my fellow brethren walk toward me
Their beautiful mouths hidden by N95 masks
Their elegant hands covered in vinyl gloves
This is the Pandemic, when safety overrides beauty
At the grocery, the line at the entrance snakes around the block
Inside, I join the line for the cashier
The woman in front of me turns around
"Social distancing," she tells me, dispelling me with her hand
This is the Pandemic, when shooing is the new social

Waiting (in Personal Prose and Poetry) During the Coronavirus Pandemic, by Jason Chetram

Note: This is the Waiting Journal entry I wrote right after our college's shortened spring break:

In the past couple of months, I feel as if I've learned more about myself that in the nineteen years that I've been alive. Partly, because in the past nineteen years that I've been alive, I did not see the point in such introspection. However, these days that seem to be mired in anxiety, stress, and copious amounts of deceiving "free time," I've come to realize that I need to start thinking about myself just a little more than before. What started the shift in my thought was the week of spring break, where familial stress, social stresses, and mental stresses all hit at once relentlessly. As a result, I became a person who became very irritable and was nearly always angry. Indiscriminate anger at anything that crossed my mind was just a commonality for me now. However, a side effect of these negative emotions was throbbing, pounding headaches, the likes of which were debilitating, and forcefully subdued me to be bedridden, as sleeping was the only way I found to suppress the pain. It was quite a while through spring break that I realized the correlation between my anger and headaches and when I finally connected the dots I felt like I had a revelation. It became as clear as day to me that all I needed to do was to not be angry, and as such, moving forward I began taking steps towards becoming someone who would not allow himself to become engulfed in anger. I began making small changes in my day to day and became more cognizant of the thoughts running through my mind. And as simple as that, the headaches subsided and I began to feel in control. However, in my mind, the initial stresses that plagued me did not up and vanish.

Something interesting that I heard recently was that the human mind will create problems when there are no current problems. As a result, at any given point, there will always be something bothering you to some degree. This is something that I find myself believing, as whenever you deal with a problem, a new one will soon take its place. The person I want to become was not one that was happy (happy in a sense of having no stress), as I felt aiming for something as that would be naive. Instead, I opted for being someone who would be able to not get angry, a very nuanced thing the more thought is given to it. However, when I finally began to achieve this state of mind a new stressor entered my mind, that is the thought of "This calmness will not last forever."

The calmness that I have achieved in my current life and mental state is something that I am proud of and is something I understand cannot remain forever. The nagging in my mind that where I am now is only temporary is something that I can accept. Ideally, I'd like to remain at where I am now for as long as possible or to reach a point where it is no longer just temporary. I am willing to wait to become that person; however, it seems impossible to become absolved from all stresses of the world. Despite this, aiming to become that person and bettering myself mentally is something I would choose over wallowing in rage, regardless of whether the end goal is attainable or not. I will never truly become the person who I want to be, but perhaps by sticking to this path, I will find something else that's just a valuable during my wait.

Waiting for Someone Who Will Never Be, Jason Chetram's poem inspired by his journal entry

One step forward two steps back
My head is splitting, about to crack
Energy with no direction gone to waste

Anger and sadness interlace
Another forward doubled back
Remains of a megalomaniac
Reached a tipping point, at the edge
Change from within is now a pledge
No steps forward one step back
Not discouraged, soon on track
Healing the damage that's been dealt
Blinding negativity begins to melt
No step forward no step back
Understanding all that I lack
Now growing from what's been destroyed
New radiant energy filling the void
One step forward no step back
Feeling content, no thoughts left to unpack
A calmness deep within my mind
A lingering feeling there's still more to find
One step forward no step back
A humble pace, but I'm on the attack
Continuing to search for what alludes me
Waiting on someone who will never be

The Great Escape: Waiting During the Pandemic, as dramatized by Trever Polk

The boy hated being at day care and couldn't stand just waiting for his mother to get out of work and come pick him up, so while they were out on the playground he slipped away and snuck out to the sidewalk. At the intersection there was, yes, the daycare, a grocery store across the street, some apartments, a church or something, and yes, a subway station.

He was only six, but the boy knew enough that the station was where he would go to get home. And now he slowly and carefully descended the staircase, making sure not to fall because of the loosely bolted step, down past the empty stands that formerly held AM New York and Metro, over to the wall of turnstiles. The boy had no MetroCard, but he knew from observation that the best way to get through was to just go under the things. So he crawled, unbothered for the moment by the dirty ground, to the other side.

There were weird circular wooden benches in a lobby-like area with a window that overlooked the tracks. The LED light with the train times stood above the window. The boy could read, but he was distracted by the fun shape of the benches. There were no other passengers, so he got up and stood on top of one of them, and then hopped over to another. On a third he got on and lay down on his back looking up at the drab ceiling. There was a downtown express train to somewhere three minutes away. The boy sprung up and went down to the platform, and he waited like he saw the adults doing: listlessly standing there, thinking about what appears to be nothing, looking at a phone, although he had to skip that part because he didn't have one.

The train arrived and he got on. The car was nearly empty—it was, after all, 12:00 on a Tuesday.

Stations passed by. He counted how many – one, two, three, until he got bored of that, and then he just waited to get off at the next stop. He got up from his seat before the train stopped, and when the conductor hit the breaks the boy fell over from the impact. He picked himself up though, unscathed except by whatever germs he'd picked up. He exited the train car and walked up the stairs towards the turnstiles.

"Hey!," a weird-sounding voice said this from behind him. The boy turned around to see where it was coming from.

"Kid! Over here!"

The woman in the box was waving at him, so it must have been her. He went over.

"Hi," he said curtly.

"Where are your parents?"

"Mommy and Daddy are at work."

"And where are you supposed to be?"

"Here."

His lying face was incredibly unconvincing.

"Really? Where are you supposed to be?"

He caved in. "Day care."

The woman sighed. "What day care?"

"I don't remember what it's called."

The woman grew more frustrated.

"Do you know your mother or father's phone number?"

"Yes," he said. He recited his mother's cell phone number and the woman dialed it inside the box.

"Hello, yes, I'm calling from the Borough Hall subway station in Brooklyn; your son was wandering around the subway and I figured you were probably looking for him. Yes. Okay. I will Buhbye."

The woman in the box hung up the phone and said through her weird circle, "Your mother is coming to get you. Just stay here."

"Okay."

So now the boy waited for this mother. No more fun than if he'd stayed at daycare and a far greater chance of getting in trouble.

Chyna Chung People-Watches as She Waits Outside on a New York City Grocery Store Line During the Coronavirus Pandemic

Ten minutes have passed and there are about 150 people in front of me. Only one at a time can go in. What to do with this time? Oh, maybe I can count all of the people in front of me. Let's see 1, 2, 3, 4 ... oh, forget it, it's too much. Maybe I'll make a list of what to get so I can get in and get out. Start off with the staples – milk, eggs, bread, water. Then move on to what is going to keep me sane for the next month – vanilla ice cream, Rice Krispies, cinnamon toast crunch. Well, what to do now? I got it.

I think the woman in front of me is a mother shopping for her kids. She wears black leggings and a long black coat, her hair tied, and a mask and gloves. She looks around the parking lot the way a protective mother would when trying to eye her kids.

Seven people in front of her is a man who is standing about ten feet from the person in front of him. I wonder if he's lost anyone in the past few weeks.

There is an older woman behind me who is with another older woman two people behind her. They might be sisters ... hmm, maybe cousins ... or just really good friends. They look back at each other and shake their heads as to how crazy the line is. The younger woman asks the older woman if she wants to leave and if the line is too much. The older woman decides to stay.

About four or five people ahead of me is a middle-aged woman standing alone with about three of those reusable bags New York City was supposed to use before the virus hit us. She waves her hand as if she is telling someone to come towards her. It's her husband. She tells him something and he goes back in their car. I see my parents in them. Dealing with this as best they can, but mainly the woman doing most of the work.

Then there is me. The only one my age, alone in this line. I feel frustrated, slightly annoyed, tired, needles in my feet from standing, but I feel ... proud. Proud to be in this line. Proud not to turn away or lose patience. Happy to help my parents. Proud that I was prepared enough to go outside and aware of the risks and not being discouraged to take them.

Waking Up and Enduring, a pandemic poem by Massiel Sanchez

Mornings are heavy
the silence of the night comes to an end
the day's worries abruptly flood in
having you wonder why you can't just stay in bed

As your dreams escape you
you wait for some sort of provocation
anything really
to help thrust yourself up, maybe find some liberation

waiting.
sunshine doesn't help from inside
the window's glass degrades its warmth

longing for what it once did provide

the uncertainty of the next moment
clouds your path forward
But don't worry, you already know your way
Maybe it's best if it is reordered

Gabriella Tuchman Writes on Playing "Waiting" Games During the Pandemic (Not Dissimilar from Vladimir and Estragon's Games in WAITING FOR GODOT)

Just as with Vladimir and Estragon in WAITING FOR GODOT, who play games with each other that bring only silence when they come to an end, during the pandemic there is not a lot for me to do at home. I feel like my emotions are only magnified, so that when I am happy, I am really happy, and when I am not, I am really not. For example, when I play what amounts to a "waiting" game with my family on a Friday night (the Sabbath), I am happy, but the second the game ends, I am no longer happy. That moment of stimulation came to a close, and so did my momentary happiness. It is very hard to stay happy when we are locked inside and scared because of a virus that is possibly deadly. I always try and remember, though, that just like happiness can disappear in an instant, it can also appear in an instant.

Christina Louie Writes the 2020 Coronavirus Pandemic Version of the Intern Vignette from the 1935 play WAITING FOR LEFTY

Dr. Barnes, an elderly distinguished man, is speaking on the telephone. He wears a white coat.

BARNES. No, I gave you my opinion twice. You outvoted me. You did this to Dr. Benjamin yourself. That is why you can tell him yourself. *(Hangs up phone, angrily. As he is about to pour himself a drink from a bottle on the table, a knock is heard.)* Who is it?

BENJAMIN. Can I see you a minute, please?

BARNES. *(Hiding the bottle.)* Come in, Dr. Benjamin, come in.

BENJAMIN. It's important – excuse me – have you seen the President's budget proposal for the 2020 fiscal year federal budget? He is attempting to cut the U.S. Department of Health and Human Services by twelve percent and the Centers for Disease Control and Prevention by ten percent! It is my job to oversee the American Public Health Association and this recommendation does not bode well for the health of the world.

BARNES. *(Dryly.)* He is the president of the United States.

BENJAMIN. He's incompetent as hell.

BARNES. *(Obviously changing subject, picks up lab jar.)* They're doing splendid work in brain surgery these days. This is a very fine specimen…

BENJAMIN. I'm sorry, I thought you might be interested.

BARNES. *(Still examining jar.)* Well, I am, young man, I am! Only remember that it is a proposal! Legislators must still vote on it.

BENJAMIN. Of course. But the consequences of this administration advocating for such allocation and cuts to expenditure in vital programs like Medicaid will surely harm our addiction and HIV efforts! Not to mention that what we need right now is funding for proper prevention with the influx of the COVID-19 virus!

BARNES. You think we're in danger?

BENJAMIN. Of course! Without the proper funding and the increasing media sensationalizing of the virus, we could be in for hysteria when we could be getting ahead of the spread here in the country! It will surely spread to our citizens and affect other sectors. Understand, Dr. Barnes, I don't mind being left unknown so long as there is not a flagrant bit of class distinction – because they're poor –

BARNES. Be careful of words like that – "class distinction." Don't belong here. Lots of energy, you brilliant young men, but idiots. Discretion! Ever hear that word?

BENJAMIN. Too radical?

BARNES. Precisely. And with the way our country is being run, some day like in Germany, it might cost you your head.

BENJAMIN. Not to mention my job.

BARNES. So they told you?

BENJAMIN. Told me what?

BARNES. With the local health departments still being down 50,000 jobs from where they were in 2008, they're looking to cut even more staff... especially those that cannot be controlled. The administration thinks it's necessary to cut losses.

BENJAMIN. Do you think it will touch me?

BARNES. Afraid it will.

BENJAMIN. But after all I'm top man here. I don't mean I'm better than others, but I've worked harder.

BARNES. And shown more promise...

BENJAMIN. I always supposed they'd cut from the bottom first.

BARNES. Usually.

BENJAMIN. But in this case?

BARNES. Complications.

BENJAMIN. For instance?

BARNES. *(Hesitant.)* I like you, Benjamin. It's one ripping shame.

BENJAMIN. I'm no sensitive plant – what's the answer?

BARNES. An old disease, malignant, tumescent. We need an antitoxin for it.

BENJAMIN. I see.

BARNES. What?

BENJAMIN. I met that disease before – in Illinois first.

BARNES. You have seniority here, Benjamin.

BENJAMIN. But I'm black!

(Barnes nods his head in agreement.)

BARNES. Doctors don't run medicine in this country. The men who know their jobs don't run anything here, everything gets decided by the insurance companies and legislators. I've seen medicine change–plenty– but not because of rich men–in spite of them! In a rich man's country your true self's buried deep. People get called inferior for the color of their skin, considered vermin for needing economic support from the nation, and dismissed from their jobs for not fitting the mold!

BENJAMIN. It is hard being stigmatized and to not be able to properly do my job because of not only the legal red tape, but the social red tape that Trump and his administration create! I wanted to see an America that has skillful leaders and properly qualified people doing their jobs. The work is not only going to be here on American soil when the virus hits our population, but also worldwide with the aid of the CDC. We must fight! Maybe get killed, but goddamn! We'll go ahead! *(Benjamin stands with clenched fist raised high.)*

Blackout.

The Pandemic Wait of Living Vicariously In Our Devices, by Paige Thorne

Crippling fear
of the world around me
Vicariously living
in our devices
Discouraged by a present I don't want to call mine
Nowhere to run
Inside
Nowhere to hide
Entertainment
Tik Tok Tik Tok
Even
Encountering
Numbness

Carolyn Reyes Writes About How She Can't Wait to Finish Writing This Journal Entry About Enduring Personal Journal Writing About Waiting

This entry in my personal waiting journal doesn't make sense to me because in the moment I don't really feel like I'm waiting for anything, although I know the whole "we're always waiting" thing. I don't think I am. Maybe I'm waiting to finish writing this entry, I don't know. Technically, I wouldn't even have to wait to finish this writing except my other personal waiting journal entries were way shittier than this and I need a good grade. Not that this is any better. How can I get credit for a "waiting journal" after clearly stating how I'm not waiting at the moment. Well, I am writing this while waiting for the train so there's that – but my other journals were on that topic and I really don't feel like boring myself even more right now. In a way, this entry is influenced by my other journal entries because I disliked them all so much that they got me to write something different.

Patrick Diaz Has the Last Word About Making It Through a Course on Waiting Literature – While Waiting Out the 2020 Coronavirus Pandemic

Throughout this course, my idea of waiting has not changed. The course has, in an indirect way, shaped how I think about my waiting. Throughout the length of this course, waiting has been a constant, sometimes overwhelming weight to bear. In the first part of the course, it was waiting eagerly to be able to discuss the readings, while also being patient enough to let my classmates who rarely spoke have the opportunity to share their thoughts. Often the end result of that waiting would be that someone shared a similar thought about the reading and I was unable to share my thoughts the way I wanted. Those moments did not leave me disappointed, though. They were reaffirming and made me wonder why it was that we shared such similar ideas. Was it some shared experience we had as students? The experience of being in the same age group, perhaps? Or maybe the universality of the experience of waiting just calls out all these mutual experiences.

I would like to think that the important thing about the latter half of this course, despite being at home and quite a lot less interactive than it was before, is that it has given us all another shared waiting experience. This experience will be something we can agree about or disagree about and have lengthy discussions about once this is all over. This time has been stressful, and rife with seemingly endless bouts of monotonous, often anxiety-ridden waiting. Because of this, and the nature of waiting, it seems like all we can do is hope for the best and do our part. Ironically for me, I have been unable to fully put my effort into my classes due to the physical and mental health of my family. I am assured, though, by the idea that somewhere there are people waiting for the world to move on from this situation, just like our classmates.

Thinking and reading about waiting has been a welcome, although sometimes sobering, experience during this extremely stressful time. It has been a distraction at times and, at others, a reminder of just how shared the emotions about this pandemic really are. I truly do hope my classmates share this sentiment and have gotten some opportunity through the literature we've studied in and out of the class to reflect on the notion that waiting is something that, in the end, brings us together. We're all in constant states of waiting, much like the characters from every piece of literature we have gone over, and that's something that we'll still share once this pandemic is over.

CHAPTER 18

The Pro and Con Wizard of "The Wizard of Oz," in L. Frank Baum's Classic 1900 Novel of Hope

During our off-campus teaching and learning experience as a result of the 2020 coronavirus pandemic, students in "The Literature Waiting" course may have been (pleasantly) surprised or (unpleasantly) puzzled by the inclusion of major excerpts (and many illustrations) from L. Frank Baum's 1900 classic THE WIZARD OF OZ as part of their required reading of "waiting" works. However, the following critical thinking and creative thinking prompts went a long way (down the yellow brick road?, up the yellow brick road?) toward addressing those reactions.

Prompts:

- *How is THE WIZARD OF OZ a novel about "expecting" as well as a novel about "waiting"?*
- *How does having a brain, a heart, and courage enable human beings to "endure waiting"?*
- *Why does its author, L. Frank Baum, both begin and end the story he tells with Dorothy at home? In what ways can it be said that while Dorothy is in the land of Oz, that house back in Kansas is "waiting for" Dorothy?*
- *What, in a non-fantasy world, do Dorothy's three companions on the yellow brick road represent? (Note: isn't "yellow" the color of "waiting"?)*
- *Can you think of a fourth companion for Dorothy to have on her journey and, if so, what would that companion represent in the real world?*

- *How might you, in a piece of creative writing, incorporate this possible fourth character into the narrative arc of Baum's story?*
- *In what ways is the wizard a con man (fake news)? And in what ways is he a font (source) of wisdom as either a soothsayer, a sage, a seer, an oracle, or a wizard (check out the meanings of all five of these natural and supernatural entities and eliminate any that do not apply)?*
- *Why might you yourself seek out the wizard? Predict what the wizard would both do for you and say to you.*
- *Why might a particular fictional character we have met in our course readings this term seek the wizard out? Predict what the wizard would both do for that fictional character and say to them.*
- *In a formal debate, which side of the following argument would you prefer to take and what specific points would you make to win the debate: the novel THE WIZARD OF OZ is nothing more than a children's book or the novel THE WIZARD OF OZ is more than just a children's book?*
- *What question or questions would you like to ask the author, L. Frank Baum, about this famous work of literature of his – and why those questions?*

So how is L. Frank Baum's THE WIZARD OF OZ a novel about waiting and expecting? Let us count the ways, said our college collaborators:

- At the start of the novel, readers find themselves in a sleepy Kansas town that itself could epitomize "waiting for something to happen"; everything is gray, Dorothy can't see for miles, and so even she is waiting for a change of scenery;
- Dorothy's foster parents – Aunt Em (Emily) and Uncle Henry – are always waiting for the next cyclone that will inevitably come and take away their farm and crop; their waiting also consists, in particular, of their building of a shelter in which to wait out a storm;
- when Dorothy is swept away in the cyclone, she waits hours for the house to land until she drifts off;
- once landed in Oz, Dorothy actively waits her way through and throughout the entire novel – her traveling along the long yellow brick road is a kind of waiting to get to her immediate goal of reaching the Emerald City and her ultimate goal of getting back home to Kansas;

- the Scarecrow, seeking knowledge and intellect, waits to be recognized as not some stereotypical unintelligent farmer without any brains;
- the Tin Woodman (the Tin Man), seeking empathy and love, waits to be recognized as not some stereotypical dehumanized industrial factory worker without a heart;
- the Lion waits to be recognized as a brave leader of others who, quite understandably, has fears and insecurities;
- Dorothy's journey with these three particular companions represents the kind of expecting and waiting known as "growing up" since as a little girl on her own, Dorothy would not have been capable of making this trip unless she came to "embody" the attributes of intelligence, compassion, and courage;
- waiting to defeat the evil of the Wicked Witch of the West and her immoral followers the Flying Monkeys shows active waiting to make it to the all-powerful Oz and, finally, to have their great expectations met;
- the color yellow (maybe not too bright) is often associated with hope, or longing, or the possibility of a promising future – all forms of waiting;
- Dorothy and her companions wait to accept themselves – through the wizard's good intentions and wisdom – as the individuals they essentially are (waiting as a process of self-discovery and self-recognition);
- the wizard continues to wait to be recognized as a sage through the wisdom of his words, instead of having to always con those who seek him out with placebos that cause them to believe in his possible supernatural powers;
- the reader of the novel waits anxiously, worried that something bad is about to happen to Dorothy and her companions on their "waiting-journey" to the not-really-Emerald City and the fulfillment of their wishes.

According to college collaborator **Chyna Chung**, a possible fourth companion for Dorothy to have on her journey could be **Aunt Em**, as she waits for the gift of youthfulness. Dorothy once discussed a time when Aunt Em was a "young, pretty wife" before the sun and wind stole the sparkle from her eyes and the rosiness from her cheeks. Aunt Em turned thin, gaunt – a sober gray woman who never smiled. Whenever Dorothy would laugh as a child, Aunt Em would be in awe, as she could not understand how such a person could find something to laugh at. Since each want of a person describes their character, Aunt Em's goal is not literal endless beauty but endless light and positivity, so much so that it radiates onto others. When Aunt Em becomes "youthful" again she will be brought back to a time in her life in which she has a sparkle in her eyes, rosy cheeks, and a smile that stretches from ear to ear. She will not be startled when others laugh or wonder how they could find something to laugh at in such trying times. She will encourage it.

College collaborator **Gabriella Tuchman** would have *a pencil without a sharpener* as a fourth companion for Dorothy. "The pencil feels useless," says Gabriella, "because he needs to conserve his point so that he can continue to stay sharp. This means that he cannot get close to anyone because the only way for him to speak is through writing. Once he has a sharpener for his point, he can write as much as he pleases and make friends with as many people as he desires because he will always have a point. This would show the necessity of everyone having one good friend – someone who you can always rely on to be by your side, someone who you can really trust. Once you have one friend, it becomes much easier to open up to others."

College collaborator **Maxine Lim** suggests *a rundown toy* as Dorothy's possible fourth companion since a toy that is rundown suggests "endurance and never giving up," qualities that Dorothy certainly demonstrated she had in her – from how she was brought up at home – as she made her way along the yellow brick road.

On the other hand, college collaborator **Patrick Diaz** believes that a fourth companion "already exists in the novel: *it's Toto!* I think Toto represents the young people of America, jumping head first into trying to fix whatever issues come up in our country, even if it's sometimes out of our depth and if we sometimes need help and protection." Patrick adds that if he were invited to be the fourth companion, he "might seek out the wizard to give me more time in my day, although he might hand me a watch and say it's to 'keep track of the time that's there.'"

And now journey back with us to the Land of Oz (through some imaginative writing by two other college collaborators) as a fourth character joins up with Dorothy and her three Baum-created companions on a quest, literally, for recognition. Oh, they're off to see the wizard, the wonderful Wizard of Oz – and be given by him that human quality they have always possessed but needed to be affirmed in.

In the Land of Oz: The Beauty of the Mirror
By Carolyn Reyes

"Well, it's my turn: I will go to the wizard next and get my beauty," said the Mirror. Now, the Mirror was a walking talking mirror who was able to show others how they looked but wanted to also see herself as beautiful.

"Oh, you have the most beautiful heart already," replied the Woodman.

"And the most beautiful way of thinking," added the Tin Man. (The Lion courageously roared his agreement.)

Super sweet and nice, the Mirror walked to the throne room and knocked.

"Enter," replied Oz.

"I have come for my beauty," said the Mirror.

"Very well," answered the little man; "allow me to get that for you." He continued on to a small flower vase, and with the same tinsmith shears cut off a lovely ruby red rose, made entirely of silk and cotton.

"Well, do you like?" said Oz.

"Yes! I love it!" exclaimed the Mirror.

So, the wizard placed the synthetic rose stem behind her ear. "You surely are a sight to look at," he said. "Now you have a beauty inside and out to envy. How do you feel?"

The Mirror raised her hand to her face to look at her reflection in it. "Beautiful," she replied with a smile and thanked the wizard kindly before returning to her friends.

In the Land of Oz: The Impatience of Golem, the Stone Creature
By Nattapat Karmniyanont

Dorothy and her four companions walked down the yellow brick road and, gradually, the forest around them began to turn into rocky fields. As it was getting to be night time, Scarecrow suggested that the group should stop for the day. However, as Dorothy sat down against a particularly large boulder, something strange happened. The large boulder suddenly started shaking and the next thing Dorothy knew she was staring at a large stone face.

"Dorothy, are you okay?" said the Lion.

"Oh," said the large rock, "I'm sorry, little friend. I almost hurt you."

"Who are you?" said Dorothy, calming the yapping Toto.

"Yes, I skipped my introduction, didn't I?" said the creature. "I am Golem, the stone creature. But I have to ask for what reasons are all of you walking through this land?" As each of the travelers told their stories, Golem listened patiently, still as a rock.

"And that's why I'm traveling to the Great Wizard Oz, so he can take me back to Kansas," said Dorothy, and Toto yelped in agreement.

"And I'm hoping Oz can give me a brain," stated Scarecrow.

"And me a heart," lamented the Tin Woodman.

"And me courage," declared Lion.

To Golem, these three individuals' hopes reminded him of Plato's idea that there are three aspects that make up a person: reason (brain), spirit (heart) and appetite or wants (courage?).

"Oh my, do you think the Great Oz can help me?" Golem said, his great stone sapphire eyes sparkling like the stars.

"I'm sure he can," stated Dorothy, "do you need to go back home too?"

"No, this is my home," replied Golem.

"Do you need a brain?" inquired Scarecrow.

"No, I think I am all right, for I have a solid brain already," returned Golem, nodding his great head.

"Do you need a heart, too?" asked the Tin Woodman.

"I do not believe I do, for I already have a great ruby heart," said Golem.

"Is it courage you seek?" spoke the Lion.

"No," replied Golem, "for nothing can make me shake with fear."

"Then what do you seek?" asked Dorothy.

"I want patience," said the stone golem, thinking to himself as he did not have the patience to explain this to the others – that what was needed to keep anyone's reason, spirit, and appetite balanced in moderation was this very quality of "patience" that he lacked.

"Patience?" the Scarecrow asked.

"Yes, for I have long been in this field," said the Golem, "but lately, I have not been able to pick a spot and sit still for more than a year, while my brothers and sisters, in character, have yet to move from theirs. Look, I'm literally made of stone, I'm supposed to be patient, but I'm not."

"Yes, for a rock monster you certainly are impatient," said Lion.

"So you see it too. Do you think the Great Oz can help me?"

"I'm sure he can," said the Tin Woodman. "He is the Great Oz."

"Wonderful," Golem exclaimed, as he stood to his full height, causing a miniature landslide of dirt and pebbles to slide off of his great body. "Let us go."

Spoiler Alert: As Golem sets off on the journey to Oz with his new companions, he often walks slower than the others, enjoying the sights and carefully listening to everyone's stressed-out talk about whether the great Wizard of Oz would even see them. He does, and wisely gives Golem a numberless watch to keep his mind off time and thus alleviate his unease about when to wait and when to stop waiting and do something else.

CHAPTER 19

What Exactly Is There Just Enough Room for in Those Rooms We Call a "Waiting Room"?

It would seem that many people (perhaps, particularly, older ones) will call out the word "room" when asked to immediately come up with a noun to follow the word "waiting." It's not surprising, then, that there are more than just a few contemporary short stories that have been given the title "The Waiting Room" by their authors. In fact, one such story, set in a hospital's waiting room, was being strongly considered for the second half of our course on "The Literature of Waiting" (the course was short on short stories) until the coronavirus pandemic struck. And so was that perhaps downer of a story (struck from the curriculum, that is).

But wait: although all these "waiting room" stories might sound at first hearing of their common title to be essentially similar, it actually all depends on how you say that title.

Said one way, the story is about a room somewhere in which one or more people (usually, more) are sitting around waiting for something to happen or not happen, or something to take place or be done, or something to be announced – either expected, hoped for, or dreaded.

But said another way, a "waiting room" story could be about a *personified* room that is patiently doing the waiting – waiting for someone to arrive or for something to occur (think of all the rooms that make up Shirley Jackson's haunted Hill House that are actively waiting for someone like Eleanor Vance to come live inside them and become (be one with) them.

Several of our college collaborators decided to write various kinds of "waiting room" stories even though the class as a whole had not read one together. To start off, here is the beginning of the "waiting room" story that **Ryan Langan** wrote.

And the end of Ryan's story? No room for it in this chapter? Not exactly, but we have, so to speak, shorted it out — in order to invite you, our readers, to exercise your own imaginative powers of "waiting room" writing and complete Ryan's story the way you expect (or would want) it to end.

The Waiting Room, the beginning of a short story by Ryan Langan

Nothing stirred in the waiting room – no breaths drawn, no sighs released, no clocks ticking. The weight of the air was such that it was nearly absent from space entirely. Had the waiting room the capacity and self-awareness to consider itself, it would surely have concluded that it was, in fact, a non-entity. That is, until Thomas Perry walked in.

He entered swiftly and closed the door behind him, at once swinging it as if to slam it, yet preventing it from doing so. He flattened his tie against his purple dress shirt, looked down, licked his thumb, lithely swung his leg so that his foot was within his thumb's reach, and then wiped a smudge from his leather shoes. Seeing no receptionist in the waiting room, he narrowed his eyes. He began a survey of the waiting room: noise-canceling wood-paneled walls, an odd, angular sofa, two tall potted ferns, a window with no shades or curtains, and a small statuette of a ballerina. He sat on the sofa and crossed his legs, immediately uncomfortable under the sharp diagonals of its structure. He did not want to be in the room, and was already waiting to get out.

Now, breaths were drawn. Sighs were released. Mr. Perry's internal clock? Ticking. Had the waiting room now suddenly sprung into consciousness, it would likely characterize itself as "impatience." You see, waiting rooms are very flexible, indeed. Unlike a kitchen or a bedroom or a living room, whose purposes are built-in to their forms, whose forms are constructed to accommodate activity, waiting rooms are built for the absence of activity. They are where activity rests, a step between a previous activity and one forthcoming. They merely become the characters they hold – they are voids to fill – liminal spaces.

As the waiting room began to take on the colors and shapes of Mr. Perry's impatience, it grew noticeably darker. Rather than being silent, it adopted strange hisses and clicks that seemed to be coming from the pipes and vents in the walls and ceiling. The ferns drooped; the angular sofa became still more angular. Time began to do that funny thing time does while one is waiting – seconds seemed to be minutes, minutes seemed to take hours. All the while, Mr. Perry, oblivious of these metamorphoses, grew ever more uncomfortable and irritable. And, of course, the waiting room began to reflect this, and became violent. Things got stranger. One of the ferns bent over and slapped our poor Perry in the face. He could hardly comprehend what had happened when the other fern, reacting to Perry's frustration, whacked him coldly upon the back of the head. The sofa, sensing all this racket, began to fold in on itself, causing Mr. Perry to pry himself out and fall over onto the carpeted floor, by now teeming with movement that caused his hands, which were resting upon it, incredible itchiness and discomfort. He flung himself upward and sought support on the statuette's podium, but by now, with the rest of the room feeling so aggressive, the ballerina was spinning, and she repeatedly kicked Mr. Perry in the head ....

Time will tell: we await your continuation and conclusion of this "waiting room" story.

The Waiting Room Where I Lose Further Touch With the Idea of Free Time, by Patrick Diaz

It's funny how easy it is to change the context of a room. My bedroom, once a safe-haven from the stresses of my daily life, free from any and all academia, is now the sole place where I experience those things. In an unbelievably quick span of a couple weeks, the entire context of my bedroom changed. I used to sit at my desk, illustrating, and writing for fun. Now, my desk has a stack of assignments and reading from Hunter College that I am behind on.

I see my computer screen perpetually logged into my Spanish homework portal with countless hours of work still left to do. Someone in the Spanish department, in a cruel joke, decided that students should have to do fifteen hours of assignments per week. Not to mention that these time values are arbitrarily assigned based on how long they THINK a student should take to finish it. These assignments routinely take me quadruple the time that they expect, and when I bring this up to my professor, all she says is to finish the work. I have spent nearly fifty hours on these assignments! Every second I sit at my computer I am losing further touch with the idea of free time. I am behind in every single class at this point because of the coronavirus pandemic, and I'm sitting here waiting for the moment where something clicks and I suddenly understand Spanish, and that moment isn't coming.

Every waking minute of my life, it seems, has been devoted to finishing schoolwork despite the fact that multiple family members, including my brother and girlfriend, are sick. I sit at home chiseling away at the mountain of assignments and it seems like I am not making a dent. The worst thing about this situation is that even sleep feels stressful. My dreams the last three nights were about sitting at my desk waiting for my assignments to be done. One of which was as follows:

> *My eyes open. The soft white glow of a computer screen to the left of my bed stings the corner of my eyes. I turn my head to see what's disturbing my sleep. I see red, gray and black, a blur of words flowing down the screen. The words continue to scroll, increasing in speed until none of them can be distinguished. I blink and rub my eyes. The computer screen seems larger now. Closer. I look down and I am in a computer chair. Compulsively, I start to try and read the words on the screen but they can't be read. The more my eyes try to focus, the blurrier the words get. I move the mouse cursor to try and figure out the issue. I can't feel anything on my hands. I look down, and my arms are stuck to the desk. I cannot tell where my arms and desk begin. The screen is now painfully bright. It begins to burn. My eyes begin burning, bubbling out of my skull, but it doesn't hurt. I feel relief. Then my heart starts to pound furiously, increasing in speed and ferocity. It builds and builds until it, too, starts to burn. This time there is no relief. It bursts from my chest erupting with black flames. I feel the screen burst into flames, engulfing my entire room.*

Then I wake up.

And, At 11:59 AM, a "Waiting Room" Poem
Created Over Time by Gabriella Tuchman

At 11:59 AM they waited:
Michael and Dianne enter the emergency room. Then they waited.
John sends in his college applications. Then he waited.
Pippa orders her favorite book series online. Then she waited.
Mark and Devon join the back of the line for the newest Star Wars movie.
Then they waited.
Phoebe makes her move in chess. Then she waited.
Leslie sends in her resume. Then she waited.
Laura writes the first word of her novel. Then she waited.
Paul prays to God. Then he waited.
Tyler auditions for the musical. Then he waited.
Maebelle breaks up with her boyfriend. Then she waited.
Dottie watches her father on the respirator. Then she waited.
Eric writes a letter to his long-lost father. Then he waited.
Ralph puts chicken in the oven. Then he waited.
Nancy calculates how much she was owed. Then she waited.
John listens to an audiobook. Then he waited.
Isaac leans in to kiss his girlfriend. Then he waited.
Nicole crawls into bed. Then she waited.
Weston lies down in the sun. Then he waited.
Bob dials a phone number. Then he waited.
Nigel answers emails. Then he waited.
Liana bakes a cake. Then she waited.
Megan sets the table. Then she waited.
Will prints out the spreadsheet. Then he waited.
Sam plants in the garden. Then he waited.
Nina leaves her clothes out to dry. Then she waited.
Rebecca walks to the bus stop. Then she waited.
Pauline parks the car. Then she waited.
Alexander cuts the baby's food. Then he waited.
Olivia snaps a picture. Then she waited.
Wendy cuts her bangs. Then she waited.
Frank copies the book pages. Then he waited.
At 11:59 AM they waited.

Although it looks like we are at the end of this chapter, before we move on to the next we'd like to now give you the ending to Ryan Langan's story set in a doctor's waiting room. (So, did you compose your own? If not, it's still not too late – just hold off on reading what you see printed next.)

As Mr. Perry grew ever angrier and more confused, so did the room. It began to quake with a frankly terrifying force, and the window smashed to pieces and allowed a frigid, violent wind to occupy the room. The ferns, now confused as well as angry, were frozen in ponderous thought. The sofa was so excited that its previously sharp and angular edges softened and melted. The carpet froze and stuck up out of the floor like stalagmites. The ballerina simply combusted. The wood-paneled walls closed in on themselves, and before Mr. Perry could as much as scream, he'd been swallowed whole by his own impatience.

"Mr. Perry?" asked a voice from the open door to Perry's left. Sweating and shaky, he shot out of his daydream and stood. "Everything alright?" the voice asked.

"Yes, Dr. Platin," he said. "Just the usual anxiety. I think I need to up my meds."

CHAPTER 20

Of Course Time Flies – But It Also Travels in Other Fantastic Ways (Especially in Alan Lightman's 1993 Novel "Einstein's Dreams")

Early in 2020 (a year that could initially have been seen a visionary) there appeared in "The New Yorker" magazine a Krugar Howard cartoon in which a parent says to a child who has come into the parent's bedroom well into the night because of troubled dreams, "Look, I'm sorry to cut you off – it's just that I <u>really</u> can't stand listening to other people's dreams." Published in 1993 (and later to become an international bestseller translated into thirty languages), the relatively short (and "brief") EINSTEIN'S DREAMS by Alan Lightman presents us with a fictional young scientist by the name of Albert Einstein as he struggles to make sense of his nightly visions – his troubling dreams – while simultaneously working on a new conception of time. Still worse, relatively speaking, Einstein is constantly being rebuffed by his colleagues in the patent office ("a room full of practical ideas") in Bern, Switzerland, whenever he tries to share his "dreams" about the universe with them.

The novel EINSTEIN'S DREAMS both opens and closes (in prologue and epilogue) on the particular day in June of 1905 that Einstein brings his handwritten manuscript on a theory of relativity to an office typist so that he can then submit it for publication.

> In some distant arcade, a clock tower calls out six times and then stops. The young man slumps at his desk. He has come to the office at dawn, after another upheaval.

His hair is uncombed and his trousers are too big. In his hand he holds twenty crumpled pages, his new theory of time, which he will mail today to the German journal of physics.

Since the middle of April of 1905 this Albert Einstein "has dreamed many dreams about time" and his dreams "have worn him out, exhausted him so that he sometimes cannot tell whether he is awake or asleep. But the dreaming is finished. Out of the many possible natures of time, imagined in as many nights, one seems compelling." Not that those other visions of the nature of time are impossible. "The others might exist in other worlds" since even in this world:

> One cannot walk down an avenue, converse with a friend, enter a building, browse beneath the sandstone arches of an old arcade without meeting an instrument of time. Time is visible is all places. Clock towers, wristwatches, church bells divide years into months, months into days, days into hours, hours into seconds, each increment of time marching after the other in perfect succession. And beyond any particular clock, a vast scaffold of time, stretching across the universe, lays down the law of time equally for all.... Time is an infinite ruler. Time is absolute.... And a world in which time is absolute is a world of consolation.

In this gem of a novel, each dream of Einstein's, as depicted by Lightman, is a vision of a noticeably different world with its own unique concept of time. For example, how about a world where:

Time is finite.

Time is infinite.

Time is circular.

Time is looping.

Time is inverted.

Time can be interrupted.

Time is without future.

Time is without past.

Time is without memory.

Might time even fly? In his both scientific and magical novel Lightman conjures up a finite (but potentially infinite) number of realities for Father Time to assume (not all of them all that fantastical), and then goes on to show us what the world and human life would look like and be like as a consequence of each possibility. Since time, in EINSTEIN'S DREAMS, operates by its own rules, one's imagination is the only limit. So, for example, in a recent short-lived off-Broadway musical version of Lightman's novel, one of the musical numbers is called "The Relativity Rag" and another, sung by a mother who yearns to *freeze time* to keep her daughter close, is entitled "I Will Never Let You Go."

In "Out of Chaos," the introductory chapter to the 2017 book MYTHOS, author Stephen Fry reminds us that there was *no there there* before there was "time":

> No one had pressed the start button on Time. No one had
> shouted *Now!* And since Time had yet to be created, time
> words like *before*, *during*, *when*, *then*, *after lunch*, and *last
> Wednesday* had no possible meaning. It screws with the
> head, but there it is.

Students in "The Literature of Waiting" course were asked to give words like those a possible meaning – to let time fly and their imaginations soar in one of two ways; either they could choose one of author Alan Lightman's "time frames" and come up with their own existential consequences for that concept of time or they could create their own "time frame" and its attendant world-view results. In other words, their own version of what "Time" is or could be, their own version of how "Time" does its fantastic "dance of duration."

Depending on how you look at it, time is an illusion
By Wardah Malik

Time is ambiguous: it could mean anything, it could refer to anything. Time zones are a manmade thing just to show us that we live in different spatial parts of the world. Time is duration: the length of time it takes something to stop or start. Time can bring out such human emotions as happiness – or fear. The saying "killing" time means that you are doing something aimlessly while waiting for something to happen.

Imagine a world where everyone lives forever
By Nattapat Karmniyanont

Imagine a world where everyone lives forever. Where the withered and aged body collapses into an unambiguous cyst. A cyst, catalyze of the Phoenix, and a new body emerges from the ruined one. Memories and experiences, will they have meanings? If we can live an infinite number of lives, will we change?

The old lady stretches in her bed and stares at the blazing sun. Her caretakers enter the room and greet her brightly. She is helped out of the bed, her tired legs not what they used to be. Aided in her morning bath and dressing. She grumbles in her chair, impatient for her food. With shaky hands and toothless mouth, she gobbles her meal, relishing the sweet flavor. Satisfied, she is placed on the couch and closes her eyes once more. A smile to conglomerate her first day in this strange place.

The children laugh as their father waddles into the room. Angrily he screams, but no fear is created. More laughter ensues. His wife smiles as she lifts up her husband. His mind boils in the embarrassment and anger. But his mouth doesn't obey. He sighs. The loop is not kind to parents.

The young man waits for his grandfather. Impatient, huddled against the cold and falling snow. Glasses fogged and nose dried, he stares sidelong at his passing classmate. Her hair is specked by the snow, ebony against ivory. The grandfather strides in his new legs and pushes back his dark mane. Smirking at his grandson he walks to the girl, suave and full of experience.

The man looks at the distant tree. The same tree that was there when he was young, the same tree that he saw when he was but an old man, and the very same three loops ago. He looks on, wondering what has changed, if anything. He wants something, something new. He reaches out for something, turns back to the tree. Closes his eyes. Raises his hand to his head. Nothing changes and nothing will change. For the only true end is with death.

The woman looks at the distant houses. The same houses that were there when she was young, and the very same four loops ago. Suffering and inactivity are abundant. Most go about without a purpose. For why do anything now if it can be done on the next loop? She wants something, something to change. She looks at the table. Cluttered. Not again. She plans her proposal. For change will not come just because of tomorrow.

He holds the knife. The block of wood in front of him shines. His hands move with a mind of their own. Ecstasy. The thrill of creation saturates his mind. Aged experience with youthful nimbleness cumulates into greatness. He fixates on his craft. The joy of his life. He smiles at his project, and critiques it, preparing for the next.

The couple sit together, fingers intertwined. Smiles decorate their faces. They reminisce about the years they've had. Laughter, as their aged memories differ. Then he looks at her. His heart swells and hammers. Years before and years after he was sure, he loved her. The giddy thumping of his heart is reminiscent of years before. He asks her to the prom. She laughs and nods, "Let's make this loop one to remember."

Imagine a world in which time is simply reversed
By Trever Polk

The dream from 2 June 1905 really struck me. At first it seemed a bit silly, talking about the peach, but when the passage got to the woman and her husband aging in reverse, and later the man burying his friend, it became quite impactful to me. Death is one topic that almost never fails to make me emotional and contemplative, and the idea of death being undone, aging in reverse, was very poetic. Time in general makes me sensitive (for lack of a better word), so a lot of these passages were interesting to me, but this one in particular stood out. Aside from the poetic-ness of it, I began wondering as I read it how exactly this system was working. Was it only applying to some people, or to everyone? For the couple it seemed to apply to both of them, but it's unclear if the man burying his friend is also aging backwards. Also, how can time go backwards if things are still progressing? Do they go back every 24 hours? Because if you were to simply reverse time, we would just act like we were on a tape being rewound.

Imagine a world in which time works backwards
By Carolyn Reyes

In a world where time works backwards, one of the existential consequences would be who takes care of whom in terms of parent and child. The child is born old, while the mother is getting younger. But because the mother had the child really young, she is closer to becoming an actual child herself. Therefore, the old lady who is really the child would have to take care of the mother who is becoming a child as she get "older." Also, a weird one to consider: would everyone now die as a baby? All the roles would be reversed between mother and child because technically the child would know more – unless you are just born old but with no knowledge, but that wouldn't make sense.

So, if they see an old person dead, they know not to mourn because that person will return as a younger person. This is like the Benjamin Button movie, and if you haven't seen it, I recommend it. This is such a sad concept of time because if time is backwards and reversed, then what if you fall in love with someone aging the reverse way as you, which would be possible because at one point you'd both be the same age at the exact same time, and the relationship would only be viable for so long. *(In a note from Carolyn: I'd just like to add a thought as a result of how we all are now living during the coronavirus pandemic: I have messed up my sleep schedule so bad that when my family is getting ready for bed, I wake up, and vice versa, so technically we get fewer hours when our awake schedules cross, and it feels like time is backwards for me.)*

Imagine a world in which there is no time, only images
By Paige Thorne

"On the count of three, everyone, say 'cheese.'"
"One ... Two ... Three!"
"CHEESE!"
Click

...

The day is, was, and will be April the Twenty-Eighth. Spending a forever in the same repetitive schedule. We are at the park. The weather is nice. The birds are chirping. Everyone is wearing the JOHNSON JOYFUL REUNION t-shirt that Aunt Maggie declared was the only way to enter. I watch her now as she grabs her Camcorder from her pocketbook. I know this day better than the back of my hand. Everyone else is excited that we have been stuck in this photograph. In this space of nothingness. Contained with this one purpose if one could call it that. I want to be free. I want to exist. Aunt Maggie is waving us all over now. It took her a while to figure out how her new piece of technology worked. I ran up to Jason and this is the moment he says ...

"Hey, little big Cuzzo, how's life?"
And this is the part where I say,
"Eh, same old, same old."
"On the count of three, everyone, say 'cheese.'"
"One ... Two ... Three!"
"CHEESE!"
Click

Imagine a world (our modern world?) in which the Clock of Time is worshipped
By Hester Milford

We live in fear of age. Getting older. Women feel their biological clocks at twenty.
"Have a baby!"
"Use this anti-aging cream!"
"Get Botox for your wrinkles!"
Men feel it too, of course.
Ticking.
Waiting.

Imagine a world in which everyone could choose "The Chance in Time"
By Anne-Lilja Rentof

Imagine a world in which every person in the world had the opportunity to use "The Chance in Time" – a choice to go back to a single point in their life and change something. A missed opportunity, something stupid that was said, something that was missed. They could only do this once. After they made the change, they would not remember anything from before the moment that they made the change, only that they had made the decision to go back. Many would jump at this opportunity and use it as soon as possible, only to discover later that they should have waited to use their chance for something more important, something of more import.

Other people would take this option and find that the results were not what they expected. After all, "The Chance" and whatever resulted from it would be exactly that – a chance. How many people would you miss out on meeting? How many opportunities or events in one's lifetime have resulted from an occurrence that was initially regrettable, but eventually led to something better and new?

The high schooler who did not get into the college of her dreams would miss out on meeting the roommate from her safety school who would have gone on to become her closest and most steadfast friend. A man who lost his job might choose later to go back to change it in order to avoid the immediate discomfort; however, he would not be thinking about the fact that that day he left the office early with his belongings was the day that he bumped into a woman on the street outside the office building who would later become his wife and the mother of his children. On the other hand, a victim of assault might be able to reverse the years of trauma they had endured had they never met their abuser. A child whose parents died when he was young might never have wound up in the foster system, and might have had a more traditional upbringing.

The multiverse would expand even more exponentially as more and more new realities were created. The butterfly effect would change so many minute details of each person's life. It would be a life full of even more anxiety: not knowing if you should use your "Chance"; knowing you used your chance and not being able to remember what it was for, or if it was worth it – what, or who, you lost. Especially if you are not particularly thrilled with your life after the Chance, you may wonder what was so bad that, hey, made you use it in the first place. Some might benefit, some might not. The only question would be whether you would be willing to take the chance.

Imagine a world in which time's drive has a reset button
By Shanya Hopkins

Suppose that time's hard drive has a reset button. A button pushed by God himself every Saturday evening at the prime of night's deadness. Imagine a world in which a person lives each week unaware that their actions, consequences, and achievements will dissipate by the end of the week, only to enter Sunday in a moment anew.

In the heart of the city lives a girl hopelessly in love with the guy she intends to marry. On Sunday morning, he stops by her home and prepares a delectable breakfast for her family. She dreams of the moment when he'll get on bended knee and ask the question she has yearned to hear, for as long as she can remember. On a midday Monday stroll, prospects for their future make home on her horizons, cementing their current memories and laying the groundwork for more. He'll propose soon, until then she'll wait.

Three days, seventy-two hours, and four thousand three hundred twenty minutes pass with no word from her love. She watches the clock as Thursday bleeds into Friday, and time slips through her fingers. On a Friday afternoon, she walks through the neighborhood, passing the boy riding on his father's shoulders on his way to school and the band of elderly women in front of the market discussing what they had for breakfast. She bumps into her love, he apologizes. He tells her it's been a busy week and he's barely had time to breathe. He promises to call her this evening and away he goes to exploit the last hours of daylight. She rushes home, unfazed by the world around her, virtually passing the fleeting minutes around her. She waits for the telephone call – the call that will ease her anxiety and reaffirm his love for her. Saturday fades in and her passion-infused hope buds seedlings of restlessness as she waits in agony for the call that would never come, whether in time or at all.

As she turns in that Sunday eve, she is a lady-in-waiting to the mercy of her love. Sunday morning rises, and the girl starts afresh – a new day, the same Sunday, filled with new chanced choices. She wakes with her waiting feelings twice removed and finds herself once again in her home, at the dining table, with her family enjoying a breakfast prepared by her love. It's as if nothing has changed, and yet, everything has. For while déjà vu, the girl has not – something feels extremely familiar and it can't be explained. In this world, time resets without interruption at the conclusion of every week. A life consists of the sum total of actions and inactions of the repeated weeks. Two types of lives to be lived – one grounded in monotonous action and emotion or a life characterized by its variability, like the reading and rereading of your choose of your own adventure novel. Even in a world in which time has a reset button, there is still room for an infinite waiting to exist.

Sweet Dreams: my take on time's travels inspired by the novel EINSTEIN'S DREAMS
By Rabeya Rahman

In this world, time travels. A girl lies in bed with her legs up fluttering in the air and making random shapes that only she can see. She has all her books and papers for her college classes spread out on the bed next to her. With Airpods in her ears and the biggest grin on her face, she talks to the boy she loves – her first love – and she prays to God that he remains her last. He makes her feel loved. He makes her feel special. She never thought she was special or worth anyone's attention. She never thought she was worth it. She closes her eyes.

The girl opens her eyes and stares up at the wall. Her cousin is lying next to her and ranting about her boyfriend. It's never a real sleepover with these two without candy, movies, and late night catchups. The girl's cousin is literal perfection. She is smart, pretty, and a social butterfly. She is rambling on about how she can't wait for her future and to get married. It was recently her and her boyfriend's anniversary and things couldn't be any more amazing. She is so lost in her thoughts that she barely even looks at the girl. She has it all planned out from the different dresses for every occasion to makeup, to the guest list, to etc. Why wouldn't she? Girls like her are destined for love. True love. God knows how dark and bleak my own future is, the girl thinks, as she continues to listen to her cousin talk. Love like that is rare. Her eyes wander to the white clock on her bedroom wall and she sees it is five minutes till 3:00 am. Thank goodness all New York City high schools are closed due to the snowstorm. She closes her eyes.

The girl can barely breathe as she tries to push off the 170 pounds of weight that holds her down. She opens her eyes momentarily. He has the biggest smile in the world with his front two rabbit-teeth sticking out as he laughs at her squirming helplessly. The girl is pushed against soft comforters in bed and can barely take in a deep breath as he continues to tickle her all over. Him being bigger and heavier and significantly more built than she is, she doesn't stand a chance. They both squirm and laugh a little longer until she forces out words of surrender and he stops and collapses right next to her. Looking around, she takes in the beauty of the bedroom once more.

The room is full of bouquets of roses, candles, and balloons that congratulated the newlyweds. It is all so surreal. She is in bed, barely out of her classical south Asian wedding dress and all the heavy jewelry, breathless from all the laughter and happy tears. She never dreamed of finding happiness as precious as this. She never dared to dream of finding someone like him and getting to the position she is in at this moment in time. She takes a deep breathe, turns to face him, looks him in the eyes, and closes her own.

The girl opens her eyes to the sound of "I love you, babe" in her ears. She drops her feet back down onto the bed, rolls over onto her stomach, and replies, "I love you too."

A world in which time has attained the status of the divine is a world unfit for human beings
By Jason Chetram

There are repercussions to the kind of world in which time has attained the status of something godly or divine. People look to God and the divine when something is missing in their earthly life, and since God and the divine are so ambiguous, people tend to keep searching; however, this does not dissuade them since it provides them with a bit of comfort as their journey is never over.

Although the concept of time on the level of an Einstein's pondering may be ambiguous, for the regular person time is not at all ambiguous. Time is objective, and time is factual. This poses an issue when confronted with ideas like "Time is the clarity for seeing right and wrong" and "A world in which time is absolute is a world of consolation." Time is cold and time is heartless. When it comes to determining such matters as what is morally right and morally wrong, it's something that must be approached humanely. Time does not forgive, nor does Time allow do-overs. Religions, on the other hand, do – and this is of help to people. Time, a scientific instrument, should not be imbued with such power to be an arbiter. The world in which time is absolute would be one which is cold, a world unfit for humans.

Chyna Chung on coping in a coronavirus pandemic world in which time is a sense

"In a world where time is a sense, like sight or like taste, a sequence of episodes may be quick or may be slow, dim or intense, salty or sweet, casual or without cause, orderly or random, depending on the prior history of the viewer" -- Alan Lightman, author of the novel EINSTEIN'S DREAMS

There is a middle-aged woman sitting on a bench near her apartment in New York. She is wearing a mask, purple gloves, and dark sunglasses. She feels the warm sun on her face and the cool breeze that follows. Her phone rings but she doesn't answer right away. She knows what is on the other end of that phone call but insists on having a glimmer of hope for what could be.

She answers. Her mind flashes through the memories of her and her husband. Their first kiss, their first trip, when she waited on him, when he waited on her. Twenty-seven years of small moments flash before her eyes like a picture she wasn't ready to take.

"Ma'am, his time of death was 7:14 am. I am so sorry for your loss. Our coordinators will have him transported to the funeral home of your choice."

"..."

"Ma'am? Are you with me?"

There is another woman who is walking down the street pushing her grocery cart. Her hair is tied and her mask is on. She is mumbling under her breath about the long day she has had. She had to wait in line to get gas, then drive to the store and wait in an hour-long line to get into the grocery store, then fight with the cashier on how the plastic bags were too expensive. After that, the paper bags ripped while she was putting them in the trunk, and she tore her finger nail. She drives back to her apartment and finds a way to manage the bags while bringing them upstairs. There is no hair salon, nail salon, spa, or any place to maintain her normal life during the shutdown. She places the bags on a bench near the door to her apartment in order to rest her hands and take out her keys. She makes a phone call on her cell and says, "This quarantine is the worst, isn't it?"

The woman she is speaking to hangs up the phone and says, "My god ... you have no idea."

A world in which time stops the moment before, by Gabriella Tuchman
(Note: adapted from the poem "Ode to a Grecian Urn" by John Keats)

In this timeline, time stops at the moment before. Time is full only of anticipation. It is full of couples about to kiss for the first time. A boy and a girl in the playground hiding from the babysitter behind the tree, slowly leaning their lips together, arms by their sides. A college-aged boy about to kiss the boy he's had a crush on since the third grade, finally ready to explore his identity. There is an artist with a brush in her hand and paint in her hair, about to complete her painting. It's a painting of the moment before because in this world what else is there to paint? It's a painting of a bird about to sing for the first time. It's a chest full of air; it's a beak open. There are moments before graduation and moments before a birth of a grandchild.

Along with these moments of joyous anticipation come moments of despair. It is the moment before a father takes his last breath and is in the middle of squeezing the hand of his young son. It is when the old grocer of the neighborhood is about to leave his shop for the last time, unable to compete with the new and less expensive chain store. A woman in the midst of the realization that her husband left her for someone else. She sees the letter on the dresser with the half-empty closet.

Some moments are simply waiting to see. When the plate that the baby pushed off the table is now inches from breaking on the floor. The moment in between flicking the switch for a light to go on and seeing light, biting into a freshly made burger and swallowing the burger, shaving off the hair on her head and seeing the hair fall to the floor.

Time in this timeline is full only of moments. It is not a continuous line in one direction, but tiny little dots next to each other. People in this timeline are waiting for the moment to occur and yet they never do. They are stuck in the waiting, stuck in the anticipation. Each person must deal with the feeling of incompleteness that emerges. Each act is never done because time is stopped right before. They soon learn to appreciate the feeling of almost as the most important feeling. The feeling of almost finishing high school, the feeling of almost sending out invitations to the wedding, and the feeling of almost having to watch their grandmother die. There is no flickering light in this world, only the moment of waiting to see if the light will go on or if the light will stay off.

Some people become disenchanted and decide to do nothing because nothing will ever be fulfilled, while others decide to do something because who knows if the moment of completeness will ever feel as good as the anticipation?

In my dreams: a pocket of frozen time, by Patrick Diaz:

I often dream that time has been frozen. For an hour, unmoving, the day does not progress. My consciousness remains in motion, progressing to the next moment, but for the rest of it all, nothing comes. My mind, losing its grip on time, fights for the next micro-second to greet me. It does not come. It is comforting, at first, and then terror takes over. My heart, frozen, does not move. Like stone, it's cold and does not feel. My lungs remain deflated, the pleasure of the next breath never comes. I await the moment when time progresses, but it does not come. My mind races, while my body is stiff. For a moment it feels as though my mind, untethered, can roam the world before I wake. Swiftly, though, the image of a white ceiling with a single cobweb, hanging from the farthest corner, drags me back. I am stuck. A moment, out of time, or a different state of it. The only thing that comes are thoughts. Of how I can do better. Of what can be done to make time move again. Fruitless, these thoughts are, as time moves for no one. We move, in time, with the hope that time will move forward. Sometimes, it stills. It decides to keep us, a boulder at the edge of a stream, just before a sharp cliff. Preventing water from flowing over and creating a wonder of the world. And then it moves again, and I awake. I feel stuck, in a different way.

A world in which time is a cosmic tapestry
By Ryan Langan

It was Nietzsche's philosophical conception that time is a flat circle, that everything we do we will do again, and again, and again, in an endless ring, rendering all things meaningless and recurring. There is merit and appeal to that conception, I'll give him that. But I don't buy it; no, I do not look out over the farm fields of Valencia where the oranges grow, or from the top of the Rockefeller building over Central Park where people move like ants in a colossal colony, and see something that has happened over and over, something that will continue to happen over and over. I see a single moment, governed by time, shaped by time. I don't see a single circle. I see infinitely many, overlapping and concentric, threaded together to create a tapestry. The tapestry is Time.

It may sound lofty and convoluted, but believe me, this is an easy thing to imagine. Let us return to the Roman Empire, when their capital buzzed much the same way Manhattan buzzes today. Just as goods from the far ends of the Empire like beads and ivory were peddled at The Forum, so today handbags and trinkets are dealt out on Canal Street. Just as ancient dignitaries and centurions laced in and out of the palaces of Palatine Hill conducting business and keeping order, so today diplomats and government officials enter and exit the United Nations upholding and facilitating foreign affairs. The same activities take place, but with infinite variation – where the character of one is defined, the character of the other becomes its own. Trends repeat; loose variations of the same melody play throughout the tapestry of time. But the fine print – the knowledge accumulated by advancement, the ever-changing interaction and exchange between minds – changes, is always changing. There is not one circle, no, and it is not flat by any means. What is done at one point in time informs another, directly or indirectly. It is all a web, a cosmic tapestry, stretched out and sewn together, bound by Time.

Not a Shadow of a Doubt in GROUNDHOG DAY

As an optional extra credit, students could also do a more academic analysis of Harold Ramis's 1993 film GROUNDHOG DAY, which starred Bill Murray as the jaundiced television weatherman Phil Connors who becomes mysteriously stuck in a time loop that causes him to repeat Groundhog Day ad infinitum: "Well, what if there is no tomorrow?" he asks. "There wasn't one today." It takes Phil thousands of Groundhog Days to become the kind of truly decent person he has to be – not only to win the love of Rita, Phil's news producer played by Andie MacDowell, but to be worthy of her.

GROUNDHOG DAY and EINSTEIN'S DREAMS
By Ryan Langan

Interestingly, I find the way time functions in the film GROUNDHOG DAY bears a relation to what I wrote about EINSTEIN'S DREAMS where I mention Nietzsche's idea that time is circular and perpetually recurring. This idea, in action, comprises the law of time that governs the film. Bill

Murray's character is stuck in a continual time loop from which he cannot escape, no matter what he does. Time has locked itself in and formed a loop – a circle – and the same day happens again and again.

Time and time again in the 1993 movie GROUNDHOG DAY
By Hester Milford

Phil Connors, played by Bill Murray, is an average weatherman covering the spectacle of Groundhog Day, a day which he is vehemently disinterested in. Phil goes about his day like any other, being a reporter with a sour attitude. Unbeknownst to him, the day February 2 is about to become an un-ending day for him – also known as a Time Loop. A time loop (or Temporal Loop) is a time where characters are subject to experiencing the same day/period of time over and over again on a seemingly never-ending cycle. This concept is similar to the societal effects of coronavirus – a never-ending cycle of mundane events that occur day to day. Phil Connors, on February 2, experiences this concept of a time loop.

There are key differences to Phil Connors' time loop than any other time loops I am aware of. First of all, Phil has subjective control over his actions during the day. In a comical sequence of actions, Phil attempts to break the monotonous loop by committing suicide, by over-eating and drinking, by robbery and by having meaningless sex. His primary motivation is his boredom, but he soon develops a crush on fellow news reporter Rita. This is when Phil decides to do something "meaningful" with his time.

With endless time on your hands, what would you do? It would take me a while to decide to do the things Phil eventually does, as human nature has demonstrated. Phil picks up a foreign language, and he learns an instrument. Having the time and endless amounts of first impressions are key to advancing this narrative. With every day Phil grows smarter and more able, and he is able to advance his skill sets. When Phil breaks the time loop, he becomes a more thoughtful and conscientious man. Instead of spitting on the homeless, he tries to save them. However this is dissimilar to life. If you are unable to be kind, or give the "right" impression the first time, you usually are not so lucky as to have a second chance.

This time loop was influential in changing Phil's life for the better, and taught him a different kind of life lesson. His good behavior was rewarded and a moral judgment was passed (but by whom? Was it "God" who broke the loop?), deeming him lovable. It seems all Phil needed to do was live up to the high standards set in place by the media industry in order to return to normal.

GROUNDHOG DAY teaches us that time is best spent with others
By Gabriella Tuchman

The movie GROUNDHOG DAY shows that time is best spent with others. When weatherman Phil Connors realizes that the same day keeps repeating, he indulges his every whim because there are no consequences; however, he soon falls into a deep state of depression because he now wakes up every day alone with knowledge that no one else can connect with. He even tries to kill himself numerous times. Until then, Phil had experienced life with everyone on the same timeline: he was able to relate to others, to talk about everything from the mundane sunny weather to the heartbreaking death of a homeless man. But because Phil now knows what the weather will be and that the homeless man will die despite Phil's best efforts, he is no longer able to connect with others. However, ultimately Phil realizes that time is something that is best spent with others (particularly his crush, Rita), and it is this realization that causes the time loop to end.

Time and time again in the 2017 Broadway
musical version of the film GROUNDHOG DAY
By Paige Thorne

In the Broadway musical GROUNDHOG DAY starring Andy Karl, weatherman Phil Connors dreads February 2 – Groundhog Day – because that is the day of the year he relives every year. The only way that Phil can be sent to February 3 is by him changing his pessimistic attitude about life to an optimistic one. What I make of this is that one cannot progress in life by being pessimistic and generally negative; these traits tend to hold one back – and so weatherman Phil Connors is stuck. It's not until this weatherman changes his attitude and completes the day in the "rightest" form that he is able to move on to February 3. I also think that this Broadway musical version of the Hollywood film wants to show that repetition of the same behaviors will always lead to the same end result but also that reliving past mistakes may be necessary for growth.

CHAPTER 21

All This Time Waiting and Waiting and Waiting for Samuel Beckett's 1953 Play "Waiting for Godot"

"Reading Plays Aloud Transforms a Sofa Into a Cozy Stage," said the headline in the March 30, 2020, edition of "The New York Times." And why would any of us in "The Literature of Waiting" course read aloud Samuel Beckett's WAITING FOR GODOT (one of nine plays recommended to be read that way by theater critic Ben Brantley) when we were scheduled to see an off-Broadway production of WAITING FOR GODOT at Theater for a New Audience in downtown Brooklyn just one month away at the beginning of May? The coronavirus pandemic, that's why.

Live theater is over and out! And so here we are in the last couple of weeks of Hunter College's off-campus online version of "The Literature of Waiting" course and we will be concluding the course with reading – not just once, but twice – WAITING FOR GODOT. (Whether it gets read out loud – a technique Mr. Eidelberg heavily promoted with a couple of other "waiting" works earlier in the semester – even one of those two times is not something he can reasonably require since he isn't allowed by social distancing to go to your home to verify.)

But why twice in any fashion? Well, each reading should be done with a distinct set of focus activities in mind – so each set of class assignments (and there will be two such sets) on the 20th-century classic WAITING FOR GODOT will be presented separately. Coming up (no waiting!): the reading, thinking, and writing set of assignments for Session 1 of our study of our final work of literature in the course.

Part One of Your Assignments During Your First Reading of WAITING FOR GODOT

Read WAITING FOR GODOT straight through, and as you read and intellectually, psychologically, emotionally, and aesthetically react to the "waiting" experience you are having, keep a sequenced list of questions you find yourself wanting to ask (and maybe even get some answers to) – and probably would ask if we were going on to discuss the play together in an actual (not a virtually online) classroom, where all of our learning and teaching colleagues were present and anxious (in both senses of the word) to engage.

WAITING FOR GODOT is a play that has always raised a great many questions and its fair share of uncertain answers. The play's title alone is filled with uncertainty; for example, who's doing the waiting?, what does the waiting consist of?, who or what is "Godot"?, why is this "Godot" the object of such expectation?, does this "Godot" wait on the waiting of those who are doing all this waiting for Godot? Uncertainty abounds. As a theater reviewer in "The New York Times" recently wrote, the play is not called GOD'S HERE, ON TIME AS USUAL.

Deirdre Bair, Beckett's first biographer (who died on April 23, 2020, at the age of 84) was quoted in her "New York Times" obituary as saying that the reason, in 1978, that she contacted Samuel Beckett for permission to write his biography was that reading Beckett's work to date – two plays, two novels – "made me want answers to a lot of questions all of which were based on the life from which the work sprang."

What I'd like to offer you now – since I've read and seen WAITING FOR GODOT multiple times (most recently, in theatrical Yiddish, which I don't speak, not even non-theatrical Yiddish – and I purposely ignored the Yiddish production's subtitles and supertitles because I decided I wanted a visual and aural experience with a play whose words I almost know by heart) – is not an assortment of my sequenced questions as I once again read the play along with you; instead, I'd like to offer a different assortment of questions, a "baker's dozen" from the many I've heard out there over the years (often from people who have *never* read the play), as well as the questions I might have run by you in class during a live-and-in-person introductory "lesson" on the play.

1. Why did everyone (everyone!) I mentioned my then prospective "waiting lit" course to immediately (immediately!) respond with: "What besides WAITING FOR GODOT do you plan for the class to read and study?" (No, I don't only associate with English teachers.)

2. Why does it make sense that you, Mr. Teacher of Literature, would end your course on "The Literature of Waiting" with WAITING FOR GODOT rather than start the course with it or teach it somewhere in the middle of the term?

3. Why are there so many cartoons out there that allude to – nay, directly reference – the play WAITING FOR GODOT (particularly cartoons from "The New Yorker" magazine – want to see my folder)?

4. Who is Godot – and why is anyone at all waiting for him, her, it, them?

5. Is "Godot" pronounced "Guh-dough," with the greater stress on the second syllable or is it pronounced "God-oh," with the greater stress on the first syllable (both pronunciations are out there)? Beckett has answered this question, but does it really matter how the name "Godot" is pronounced?

6. Does all this waiting matter? And does it matter who is doing the waiting – who they are, how different or alike they are, that there are two of them of the same gender and not three or more in varying combinations? Why not one "waiter"? And, while we're at it, is Godot doing any waiting?

7. Have the following authors of recently published illustrated children's books read their Beckett? In WHAT ARE YOU WAITING FOR?, Scott Menchin has a larger animal of one species converse with a smaller animal of another species:

What are you doing up so early?
I'm waiting.
What are you waiting for?
Wouldn't you like to know.

And in Kevin Henkes' illustrated children's book WAITING, a pig with an umbrella is waiting for the rain, a bear with a kite is waiting for the wind, but a rabbit with stars wasn't waiting for anything in particular. He just liked to look out the window and wait.... Waiting to see what would happen next.

8. Why did Beckett, an Irish Protestant whose native language was English, originally write the play in French? What does the French title EN ATTENDANT GODOT best translate as? How did French audiences and the French theater critics greet the play?

9. Why was the American premiere of WAITING FOR GODOT in a city in Florida rather than on a Broadway stage in New York City? What was the critical reception and what was the audience response to that first American performance?

10. If I've read or seen Harold Pinter's 1960 play THE DUMB WAITER (as all of us have) or Tom Stoppard's 1967 play ROSENCRANTZ AND GUILDENSTERN ARE DEAD (as several of us have) how, specifically, will it be clear to me that both these playwrights not only admired Samuel Beckett's new approach to theater but were influenced, in particular, by his 1953 play WAITING FOR GODOT?

11. How good or bad is Mr. Eidelberg's timing in "teaching" WAITING FOR GODOT during the 2020 coronavirus pandemic? (When Mr. Eidelberg first taught WAITING FOR GODOT to 12th-graders back in the late 1980's, a young lady who was born in Vietnam in the mid-1960's and went on to be her graduating class's valedictorian, complained to him that he should never have taught such a depressing play to young high school students.)

12. If it is true (and it is) that Beckett considered his 1950's play WAITING FOR GODOT to be a tragi-comedy (very much unlike Eugene O'Neill's 1946 dark and nihilistic play THE ICEMAN COMETH), can WAITING FOR GODOT still be considered a tragi-comedy in today's world?

13. The play's absurd, right?

Part Two of Your Assignments During Your First Reading of WAITING FOR GODOT

Go back through the entire play and find one (just one!) representative "scene" between Estragon and Vladimir (a "scene" in this two-act play would be a somewhat extended exchange of dialogue between these two men) that you would choose to show as the movie "trailer" for a upcoming general release "R"-rated film version of WAITING FOR GODOT that accomplishes all of the following: (a) intrigues the trailer audience enough to consider paying good money to see the full film when it comes out, (b) honestly captures what you believe WAITING FOR GODOT to be thematically "about," (c) accurately represents the writing and production style of this "tragi-comedy" (as it is actually labeled by Becket in his own English translation of his original French version), and (d) fairly well presents Beckett's modernist viewpoint on human life as it is lived. In a formal piece of writing, describe "the scene" only as you use various elements of it to make your convincing argument that the scene you chose representatively accomplished a, b, c, and d.

An Assortment of Pressing Questions (Awaiting Answers?) Raised by Our College Collaborators During Their First Reading of WAITING FOR GODOT

o   *Would the play WAITING FOR GODOT be different if the characters were all female instead of male?*

o   *Why is the play in two acts?*

o   *Why are immobility and inaction so monumental throughout the play?*

o   *What is the role of memory in the play? Why is it that there is so much forgetting of what happened previously and confusion about what happened "yesterday"?*

o   *What is the importance of all the repetition, and why do the characters ask so many questions of each other? Am I the only one frustrated by the play?*

o   *Have both men always possessed such a strong relationship with inaction? Why are they so damaged? Are they related or friends over a long period of time?*

o   *Are both of them truly mad or have some kind of mental disorder? What are they suffering for? How reliable are they? Why doesn't Vladimir ever want to hear Estragon's dreams?*

o   *Why are they waiting for Godot?*

o   *Where had Vladimir been before the very start of Act One? Are both of them homeless?*

o   *What does Vladimir "feel...coming on"?*

o   *Is Vladimir meant to be so impressionable?*

o   *Why did Estragon sleep in a ditch?*

o   *Why did Estragon get beat up – and who is the "they" that did it?*

o   *Why does Estragon often repeat himself in a string of sentences, and why is the conversation between the two men (who are how old?) so choppy?*

o *What is the nature and symbolic meaning of the relationship between Estragon and Vladimir? Are they really friends, or is their relationship an odd couple farce?*

o *Why do they consider, so casually, hanging themselves to pass the time?*

o *Why do they remain unmoved at the end of every important section of the play?*

o *Why and how did they "[give up their] rights"?*

o *Why the use of bowler hats as a prop?*

o *Who is Pozzo, and is he actually in control of Lucky in their power relationship?*

o *Why does Pozzo break down over having had a slave so long?*

o *Is Lucky (ironic?) a human? If so, why is he treated like a pack mule?*

o *Is Lucky's baggage "human baggage" carried throughout life?*

o *What is the symbolism behind his wearing a rope – and is the rope connected to Estragon's and Vladimir's conversation about hanging themselves?*

o *Why isn't Lucky nice to them when they tried to help him?*

o *Why can Lucky only think with his hat on?*

o *Is there any actual meaning to what Lucky says?*

o *Why doesn't Lucky leave after Pozzo goes blind, and why and how did Pozzo go blind?*

o *Are Lucky and Pozzo merely visible physical manifestations of their waiting?*

o *Did Estragon attempt suicide (based on the reference to his having jumped in the Rhone River once)?*

o *If they used to live in France (I looked up what Macon country is), where are they now? Google says that "Cackon country" was a play on "caca," that is, shit, but where is it?*

o *Why the recurring use of "pig" as a form of address?*

o *Why does Vladimir keep singing?*

o *What is the significance of Vladimir's use of that Latin phrase in the second act?*

o *Who did Estragon see coming that they had to hide from?*

o *Why was being called "critic" the worst insult?*

o *What's wrong with Pozzo? What game is he playing with Estragon and Vladimir?*

o *Why does Estragon use "Abel" as his first guess (and, logically then, "Cain" as his next guess for Lucky's name)?*

- o *Why does Estragon hurt his foot again? What's the significance (especially given the motif of his boots)?*
- o *What is the significance of the shorter rope? Why do Estragon and Vladimir think of hanging as such a light thing, as though they could return afterwards?*
- o *What is the significance of the boy's saying Godot does not beat the boy who minds the goats but instead beats his brother who minds the sheep? What is the actual relationship between these boys and Godot?*
- o *Who really is Godot? What does he represent (since he doesn't seem to actually be providing any service of value to Vladimir and Estragon)?*
- o *Is Godot supposed to represent God – why the French name "Godot" with the English word "God" as a part of it?*
- o *Why don't Estragon and Vladimir leave each other? Does one actually need the other?*
- o *Is the play just a pull-out moment in an endless repeating cycle of waiting moments?*
- o *What was Beckett's point? What is the significance of the play's never-ending conversations about "nothing" that fill the time while waiting for someone who will never come? And why doesn't Godot ever make an appearance?*
- o *Does the play show that we should just live our lives instead of waiting for something?*
- o *What is the playing saying about "the absurdity" of existing?*
- o *What would Estragon and Vladimir do during the 2020 coronavirus pandemic?*

An Assortment of Movie Trailers From Our College Collaborators For Enticing an Audience Into Going to See the Full Film Version of WAITING FOR GODOT

Trailer scene choice from Shanya Hopkins:

My trailer "scene" of choice would be *a moment very early on in the play (pages 5 to about 11 of my edition)*. The exchange between Vladimir and Estragon is one that would be very entertaining and comical for movie audiences, but also an extremely insightful foray into Beckett's approach to existential waiting and the meaning of existence. Two older scraggly men, standing in the middle of an open natural landscape, discussing erections would be more than intriguing for even the simplest viewer. The humor and mastery of the "scene" is apparent in how serious the two men take themselves, almost completely dissociated from the absurdity of their streams of consciousness and never-ending cycle of decisiveness and subsequent inaction. Their dialogue, though minimal in language, is immensely telling – and the lack of tangible possessions on the part of both men is symbolic of the internal emptiness they both experience.

The "scene" captures the essence of what the play is truly "about": on the surface Vladimir and Estragon present as two mindless "waiters," spending their lives indulging in mindless waiting with no tangible sense of control over their lives or their fate. Simply put, two men immobilized by inaction. Yet, though they might not know it themselves, the two men seem to be searching for some meaning to their lives, meaning they hope to get from the notorious Godot. Their pursuit of meaning is reflected in their busied waiting, a waiting that simply exists as a means to pass the minutes and the days until they meet that which they most desire. The culmination of dialogue and inactions in this chosen "trailer scene" exists in the sphere of tragi-comedy – while Vladimir and Estragon's repetitive exchanges are amusing in their complete and utter idiocy, their lack of fruitfulness and existential value is deplorable. This moment in the play reflects Beckett's critique of human existence and his suggestion that humans partake in an act of waiting, also known as "living," for the sole purpose of finding purpose.

Trailer scene choice from Hester Milford:

Seeking meaning. What does Godot represent? The two men who ramble on and on, filling the time with frivolous conversations about nothing, are the play's key elements – but my favorite part is when Lucky speaks, "given the existence as uttered forth...." Still, all the men have meaningless conversations that drive forth the point of this play: life is meaningless, we are all clinging to old baggage, what we are waiting for shall never arrive. If I were to create a trailer for this play, I would use *the start of Act Two, "Next day, same place," when the tree has grown 4-5 leaves.* I think this is a symbolic representation of life. Into the act, the same events take place, the same sayings are uttered. Vladimir and Estrogen's friendship is established, and Lucky is now an essential aid to Pozzo. I was upset reading Pozzo's treatment of Lucky in Act One, undeserved and creepy. At least when Pozzo goes blind, his condescending nature is quelled – or at least mocked. Lucky, his submissive servant, becomes his new eyes, while still allowing himself to be mistreated.

Trailer scene choice from Massiel Sanchez:

VLADIMIR: Perhaps we should help him first.
ESTRAGON: To do what?
VLADIMIR: To get up.
ESTRAGON: He can't get up?
VLADIMIR: He wants to get up.
ESTRAGON: Then let him get up.
VLADIMIR: He can't.
ESTRAGON: Why not?
VLADIMIR: I don't know. (*Pozzo writhes, groans, beats the ground with his fists.*)

Vladimir and Estragon's conversation drifts into the same existential line of questioning it always does: what is there to do next, and why? This scene captures the main theme of the futile search for meaning in human life.

Trailer scene choice from Trever Polk (the same scene as chosen by Massiel Sanchez):

I would use *the scene in the second act when Pozzo returns and has fallen, and Estragon and Vladimir debate picking him up.* My copy of the play for whatever reason labels every two pages as one, so this would be from about page 50 to the second page of page 52 (weird way of saying it, I know). The first page of page 50 shows some action that would get people's attention: they talk about waiting for Godot, not revealing yet that he never actually comes; the scene also shows them debating actually doing something, which by the end of this section they do. Then, on page 51, Vladimir and Estragon wax philosophical on boredom, madness, being needed, and the purpose of life, all major themes of the play that also indicate, to an extent, how Beckett views the way we live life. There's also the comic back-and-forth repetition when the two characters debate what to do, which, combined with the aforementioned somewhat bleak philosophical musings, shows the tragicomic nature of the play.

Trailer scene choice from Rabeya Rahman:

In *the ending scene of Act Two of WAITING FOR GODOT by Samuel Beckett, the boy returns and Vladimir knows exactly what the boy will say* because it has happened multiple times before, due to the repetitiveness of the story. They are told that Godot cannot come today but will show up tomorrow. Skipping to after sunset, Vladimir and Estragon discuss leaving and returning the next day for Godot, but if he doesn't show up, then they'll hang themselves.

This scene can be used for an attention-grabbing movie trailer because it incites curiosity in the audience as to who this Godot figure might be and why he is significant enough for the two characters to want to hang themselves if he does not show up. If filmed properly with the right videography, acting, and such, this scene can attract viewers to consider seeing the full film when it comes out.

In addition, this scene captures what the play is thematically about – holding onto hope and a belief in a superior power. The Godot figure who never seems to show up physically can be interpreted as God, who is present but cannot be literally seen. Vladimir and Estragon try every single day to see Godot, but he never shows up. They don't know how he even looks or anything and yet they persist in waiting. The wait for Godot is associated with holding onto hope that he/it will come eventually. They have proof that Godot is real because the boy character has come in contact with him, whether directly or indirectly.

The ending decision that the two characters will resort to hanging themselves if Godot does not appear the next day can be taken as impatience and loss of hope after repeatedly being let down in Godot's failure to show up in person time and time again. This one scene does not explain everything to viewers of the movie trailer, but it has enough to at least hint at this struggle to hold on to hope. This ending has signs of the tragi-comedy that this play is because of the intriguing conversations between the two characters (albeit other scenes do exist with more humor) and the tragic aspect of it – the possibility of resorting to death from Godot's lack of appearance.

This scene and the play in general can be interpreted as Beckett's commentary on the human tendency to find hope, excitement, and comfort in a superior power or being – God. He does not show up literally and, at times, people fail to see the literal signs of His existence, but He is there; those who fail to understand this, resort to shocking measures because it is associated with loss of hope. Vladimir and Estragon, however, dedicate their time and energy as if it is their life's purpose to meet up with Godot – a depiction of humankind's finding purpose and value in religion.

Part One of Your Assignments During Your Second Reading of *WAITING FOR GODOT*

Although we are, at this writing, less than a half a year into 2020 (and more than 65 years since WAITING FOR GODOT first appeared on the theatrical scene), Samuel Beckett's twentieth-century masterpiece continues, to this day, to both stimulate and to stimulate comment. As you do a second reading of WAITING FOR GODOT, keep these comments that I'm sending to you in mind, and react, via email, to as many of them that get you going or set you off.

An Assortment of Our College Collaborators' Reactions to the Bold-Faced Items

"The proper method of philosophy consists in clearly conceiving the insoluble problems in all their insolubility and then in simply contemplating them, fixedly and tirelessly, year after year, without any hope, patiently waiting." – Simone Weil (1929 - 1943), religious philosopher, dramatist, poet, social critic and political activist; author of, among other works, WAITING FOR GOD

From Carolyn Reyes:
Interesting viewpoint expressed by Simone Weil because no one really has any answers to the greatest questions of philosophy. They are simply brought up and further explained, analyzed, discussed, and thought about without a soluble answer to them – just raising more problems and questions under the main problem: trying to find a solution knowing there isn't any. Similar to the two characters in WAITING FOR GODOT, who year after year, it seems, wait for the answer or solution to the problem, and they just wait and think and wait. It makes sense why the characters seem a little mentally unstable after waiting for so long: only contemplating life's meaning or answers for so long in your head is enough to drive anyone a little crazy. It also makes some sense why they wait: they want answers just like anybody else would; maybe we read and judge them for waiting, but maybe if anyone was willing to wait and dig deep for so long, there'd be answers. Their life seems to be wasted by waiting, but so is everyone else's; we just seem to have more activities to keep us busy while we do and we don't claim to be waiting for Godot to everyone who passes us by. But we all wait and contemplate on something that never shows – and quite possibly will never show – because nobody has all the answers.

From Massiel Sanchez:
Humans are essentially clueless, and powerless. There are some questions we simply do not have the answers to. Vladimir and Estragon remained waiting, in constant contemplation for the answers.

From Paige Thorne:
I think that this quote of Simone Weil's mainly connects to the last part of the play in which, I now think, Vladimir realizes that Godot will not be coming, as the boy once again tells him that Godot will see him tomorrow and he realizes that the boy had said the same thing to him before. I'd have to disagree, though, that there is no hope because Vladimir and Estragon are still waiting at the end of the play. I think that if they truly believed Godot was not coming, they would have left, but maybe this is due to them not having anything else better to do – and maybe this waiting is a form of waiting for another thing. Instead of "without any hope" I'd substitute "without satisfaction." I think the lack of satisfaction is what keeps people waiting, or maybe it's the running around in circles.

"Shouldn't we wait until after the pandemic to fill out the census?" – "dark" joke quoted at the start of a New York Times news article entitled "Don't Feel Guilty. It's OK to Laugh At Some of This."

From Trever Polk:
I don't think there's anything morally objectionable about this joke, and in fact they actually have kind of a point. However, I think it's a lot more direct than the darkest humor in WAITING FOR GODOT, namely the times that they contemplate suicide. In that case, the darkness is more abstract – real, yes, but not as much of an imminent threat as a joke about the pandemic.

From Jason Chetram:
This sort of dark humor is scattered throughout the play WAITNG FOR GODOT. In times of crisis or of great anxiety, as is the case with WAITING FOR GODOT, humor is a great weapon to combat the negativity. The title of the article is interesting, also, because it implies that there would be a reason to feel guilty for laughing. The only time it would be bad to laugh at something would be if it's insensitive or at the expense of another. The joke about the census is humorous to the many who aren't affected directly by the pandemic. However, in regards to those who have family members in the hospital, unsure if they could make it or not, the joke may

cross the line. But does putting a smile on the faces of the many at the expense of the few who are hurt by the joke make it justified?

From Gabriella Tuchman:
Beckett uses dark humor in his play to both underscore and understate the tragedy. For example, in the beginning of the play, the scene about Vladimir and Estragon hanging themselves in order to get an erection but, obviously, it is sad because they are contemplating suicide. The scene emphasizes the fact that the mundanity of their days brings them into a state of depression and the individual moments that make the two men laugh. Being able to laugh in the face of a terrible situation is an important skill to have; it allows us to step back from the terrible situation and appreciate the absurdity of life, to smile in the fact of it, and maybe have a little bit of courage to continue without feeding despondent.

"Bruce Handy (one of several authors writing about the Charles Schulz comic strip "Peanuts" in a newly published book THE PEANUTS PAPERS) writes an analysis that could apply to Sartre or Beckett: 'What I took away from Schulz is that life is hard, people are difficult, at best, unfathomable at worst, justice is a foreign tongue, happiness can vaporize in the thin gap between a third and fourth panel, and the best response to all that is to laugh and keep moving, always ready to duck." – New York Times news story on the book THE PEANUTS PAPERS

From Chyna Chung:
This quote is relatable and true as to what it means to live life and push through struggles. In Samuel Beckett's play WAITING for GODOT, Vladimir and Estragon always find ways to find a comedic aspect and keep themselves occupied. My personal favorite part of this quote of Bruce Handy's is "The best response to all that is to laugh and keep moving." Life never truly stops being hard, you just have to learn to cope. Diffferent people cope in their own way. Vladimir and Estragon always found ways to keep their minds off of waiting for Godot, whether it be talking to Pozzo, or being entertained by Lucky, or even describing what they see around them. Pozzo probalby went blind trying to live Estragon's and Vladimir's life but not coming up with a way to cope with it.

From Hester Milford:
The Charles Schulz comic strip "Peanuts" was a comic I grew up reading and loving. Simple-minded characters, with easily solved problems and

relaxing voices. The adults/parents portrayed in the comic strip, when aired, are garbled authoritative voices: "womp ... womp ... womp." Bruce Handy's quote applies to both Schulz, and Beckett in an odd way. Schulz is clearly writing for children, and Beckett attempts to wow adults with his psycho-babble. Why not. Beckett's characters, Vladimir and Estrogen, are often forgetful and unmoved, sticking to their ill-informed theories, and entertaining Pozzo. Most of the time I really am not sure what they are talking about. "Peanuts," on the other hand, is very straightforward. Lessons are taught in the span of a few boxes.

From Paige Thorne:

A comment I would like to make about this quote of Bruce Handy's is that life is hard because we are waiting for the unknown, but also because we have to entertain ourselves as a distraction for it and from it. The part about people made me think back to how Vladimir and Estragon wanted to treat Pozzo poorly when they noticed he was blind and helpless – having power over or being in control of a person is an entertaining enough method for someone to wait. This also reminded me of Lucky's purpose to Pozzo, as Pozzo gained empowerment at the expense of another human and was greatly entertained by it. The idea of justice makes me wonder whether Handy is talking about justice between humans or justice between mortals and higher beings. In both cases in WAITING FOR GODOT, I think there is none – no justice – since throughout the play humans are at the mercy of themselves and other humans and their own purpose disappears once they acknowledge their waiting.

"Samuel Beckett, when asked one beautiful spring morning whether such a day did not make him glad to be alive, responded: 'I wouldn't go as far as that.' Life is a predicament, death the elephant at the horizon that looms larger as the years pass." – The opening paragraph to a New York Times op-ed piece by columnist Roger Cohen, on the recent deaths of two of his professional colleagues, entitled "Two Deaths and My Life"

From Nattapat Karmniyanont:

Is life rendered meaningless because of its end? I wouldn't put it that far; after all, it's about perspective. If you are constantly anxious about the approaching hand of the reaper and live your life trying to outrun the chill rolling down your spine, then certainly life can be a bit of a downer; otherwise it's pretty good. In saying that I do agree with Samuel Beckett that a spring day, no matter how beautiful, certainly wouldn't engulf my heart with joy causing me to scream at the top of my lungs "Oh, what joy it is to live! I'm glad I am alive on this wonderous day!" because I'm too self-conscious to yell out something like that in a public setting. I've been happy that I'm alive many times, especially reading books I like and looking at things that are blue friends (some might say I'm obsessed with the color blue but I would say I admire the color), playing games, and occasionally talking with people. However, it's hard to say that I am glad that I'm alive because of a beautiful day. But in saying that I can see why Beckett said what he did. Although I now have a question: is being glad to be alive, the same as enjoying living?

From Massiel Sanchez:

Although there are some undeniable truths that derive from nihilist thought, such extreme nihilism is misguided. Yes, we are meaningless. We live, we struggle all for nothing, yes I agree. But being insignificant doesn't make life completely unredeemable. As insignificant as we are we still feel! Love. Anger. Joy. Sadness. The world is so big, there is so much to feel. If we are as insignificant to the universe as a rock or a pair of socks, then let's at least be grateful we exist in such lively vessels. We can walk on the shore and swim in the ocean on a warm summer day. We can experience a very good film, or a good book. We can experience our favorite foods, experience a good joke, experience others, experience big bustling cities and so on and so on. Knowing that one day it will end shouldn't make these things less enjoyable, but instead should give us permission to live fully, experience these things fully. As miserable as life can be at times, there is always still hope for the beautiful things to prevail. At the end, we should be more grateful than indignant for the time we have been granted here.

From Shanya Hopkins:

Beckett's characterization of life is evidenced by the waiting actions of Vladimir and Estragon in the tragicomedy that is WAITING FOR GODOT. Through the frustration and absurdity of waiting exhibited in this two-act play, Beckett makes the existential argument that life is one extensive difficult situation, a situation comparable to that of a hell. Beckett marries the concepts of existing and waiting, birthing a symbiotic relationship and exhibiting the difficulties of having one without the other. The life of each "waiting" man could be attributed to one massive horrible circumstance unfazed by hope or the arrival of meaningful prospects. A circumstance in which the only end to waiting is death, and the only purpose of waiting is for death. As such, the lives of Vladimir and Estragon were truly major predicaments.

"For those of you feeling that life is indeed an endless waiting game these days and are brave enough to take on the ultimate literary evocation of that feeling," theater critic Ben Brantley on March 30th recommended reading the play WAITING FOR GODOT during the coronavirus pandemic's stay-at-home regulations. **"Not exactly escapist fare,"** added Brantley, **"but a lot funnier than you may remember."**

From Hester Milford:

The coronavirus pandemic has put a stop to all activity. Even gang violence is down. Why not read WAITING FOR GODOT? WAITING FOR GODOT is not really an escapist play. It asks a lot of hard and uncomfortable questions. However, it highlights the absurdity of life, in a way the coronavirus has exposed. Without all of our systematic coping tools/mechanisms, our educational programs, sports, entertainments, we are left with very little to do. This space in time, when we are not filling our brains with meaningless riddle, to fill this gap .... What have we become? Americans are reportedly drinking excessively, smoking pot, playing video games, watching TV – anything to distract ourselves from ourselves. This is the escapism we seek. "A lot funnier than you may remember," Brantley says. But not really.

From Nattapat Karmniyanont:

I agree that life is an endless waiting game even before the quarantine forcibly flaunted this realization in the faces of many. However, I don't necessarily see this as a bad thing, waiting – at this point – might as well be a synonym for life: to have life is your waiting action and to have death is what you are waiting for (although not quite in the sense that death is what we yearn for, it's just what we are aware of). In that sense, just as there are ups and downs in life, fun parts and the mundane, so too our waiting can have ups and downs. Thinking this way, WAITING FOR GODOT is somewhat more enjoyable as we can take the time to enjoy the insanity that is brought out of us through mindlessly waiting. Looking at Gogo's and Didi's relative freedom from forced waiting, it is quite funny in comparison to our situation where we are forced to wait – both waiting for Godot and, in our case, Godot's last name: "L'tusout."

From Rabeya Rahman:
I can see why Brantley would suggest reading WAITING FOR GODOT during quarantine. I wasn't much of a fan of the humor in the play, maybe because the writing style and structure are not my taste, but I can see people finding it funny. What I can agree on is that this play is relatable to the current events. Like Vladimir and Estragon and their never-ending wait for "Godot," we are stuck in quarantine waiting endlessly for the virus to be contained. I haven't been out and about for two months and six days now and I. AM. ANNOYED. Reading this play during the coronavirus pandemic can make one feel like they are not alone.

From Shanya Hopkins:
For the two men in Beckett's WAITING FOR GODOT life can be indeed be attributed to an endless period of waiting. Vladimir and Estragon's humorous repetitive daily cycles of waiting mirror one's cycle around a game board – and yet, their game is both figuratively and literally never-ending. In this game their opponent is time, there is no end goal for the men, no grand prize, and no prize. This waiting game has no bounds and thus lacks reason. Analogous to the lives of the men, the "waiting" is aimless and flounders under the concept of meaning. Like Vladimir and Estragon, the world has found itself picking up the game pieces and making our cycles around the waiting board, and no matter how many times we pass go, we do not collect two hundred dollars. In the midst of a global pandemic, there is no end to waiting on the horizon. Home we reside, stuck in a vortex of waiting, where one "wait" always precedes another.

"The novelty of waiting in GODOT is not, I suggest, in how we pass through waiting but how we are in it, not in the expectation of the end of waiting but in the quality of waiting as such.... Waiting in WAITING FOR GODOT is without the preposition 'for.' And yet ... it is difficult to conceive of waiting in WAITING FOR GODOT without invoking, conceptualizing, indeed expecting Godot – even the Godot who won't come, even the Godot under erasure. For, how can we wait without invoking Godot as a makeshift remedy for the endlessness of waiting? How, in other words, could we wait in WAITING FOR GODOT without waiting for Godot? .... When we say that in GODOT we just wait, we mean that waiting has been emptied of all practical, philosophical, or theological resonance. Beckett's genius is simply to make waiting nothing more than time ... as nothing other than the endurance of time. For this is not waiting for something that

would validate, cancel, or fulfill waiting. This is the kind of waiting we fear that waiting – or living – might amount to: just waiting." – Scholar Harold Schweizer in the 2008 book ON WAITING (part of the "Thinking in Action" series published by Routledge)

From Jason Chetram:

The definition of waiting here as the endurance of time is one that is painful to experience in life. This type of waiting is of the kind where there is no end goal that would signify that the wait is over and it could easily continue at Infinitum, somewhat similar to the looping and repetition seen in the play WAITING FOR GODOT. Obviously, when looking at this type of waiting it is easy to say that we would clearly avoid it and take no part in it. The scary thing is that we undergo this type of waiting without realizing it initially. A multitude of factors could lead us to be trapped in the loop of endless, fruitless waiting, much like with Estragon and Vladimir. The factors that got them happened to be a "Godot" with seemingly no intention of showing up as well as the men's inability to take action. The play is definitely a cautionary tale to keep mindful of as we undergo any type of waiting, so as to not end up waiting for a "Godot" of our own.

From Massiel Sanchez

I agree that Beckett makes waiting "nothing other than the endurance of time." In the play WAITING FOR GODOT, Vladimir and Estragon spend their waiting searching for things that will help "pass time." Everything they do, and everything that happens, they make sense of as merely something to help them pass time. But what they're deeming a way to pass time is really them existing, them being. Without the "makeshift remedy" that is Godot, there would be no other way for them to make sense of these things (their actions). Without Godot, if they dance for example, it wouldn't be "dancing as a way to pass time as we wait for Godot," instead it would have to be "dancing just to dance." This forces them to question why they are dancing and subsequently face the truth that there is no real reason. This will be unbearable, because if there is no reason, then why am I doing it? It would just lead to dread. It would leave them without the drive to do anything (to exist).

In one of his lectures psychoanalyst Jacques Lacan said, "Death belongs to the realm of faith. You're right to believe that you will die. It sustains you. If you didn't believe it, could you bear the life you have? If we couldn't totally rely on the certainty that it will end, how could you bear all this?" Lacan points out that without death, without knowing that it will end, how can one endure the routine and the tasks of everyday life, how would one find the drive to do things. Similarly, without the pretense of waiting for Godot, how would Vladimir and Estragon endure the time and the endlessness of waiting.

Part Two of Your Assignments During Your Second Reading of WAITING FOR GODOT

Choose one of the following five inspirations for a piece of *creative writing* based on your two readings of WAITING FOR GODOT (if your creative juices are gushing and you absolutely have to do two, I will enter the second piece as extra credit); submit your piece to me online by May 7, the last official session of our course on "The Literature of Waiting" because all good things must come to an end – if you wait long enough.

1. Just as we did with the "waiting" prose in the first chapter of Henry James's novel THE WINGS OF THE DOVE (remember that?), go back through both acts of WAITING FOR GODOT to *select* words, phrases, sentences, snatches of dialogue, props, and stage directions to use for a "found poem" you will create (of any length) to be entitled "Waiting." You may use the language (diction choices and their tones of voice) of any and all of the play's five characters (six, if you believe it is two different boys that appear in the play) and in any sequence of your choosing. You may also use repetition of words (a technique that Beckett himself makes frequent and purposeful use of throughout his play). You may *not* use anything that does not appear in or get said in Beckett's play.

2. Study the famous (infamous?) speech (not a soliloquy but a monologue, since it is meant to be heard by other characters in the work of literature) that Lucky (lucky?) makes in the first act of this two-act play. Commanded to "think" by Pozzo, Lucky proceeds (once he has the hat on – hats figure in this play) to perform a verbal and visual dance, whose rhythm speeds up (out of control?) as it works its way to its end (conclusion?). This stop-the-show "bit" is always something to see and hear in the theater and, thanks to Lucky's repeated use of certain catch lines and phrases, sometimes actually seems to have a structure in the service of an important and meaningful message (and sometimes, not). Be both creative and faithful to what you think is on Beckett's mind in the entire play and write out the *coherent* speech that the actor playing

the role of Lucky will need to memorize (a much easier task than memorizing what Beckett has actually put into Lucky's mouth!).

3. Officially, WAITING FOR GODOT has two acts. Some critics say that it has only one – an act that is pretty much repeated, with certain variations as in a musical piece, and called Act Two. But what if WAITING FOR GODOT is actually a three-act play? No, it's not what you may be thinking – an act after Beckett's Act Two – but a play that begins with an act that has been lost to time, lost back in the early 1950's, lost in translation from the original French. Your mission, should you accept it, is to miraculously find Beckett's English-language version of the lost Act One and publish it for a world that did not even know that this is what it was waiting for. (Or, think of your "Act One" as the *prequel* to the 1953 version of Beckett's published play, which he decided to discard, and write it to be performed in Hunter College's Sylvia and Danny Kaye Theater "some day.")

4. Rewrite "a section" of Beckett's WAITING FOR GODOT with only one production change: the "scene" now takes place during the current coronavirus pandemic, so instead of the play's being set in a barren outdoor space with only one visible tree (sometimes with, sometimes without, a few leaves), your rewrite takes place indoors somewhere (indicate where in your stage directions), with one or more of Beckett's characters quarantined in place (with props?).

5. Being critically negative, some commentators have called Beckett's play "reductive." Think about what that might mean, and then do something creative with the following:

The play WAITING FOR GODOT is a play about waiting for Godot.
The play WAITING FOR GODOT is a play about waiting for.
The play WAITING FOR GODOT is a play about waiting.
The play WAITING FOR GODOT is a play about.
The play WAITING FOR GODOT is a play.
The play WAITING FOR GODOT is a.
The play WAITING FOR GODOT is.
The play WAITING FOR GODOT.
The play WAITING FOR.
The play WAITING.
The play.
The.

Two poems inspired by WAITING FOR GODOT, by Wardah Malik

Waiting

It's only the beginning
     It's awful.
We were to wait
We will come back tomorrow
And then the day after tomorrow
     Silence ...
I hear nothing.
Who believes them?
You took me from him!
We didn't intend any harm.
     Silence ...
Look!
We are not beggars
It's not over
     Trembling ...
     All the dead voices
Make a noise like wings
     Trembling ...
They talk about their lives

Endurance

Waiting is the endurance of life
     We wait and wait
     for what?
For one little flicker of hope and a
     sense of purpose
Time
     moves slowly
     thoughts
race through your head
     while you wait
We keep going backwards thinking
     Going back to the old ways
        will fix things
     But awareness is awareness
that waiting is a never-ending marathon
     Time passes but you are still waiting

An earlier meeting between Vladimir and Estragon from an imagined prequel to the Samuel Beckett play WAITING FOR GODOT By Gabriella Tuchman

Vladimir is pacing back and forth by the tree.
Vladimir: I must stay, linger, pause, halt, remain. *Silence.* I can go, leave, depart, embark, elope. *Silence.* No, I'm waiting for Godot. *Silence.*

Vladimir continues to pace and whisper to himself. Then, he stops and contemplates the tree.

Vladimir: I bet I can climb this tree. Get to the top of this tree. Reach for the sky from this tree. Spend the night in the tree. Wake up in the tree. Die in the tree. All I must do is start climbing the tree. Not come down from the tree. Perhaps I can see Godot in this tree.

Vladimir stands still and stares at the tree. Then he starts circling the tree and it seems like he's looking to see how best to start climbing. He approaches the tree, then steps away. He seems defeated.

Vladimir: I can wait from the ground. I don't have the tools, the equipment, the materials to go up to climb up the tree. Why should I go up the tree?

Estragon appears on the stage limping. He is mumbling to himself.

Estragon: There were at least twelve of them. I was just sleeping. Doing nothing. Minding my own business. When they attacked. They attacked. They attacked me! I could really use a carrot. Or a nap. Or a carrot and a nap. I'd even settle for a turnip and a nap.
Estragon: Gogo?
Vladimir: No. Godot. You're not Godot.
Estragon: No. Who's Godot?
Vladimir: Well, you see, I um … I am waiting for Godot. I'll know him when I see him. Who are you?
Estragon: Estragon.
Vladimir: Estrogen?
Estragon: Es-tra-gon!
Vladimir: Ohh. Estragon. Mind if I call you Gogo? Why're you limping, Gogo?

Estragon: I could really use a carrot right about now. You happen to have any carrots?

Vladimir: No, but I do have some turnips. What happened to your leg?

Estragon: Oh man, I don't want a turnip. You sure you don't have any carrots?

Vladimir: No carrots. But what's wrong with your leg? You are limping, hobbling, staggering.

Estragon: No carrots, you hear that, no carrots. He thinks he can feed me a turnip when I'm asking for a carrot.

Vladimir: No carrots, and I offer Gogo some turnips and he turns me down. He says no. I offer him food and he declines. You know what? No turnips for you. I refuse.

Estragon: Gogo? Who's Gogo? That guy you were waiting for?

Vladimir: No, you're Gogo. I'm waiting for Godot. Don't you remember?

Estragon: Remember? I don't remember. Who are you again?

Vladimir: Vladimir. Vladimir. You never asked. Why're you limping?

Estragon: Want to help me take off my boot? It's stuck. I can't take it off. It's stuck.

Estragon sits. He leans back as Vladimir pulls on his boot. Vladimir shakes the boot. Estragon grabs onto the heel of the boot and helps pull the boot. The boot pops off. Vladimir stumbles, then regains his balance.

Estragon: You mind if I sit with you? I think I might take a nap.

Vladimir: Relax.

Estragon: Rest.

Vladimir: Lie.

Estragon: Nap.

Sheltered Together At Home During the 2020 Coronavirus Pandemic While Living Out a Kind of WAITING FOR GODOT
By Rabeya Rahman

Stage Directions: Estragon and Vladimir live in a small street-level apartment in a brownstone in Brooklyn, New York. Pozzo and Lucky visited recently, before the city's sheltering-at-home rules went into effect. Because of the health crisis, the Beckett character of the little boy is now a young delivery guy. Having been quarantined for a while, Estragon and Vladimir are a bit crazed. The noise of ambulances announces that someone in the neighborhood is probably sick. Vladimir goes towards

Estragon, who lies asleep in bed; he contemplates him a moment, then shakes him awake.

Estragon *(Wild gestures, incoherent words. Finally.)*: Why will you never
    let me sleep?
Vladimir: I felt lonely.
Estragon: I was dreaming I was happy.
Vladimir: That passed time.
Estragon: I was dreaming that –
Vladimir *(Violently)*: Don't tell me! *(Silence.)* I wonder if we'll get out of this
    situation soon.
Estragon: Situation?
Vladimir: Situation.
Estragon: Soon. In my dream, we did.
Vladimir: You dreamt it? *(Pause.)*
Estragon: I dreamt it.
Vladimir: In your sleep?
Estragon: In my ... Was I sleeping? While others suffered? Am I sleeping
    now? Tomorrow, when I wake, or think I do, what shall I say of
    today? That with Vladimir my friend, at this place, I waited for this
    virus pandemic to end? That Pozzo called on Facetime, with his
    carrier, and that he spoke to us? Probably. But in all that, what truth
    will there be?

Estragon begins to doze off again. The doorbell rings. Vladimir turns his head towards their apartment's front door and hears, on the other side, someone speak through the door.

Guy: Mister ...
Vladimir: Oh my! The newspaper guy is here! *(He takes out his face mask
    and gloves and puts them on. He walks over to the door and opens it.)*
Guy: Mister ... Mister Michael ....
Vladimir: Off we go again. *(Pause.)* Do you not recognize me?
Guy: No, sir.
Vladimir: It wasn't you came yesterday?
Guy: No, sir.
Vladimir: This is your first time?
Guy: Yes, sir.

Silence.

Vladimir: You have any updates?
Guy: Yes, sir.
Vladimir: Things are still bad.
Guy: Yes, sir.
Vladimir: People are still dying.
Guy: Yes, sir.
Vladimir: Are you affected by it?
Guy: No, sir.
Vladimir: Your ... coworkers?
Guy: I don't know exactly, sir.

Silence.

Vladimir: Is it really that contagious?
Guy: Yes, sir.
Vladimir: Treatable, no?
Guy: It should be, sir.

Silence.

Vladimir: Christ have mercy on us!
Guy: Any last words before I go, sir?
Vladimir: Tell the frontline workers ... *(He hesitates.)* ... tell them THANK
     YOU! Tell them I said "Thank you." Since you are out and about ...
     be brave, and be sure you saw me. You won't come and tell me next
     time that you never saw me!

*Silence. Vladimir makes a sudden spring forward to hug the guy, but the
guy avoids him and exits running.*

**Vladimir and Estragon have stopped counting the weeks they have
been in quarantine together, an additional coronavirus pandemic
scene for Samuel Beckett's play WAITING FOR GODOT, by Chyna
Chung**

*Stage directions: Vladimir and Estragon got into an argument over not
giving each other enough space. Estragon felt as if he was better off alone,
in his own space, enjoying his time without anyone else. Vladimir felt as
if they should remain together during the pandemic. Estragon stormed
off due to his "need" to be free from Vladimir, but then comes back the
next day.*

Vladimir: You again! Come here till I embrace you.

Estragon (Voice gets higher while he walks away from Vladimir): Don't touch me.

Vladimir: Do you want me to go away? Gogo!

Estragon: Don't touch me! Don't question me! Don't speak to me! Stay with me!

Vladimir (Matches his tone): Did I ever leave you?

Estragon: You let me go.

Vladimir: Look at me! Will you look at me!?

Estragon: What a day! Another day done with.

Vladimir: Not yet.

Estragon (Calms down and moves closer towards Vladimir): For me, it's over and done with no matter what happens. I heard you singing.

Vladimir: That's right, I remember.

Estragon (Begins to reflect on his relationship and what he has done to make Vladimir feel such a way): That finished me. I said to myself, he's all alone, he thinks I'm gone forever, and he sings.

Vladimir (Tries to prove Estragon wrong): One is not a master of one's moods. All day I've felt in great form. I didn't get up in the night, not once!

Estragon: You see, you piss better when I'm not there.

Vladimir: I missed you ... and at the same time I was happy. Isn't that a queer thing?

Estragon (Shocked): Happy?

Vladimir: Perhaps it's not quite the right word.

Estragon: And now?

Vladimir: Now? ... (Joyous) There you are again ... (Indifferent) There we are again ... (Gloomy) There I am again.

Estragon: You see, you feel worse when I'm with you. I feel better too.

Vladimir: Then why do you always come crawling back?

Estragon (Thinks about telling the truth but claims otherwise): I don't know.

Vladimir: No, but I do. It's because you don't know how to defend yourself.

Estragon turns away and thinks on what he has heard. On how much is true from experience and how much is false but seems true from emotion.

After several hours of "mind-numbling but interesting" work, this speech of Lucky's "luckily came to me," says Nattapat Karmniyanont about his several-times-revised interpretation of Lucky's famous monologue

God. Oh, how He loves us so, with the divine love of his impartiality and, a father ever silent, ever present. But why does this love disappear at moments? This loveless love leaving … dread. The dread that can only be cured with a glimpse of the heaven oh so high above with its splendor, but then the towering inferno of the depth reaches out of the mist and strangles it. Although for a time everything is calm. The works of men reassure us, with their measurements and numbers and inches and miles and hertz, saying that to a high degree of certainty that it is all right for Him to lay down and He is the right one. Thus he gives us so many things to do, so so much, hitting a ball back and forth back and forth, oh so fun. How about jumping, flying, skipping, shooting, dilemmas and quizzes, and asphyxia and phobias and games. Yet, it lingers, this feeling that with words that reached the moon, that reached the stars and pierced His heart fails to convey, not a caress, not a skim, not a graze, not a glance, not a touch to this … dread. This dread shrinking he and her, they and thems, into a ball. But wait, no, we can look deeper, by miles? Deeper, by feet? Deeper. By inches? Centimeters? Millimeters? Nanometers? Atoms? Electrons? Planck? Yes, that must be it, that must be why this … dread is still there. It's still there. It must be in the imagination then. It must not exist. Play more games, look at more things, hit more, thrust more, laugh more, smile more, speak more, jump more, shout more, scratch more, bash more. It's still there. Godot, help me.

The Play WAITING FOR GODOT is. The Play Waiting.
Reductive manipulations by Shanya Hopkins

> The play WAITING FOR GODOT is a play about waiting
> for Godot.
> The play WAITING FOR GODOT is a play about waiting.
> is a play about waiting.
> is a play about waiting for Godot, the play WAITING?
> The play WAITING FOR GODOT is a play about.
> The play WAITING FOR GODOT is a play about waiting
> for Godot.

The play WAITING FOR GODOT is a play about waiting
for. The play WAITING FOR GODOT is a play about
waiting for.
The play WAITING.
The play WAITING FOR GODOT is a play about. The play
WAITING FOR.
The.
The play.
The play WAITING FOR GODOT is a play about waiting
for Godot.
The play WAITING FOR GODOT is a play.
The play.
The play WAITING FOR GODOT is a play about w*aiting*.

**Comments by College Collaborator Ryan Langan on "Reduction in
Samuel Beckett's Play WAITING FOR GODOT" (and, Indirectly, on
Colleague Shanya Hopkins's "Reductive Manipulations" Piece That
You've Just Experienced)**

If there were any piece of literature in existence to be examined through
the lens of reduction, WAITING FOR GODOT is it. While I understand
that the attribute "reductive" is meant to be critically negative, I find that
application to be a shallow one. While it's true that its definition is listed on
Google as "tending to present a subject or problem in a simplified form,
especially one viewed as crude," there is more to the idea of reduction
than this. I see reduction in WAITING FOR GODOT as meaning something
roughly equivalent to distillation – rather than the simplification of an
idea, the concentration of one. And this can be understood by the series
of sentences that were posted by Professor Eidelberg in his Blackboard
announcement about reductive creative writing. "The play 'Waiting for
Godot' is a play about waiting for Godot" is a sentence that, more than
being redundant, simply states the obvious. In fact, it is the reduction
(concentration) of this sentence that actually brings about its meaning
more clearly: "The play 'Waiting for Godot' is a play about waiting."

Because Godot is an abstract and absent figure in the play, it isn't really
a play about waiting for him as much as it is about waiting in general.
Godot is merely an allegory for the broader idea of a "something that is
waited for." The play examines not what is being waited for but the act
of waiting itself. In so doing, it is further reduced. Now that Godot is no

longer the center, and now that the act of waiting is, the broader themes of existential questioning can be brought to light....

WAITING FOR GODOT is, at bottom, a play. It *examines* the act of waiting itself, but it is not *in* the act of waiting itself. The play exists. The characters within the play exist because it exists. And the play is a representation of our world – the world exists, and we exist within it because it exists. See what happens when we trim down? We arrive at the point of questioning existence itself. "Reduction" is the very mechanism by which WAITING FOR GODOT allows its audience into its themes and by which it has achieved such success and merit.

A found "Waiting" poem, inspired by and composed from WAITING FOR GODOT
By Shanya Hopkins

Help me!
What am I to do?
How does it fit me?
What?
... waiting?
Neither more nor less.
[silence]
I'm in hell
It is not sufficient.
... waiting?
I'm in hell.
It hurts?
Hurts!
It's too much for one man.
It hurts?
Why don't you help me?
Shall we go?
[they do not move]
You know I can't bear that.
Pass the time.
I'm tired.
Tell me what to do.
[pause]
Do you think God sees me?
It hurts?

God have pity on me!
Calm yourself.
[exasperated]
Try as one may ...
The best thing would be to kill me.
It is not sufficient.
That's enough, I'm tired
You'll never see me again.
[he does not move]
But I can't go on like this!
While waiting?
Hell.
How does it fit me?
[pause]
It fits.
You think?
I think.
Ah.
Ah?
Ah!
Why don't you help me?
Tell me what to do.
I'm going.
Wait!
[he does not move]
At last!
He comes ...
Godot?
[pause]
Godot?
Imbecile!
Death.
[pauses]
Don't be afraid
Now our troubles are over.

A poem found in WAITING FOR GODOT
By Hester Milford

A crust of bread
Beat him till he was dead

Where did you spend the night?
You better tell me
You piss better when I'm not there.
(They murmur)
This is awful!
(Another of your nightmares ...)
Show me your leg, pull up your trousers.
Bloody radish
You're merciless! (The horror!!)
It's a turnip!
A carrot?
I could've sworn ...
(A cretin. A halfwit! The slobber. A goiter!!)
You're making me nervous
Oh, just get rid of him

"Waiting": a poem created with Samuel Beckett's words
By Jason Chetram

Note from Jason: Unless I made a mistake, my poem used every sentence of WAITING FOR GODOT in which the word "wait" or "waiting" was said by a character, except one. In the end, I omitted the sentence "Wait, there's my belt" because I felt it really did not fit in with the last stanza. The sentences are also in the order in which they were said in the play.

What do you expect,
you always wait till the last moment.
We're waiting for Godot.
That we were to wait.
That we were to wait.
Wait. Yes, but while waiting.
Let's wait and see what he says.
Let's wait till we know exactly how we stand.
Wait, I have it. That's to say
. . . you understand . . . the dusk
. . . the strain . . . waiting . . . I confess
. . . I imagined . . . for a second . . .
Waiting? So you were waiting for him?
You couldn't have waited?
Wait a little longer, you'll never regret it.
He might have waited!

I'd wait till it was black night before I gave up.
Simply wait. Wait. Wait.
Wait! Wait! Wait!
What's he waiting for?
Wait! We're waiting for Godot.
Then all we have to do is to wait on here.
Wait!
Wait for Godot. Wait for Godot.
Wait . . . we embraced
. . . we were happy . . . happy
. . . what do we do now that we're happy
. . . go on waiting . . . waiting
. . . let me think . . . it's coming
. . . go on waiting . . . now that we're happy
. . . let me see . . . ah! We're waiting for Godot.
Wait. We're waiting for Godot.
Wait till I see. While waiting.
While waiting. We are no longer alone,
waiting for the night, waiting for Godot,
waiting for . . . waiting.
We're waiting for Godot.
We are waiting for Godot to come –
We wait. We're waiting for Godot.
What are we waiting for?
What is he waiting for?
What are you waiting for?
I'm waiting for Godot.
We wait till we can get up.
That with Estragon, my friend,
at this place, until the fall of night,
I waited for Godot?
To wait for Godot.

"Waiting" (much, much longer): an extended poem from the language of Samuel Beckett
By Carolyn Reyes

And I resumed the struggle.
I thought you were gone forever.
When I think of it . . . all these years . . . but for me . . . where would you be. (*Decisively.*)

You'd be nothing more than a little heap of bones at the present minute, no doubt about it.

We should have thought of it a million years ago, in the nineties.

It'll pass the time.

I'm going.

We're waiting for Godot.

That we were to wait.

No more weeping.

We'll come back tomorrow. And then the day after tomorrow. Until he comes.

We came here yesterday.

Nothing is certain when you're about.

That we were to wait. Let's stop talking for a minute, do you mind?

I was asleep! (*Despairingly.*) Why will you never let me sleep?

I felt lonely.

Wait.

Yes, but while waiting.

What about hanging ourselves?

Let's hang ourselves immediately! Let's wait and see what he says.

I'm curious to hear what he has to offer. Then we'll take it or leave it.

Take your time.

I'm hungry! I asked you a question.

Waiting? So you were waiting for him?

Can't you see he wants to rest?

You couldn't have waited?

Unless I smoke another pipe before I go.

Wait a little longer, you'll never regret it.

Will night never come?

It's only beginning. It's awful.

Oh! He's gone! Without saying goodbye! How could he! He might have waited!

Will night never come?

All three look at the sky.

You don't feel like going until it does?

I'd wait till it was black night before I gave up. (*He looks at the stool.*) I'd very much like to sit down, but I don't quite know how to go about it.

Time has stopped.

So long as one knows.

One can bide one's time.

One knows what to expect.

No further need to worry.

Simply wait.

We're used to it.

He picks up his hat, peers inside it, shakes it, puts it on.

Wait.

No matter! What was I saying? (*He ponders.*) Wait. (*Ponders.*) Well now isn't that . . . (*He raises his head.*) Help me!

Wait!

Wait!

Wait!

All three take off their hats simultaneously, press their hands to their foreheads, concentrate.

(*Triumphantly*). Ah!

Nothing happens, nobody comes, nobody goes, it's awful!

Tell him to think.

Give him his hat. His hat? He can't think without his hat.

(*To Estragon.*) Give him his hat.

What's he waiting for?

I don't seem to be able . . . (*long hesitation*) . . . to depart.

That passed the time.

It would have passed in any case.

Yes, but not so rapidly.

Pause.

What do we do now?

Let's go.

We can't.

Why not?

We're waiting for Godot.

(*Despairingly.*) Ah!

Pause.

That's the idea, let's make a little conversation.

We've nothing more to do here.

Nor anywhere else.

Ah, Gogo, don't go on like that. Tomorrow everything will be better.

Then all we have to do is to wait on here.

Remind me to bring a bit of rope tomorrow.

Wait!

I'm cold! Wait! (*He moves away from Vladimir.*) I sometimes wonder if we wouldn't have been better off alone, each one for himself. (*He crosses the stage and sits down on the mound.*) We weren't made for the same road.

Next day. Same time. Same place.

Lucky's hat at same place.

The tree has four or five leaves.

Enter Vladimir agitatedly. He halts and looks long at the tree, then suddenly begins to move feverishly about the stage. He halts before the boots, picks one up, examines it, sniffs it, manifests disgust, puts it back carefully. Comes and goes. Halts extreme right and gazes into distance off, shading his eyes with his hand. Comes and goes. Halts extreme left, as before. Comes and goes. Halts suddenly and begins to sing loudly. He stops, broods. Softly.

And dug the dog a tomb . . .

Another day done with.

I missed you . . . and at the same time I was happy. Isn't that a strange thing?

Now? . . . (Joyous.) There you are again . . . (Indifferent.) There we are again. . . (Gloomy.)

There I am again.

What do we do now, now that we are happy?

Wait for Godot. (Estragon groans. Silence.) Things have changed here since yesterday.

The best thing would be to kill me, like the other.

We have our reasons.

All the dead voices.

Wait for Godot.

Ah!

Silence.

This is awful!

Sing something.

That's the idea, let's contradict each another.

Impossible.

You think so?

Wait . . . we embraced . . . we were happy . . . happy . . . what do we do now that we're happy ... go on waiting . . . waiting . . . let me think . . . it's coming . . . go on waiting . . . now that we're happy . . . let me see . . . ah! The tree!

(Having tried in vain to work it out). I'm tired! (Pause.) Let's go.

We can't.

Why not?

We're waiting for Godot.

Ah! (Pause. Despairing.) What'll we do, what'll we do! There's nothing we can do.

But I can't go on like this!

This is becoming really insignificant. I've tried everything.

We're waiting for Godot.

Estragon takes Vladimir's hat. Vladimir adjusts Lucky's hat on his head. Estragon puts on Vladimir's hat in place of his own which he hands to Vladimir. Vladimir takes Estragon's hat. Estragon adjusts Vladimir's hat on his head. Vladimir puts on Estragon's hat in place of Lucky's which he hands to Estragon. Estragon takes Lucky's hat. Vladimir adjusts Estragon's hat on his head. Estragon puts on Lucky's hat in place of Vladimir's which he hands to Vladimir. Vladimir takes his hat. Estragon adjusts Lucky's hat on his head.

What about a little deep breathing?

I'm tired breathing.

Let us do something, while we have the chance! It is not every day that we are needed. Not indeed that we personally are needed.

What are we doing here, that is the question. And we are blessed in this, that we happen to know the answer. Yes, in this immense confusion one thing alone is clear. We are waiting for Godot to come –

Or for night to fall. (Pause.) We have kept our appointment and that's an end to that. We are not saints, but we have kept our appointment. How many people can boast as much?

Help!

Let's go.

We can't.

Why not?

We're waiting for Godot.

Ah! (Despairing.) What'll we do, what'll we do! what are you waiting for?

I'm waiting for Godot.

Why will you never let me sleep?

I felt lonely.

I was dreaming I was happy.

That passed the time.

Was I sleeping, while the others suffered? Am I sleeping now? Tomorrow, when I wake, or think I do, what shall I say of today? That with Estragon my friend, at this place, until the fall of night, I waited for Godot? That Pozzo passed, with his carrier, and that he spoke to us? Probably. But in all that what truth will there be?

At me too someone is looking, of me too someone is saying, He is sleeping, he knows nothing, let him sleep on. (Pause.) I can't go on! (Pause.) What have I said?

He goes feverishly to and fro, halts finally at extreme left, broods. Enter Boy right. He halts. Silence.

I don't know.

Silence.
Where shall we go?
Not far.
Oh yes, let's go far away from here.
We can't.
Why not?
We have to come back tomorrow.
What for?
To wait for Godot.
Ah! (Silence.) He didn't come?
No.
Why don't we hang ourselves?
With what?
You haven't got a bit of rope?
No.
Then we can't.
Silence.
Let's go.
Well? Shall we go?
Yes, let's go.
They do not move.

A CONCLUSION (TIMELY BUT UNEXPECTED) TO SOME DAY

Hunter College Collaborator Fawzi Saleh Tells an Original Composite "Waiting" Story That Assembles a Cast of Characters From a Dozen Works of Literature Studied During the Coronavirus Pandemic Term of Spring 2020 in Robert Eidelberg's Hunter College Course on "The Literature of Waiting"

The Dozen Literary Works Alluded to in Order of Appropriation

- ➤ the novel WAITING by Ha Jin
- ➤ the novel THE TRIAL by Franz Kafka
- ➤ the novel THE WINGS OF THE DOVE by Henry James
- ➤ the essay MY MOTHER'S CALENDARS by Carol J. Adams
- ➤ the children's book WAITING IS NOT EASY! by Mo Willems
- ➤ Dr. Martin Luther King Jr.'s Letter from Birmingham Jail
- ➤ the story of Jacob and Rachel in the Hebrew BIBLE
- ➤ the novel EINSTEIN'S DREAMS by Alan Lightman
- ➤ the one-act-play THE DUMB WAITER by Harold Pinter
- ➤ the short story A TELEPHONE CALL by Dorothy Parker
- ➤ the memoir GROWING UP by Russell Baker
- ➤ the one-act play WAITING FOR LEFTY by Clifford Odets

The alarm rang and broke the silence of Lin Kong's bedroom.

Lin's black, hazy vision was soon replaced with the sight of his bed sheets as he slowly opened his eyes. He removed the blanket over his head and turned off the alarm sitting on the drawer next to his bed: 6:30 am it read. Lying next to him, Shuyu stirred and then also removed the blanket covering her face. Unlike him, she did not have slow, monotonous movements. "Good morning," she murmured and then quickly headed to the bathroom.

Still lying in bed, Lin turned around and stared up at the ceiling. He had been dreaming about Manna, as he frequently did. It was not about her last moments in hospital but rather her younger years, before they were married and simply comrades in the hospital. He thought of their long walks and their meals together in the hospital cafeteria. He remembered talking with her about the patients, nurses, and doctors while she listened eagerly, her radiating eyes and her beautiful complexion soothing his eyes.

The bathroom door abruptly opened and Shuyu stepped out. "I'm making eggs and toast," she said, as she exited the room. Lin showered and dressed and then went to the kitchen. His breakfast was waiting for him at the table, as well as that of Shuyu and the children. None of them were present, though. He glanced at the clock and saw that it was ten minutes before 7:00. Shuyu had most likely gone to wake them. Well, he thought, at least American schools started at 8:00. He remembered in China they began at 7:00 o'clock and sometimes even earlier.

Coming to America had not been easy. First, there was his job. He had been a physician in China for many years and he felt a duty to care for his patients. Then there was his wife. Shuyu had spent most of her life in China and probably would not agree to move to a foreign country.

Despite these hardships, however, he knew he couldn't stay in China. The political atmosphere had turned grave. The communist government had grown in strength and it demonstrated its power by putting down rebellions with extreme force.

An oppressive government was the last thing Lin wanted his children to live under. Also, he had found some books authored by radical minds. Books like this were usually censored, but he had been lucky to meet a colleague who had a few. Within a week, he had finished all of them. He had never taken a firm stance in politics, but these books instilled a love for democracy in him. One specifically talked about America and the American dream. Lin knew this was the country he wanted his kids to grow up in.

Still, for a while, he did nothing. The idea seemed too bizarre. But then he began talking with Shuyu about it. She resisted at first, as he expected, but she too clung to the idea for a better life, away from the constant violence that had been plaguing their country. Then the Tiananmen massacre happened, and that was the last straw for both of them. Lin applied for a visa and resigned as a doctor. This meant he could never practice medicine in China ever again.

Within a few months though, Lin received his visa and his family moved to America. Their difficulties didn't end there. In order to practice medicine, he needed to pass several board exams. At the same time, he had to work odd jobs to support his family. Lin was resilient, however, and after about a decade of hard work, he was able to obtain an American medical license.

It took about five minutes for Lin to completely finish his breakfast. He quickly chugged the orange juice, put on his white coat, and rushed out the door. The hospital was only a few blocks away.

*****

Approaching the hospital, Lin noticed a security guard at the door. That's weird, he thought, he had never seen a guard at the entrance before. And as he reaches the entrance, the guard tells Lin that he cannot grant him entry just now. Lin ponders this and asks why not. "As you probably already know, there is a virus going around, Anypomonisía-19, or APM-19, and so access is strictly limited and even employees need to present their IDs," the guard explained. Lin asks if he will be allowed in after presenting his ID. "It's possible, but not until I see it," the guard replied.

Lin quickly searched his coat pockets for his ID but his search proved fruitless. He then looked over the shoulder of the guard and saw a fellow colleague of his walking down the hall. He thought of waving at him and calling him over. The security guard read Lin's thoughts and chuckled. "If you want it so badly, just try to get in against my expressed orders. But remember, I'm powerful, and I'm just guarding the entrance. There will be security guards in every hall, each more powerful than the last," the guard explained.

Lin didn't expect such difficulties; surely the hospital should be accessible to doctors at all times. Nevertheless, Lin saw the gun in the guard's holster and he decided he'd better wait until he had his ID. The guard gave Lin a chair and let him sit down on one side of the entrance as he pondered about how to get his ID. In Lin's mind, the minutes seemed to turn into hours, which turned into days and weeks, and then into months and years.

Unable to withstand the prolonged waiting, Lin said, "I left my ID at home, but I'm a doctor," pointing to the name tag on his white coat which read, "Dr. Kong." The security guard smiled. "I'll agree so as to make sure that you don't think you haven't tried everything," the guard said.

Lin slumped back into his chair. Once again, waiting took a toll on his mind, and the few minutes that passed seemed like years. Eventually, his eyesight began to fail as he became drowsy yet he could still clearly see the light shining from the entrance.

Shortly before he was about to take a nap, he thought to ask a question: "Isn't it true that everyone strives to get into the hospital?" Lin asked the guard. "How come, then, that in all this time waiting no one else has requested entry to it?" To which the guard responds, "Nobody else could have been granted entry here, for this door was made for you alone. Now I will go and close it." The guard then turned around and reached for the door handle to close the door.

"Wait!" Lin exclaimed. The guard calmly turned back to Lin. "I have patients inside waiting for me. I have to be inside before 7:00 am and I'm already a few minutes late. Please, for the sake of my patients, please let me in," begged Lin.

The guard did not seem satisfied with this response. He crossed his arms and bore daggers into Lin's eyes. "Had you truly cared for your patients, had you truly wanted to be on time for them, why didn't you disregard me and go inside? What were you afraid of?" asked the guard. Lin lowered his gaze, and unconsciously, he glanced at the guard's holster before staring at the floor. The guard frowned. "My gun? You were afraid I was going to shoot you?" asked the guard.

Lin continued to stare at the floor. "If you really are who you say you are, a doctor, then why would I shoot you? My job is to only prevent anyone who is unauthorized from entering, and thus I was testing you. Your passive behavior made me not trust you. Why did you just sit there? Why did you not go and get your ID? Why did you not call someone to bring your ID, or at least call someone from the hospital, like your superior, to help clear up the situation? There were so many things you could have done to get past me, yet you chose to wait, hoping the situation would solve itself," the guard said.

Lin didn't know what to say. The guard mistook Lin's silence for seriousness, and so he decided to lighten the mood. "Besides, if I did shoot you, where would you end up?" the guard asked. What a strange question, Lin thought. "Um... Heaven?" Lin asked.

The guard was taken aback. "Well no, I mean, what I meant was the hospital," the guard said. Lin remembered the patient he treated last week who had been shot six times. "Oh right," he said. The guard sighed. "Alright you can go in. I was just making sure you were a doctor, and you..." the guard paused as he squinted at Lin's name tag, "....appear to be a doctor so I'll let you through," the guard finished. The guard stepped aside and Lin entered the hospital. The guard stared at Lin as he walked down the hallway. Doctors these days, the guard thought.

*****

Lin entered the hospital and went to the 13th floor, where he was stationed. He reported to his superiors and explained his lateness by saying he had awoken late. Since he was always on time, his lateness was excused and he was told his first patient was already here and waiting for him.

Lin rushed to his room and as he was doing so, he passed by the patient lounge. He couldn't help but notice it was completely empty except for one girl. He stopped and stared at her. She was sitting on the couch and there was a small table in front of her, its edges a few inches from her knees. The table had a purplish cloth and on top of it sat a lonely magazine. The girl stared at the magazine, she seemed to be sad, so as not to be angry, but he could tell she was becoming angry at the fact that she couldn't be sad.

"Hello, I'm Dr. Kong, sorry I'm late," he said. The girl quickly looked up at him, surprised by his voice. "Hello Dr. Kong," she replied, and then she looked back at the magazine. He was hoping she would say a bit more, but she remained quiet. "Well uh, let's get going to my room," he said. The girl looked at him, puzzled. "Your room, what for?" she asked. Lin exhaled and tried to hide his annoyance. First he had to deal with a detective and now a clueless patient.

"You were waiting for me, right? Well I'm here, let's go," he said. The girl now understood what he meant and blushed out of embarrassment. "Oh no, I don't have an appointment, I'm here to make an appointment," she explained. "Oh I see," Lin said. "In that case you should go to the front desk to make one, this is the patient longue for people who already have an appointment," he said. "I understand doctor," she replied but she did not move from her place, and simply kept staring at the magazine.

Lin wasn't sure what to do. He could easily walk away, but he felt pity for this girl. She seemed so depressed that he didn't want to leave her like this. A brief moment of silence passed as he looked around the room. He then slowly walked over to her and sat down on the couch next to hers.

"Tell me, what's wrong?" he asked. For a moment she said nothing, but then she closed her eyes and clasped her face with her hands and broke out into sobs. "Oh doctor, please help me, I don't know what to do," she said in a crying, muffled voice. Lin thought of embracing her but then remembered the virus and changed his mind.

"My father, Lionel Croy, has told me he is sick but I'm not sure what's wrong with him and whether he's actually telling the truth. Also, my aunt, Aunt Maud, is asking me to live with her but only on the condition that I break all relations with my father and never talk to him ever again. She wants me to marry a rich man but I'm already in love with someone, although he is not very wealthy," she said while sobbing and wiping tears off her face.

Lin grabbed a box of tissues from the top of a small table in the corner of the room and handed the girl some tissues. "What's your name?" he asked. "Kate, Kate Croy," she croaked. "Alright Kate, listen to me, everything is going to be okay," he said. He then thought about her family situation and pondered about what to say next. Kate meanwhile had calmed down. Her rhythmic exhaling and inhaling, occasionally interrupted by sniffs, was slowing down, and she was no longer sobbing.

"So, your father is sick and you came here to make an appointment for him? You did the right thing. I'm not sure what's going on between your father and your aunt, but it seems that they had an argument. As for your lover, I think you should marry the person you love and not the person who has more money," he explained.

Kate blew her nose with a tissue. "I think so too, but my father is encouraging me to follow my aunt's advice, and then give him some of the money I receive from my wealthy husband," she said in a nasally voice.

Well, Lin thought, he had always blamed himself for not being a good enough father, but this Lionel guy was on another level. Not only was he so horrid that his sister wanted his daughter to break all relations with him, but he actually encouraged his daughter to listen to his sister for his own benefit.

Despite the complicated situation Kate was facing, Lin wanted to help her. She reminded him of his daughter, Hua. Hua had gone through a similar situation, but in her case she had to choose between the man she loved and her family. In the end, they all decided that she should stay in China. She had been engaged and had already started living with the family of her fiancé so she was financially taken care of. And while it was true that China's government was going through a tumultuous time, Hua's fiancé was an officer in the army, thus she had somewhat better protection from the violence that was ensuing there. Nevertheless, it had been difficult for Lin to let her go, and even more so for Shuyu. They were not even able to get her married because both families were going through hard economic times.

"Alright Kate, if you can't live with your aunt because she's upset with your father, then for the time being just live with you father. In the meantime, bring him to the hospital so we can figure out what's wrong with him and also discuss his issues with your aunt," said Lin.

Kate shook her head. "I went to him, but he wouldn't accept me. My aunt is the same too, she said she will only accept me if I promise never to speak with my father again," she said.

Lin signed. He had run out of options. Kate had no place to go as she was barred from both her father and aunt. She could technically stay with her lover, but given the fact that he was not wealthy, Kate would most likely be a burden financially and their love could take a wrong turn.

"Okay, I'm going to go talk to my superiors, I'll explain to them your situation and we'll see what we can do," Lin said. "It's quite alright Dr. Kong. You've helped me enough, you don't need to go that far. I'll figure something out," she said as she got up and collected her tissues off the table.

"Are you sure? Where will you stay?" he asked. "I'll persuade Aunt Maud to let me stay with her. If my father really doesn't want me to stay with him, and he only values me for money, perhaps it really is best that I stay away from him," she explained. Lin smiled. If he were in her position, he too would do the same.

"Well, that sounds good. It was nice talking to you Kate. Take care of yourself," said Lin.

Kate beamed. "I will. Thank you for everything," she said. And with that, she threw the tissues in the trash and exited the lounge.

Lin exhaled a sign of relief. Well, her father-problems were over. He just hoped she could work something out with her lover. Hopefully they would have a happy ending. It would be a shame if her lover were to somehow obtain a large sum of money, stating that if she married him, he would turn down the large sum of money he had obtained, and if she rejected him, then he would give her all the money.

*****

He finished his patient rounds around 3:00 in the afternoon. He was technically not done, as he had only finished the first of his two shifts. However, he had a lunch break until 4:00, so he was heading home. When he came home, it was as lively as ever. In the kitchen, he could hear the cooker whistling on the stove. Shuyu was in the living room on the couch watching TV while the kids were sprawled on the floor working on a worksheet. As soon as the front door closed behind him, his family came to greet him.

"Dad! You're home early," said Lake.

"How many patients did you see? Did anyone die from the virus?" asked River.

Lin laughed while Shuyu slapped River on the shoulder. "I made chicken and rice with fried vegetables. There's also some salmon left over from yesterday," Shuyu said.

"I'll take everything, I'm starving," Lin replied, and Shuyu nodded and went to the kitchen.

Lin then went to the living room and sat on the couch with his sons. He usually would talk about his patients with his sons. He wanted both to become doctors, and so he thought it was best to instill a love of medicine into them early on.

"I have a short break to eat, what about you guys, you just came from school?" asked Lin.

"Today was a half-day, so we came home around 12:00," said Lake.

"Yeah, we played in the park before we came home," added River.

"Lucky you. What about your homework?" asked Lin, staring at their worksheets on the floor.

They all stared at the floor. "You know I want your homework done before I come home," continued Lin.

"But you came home earlier than usual today, and school might be cancelled because of the virus," protested Lake.

Lin shook his head. "You are in 5th grade. It should not take more than one hour to finish your homework, regardless of whether you have school tomorrow or not," replied Lin.

"He wanted me to play video games with him," said River, pointing at Lake.

"Liar! You started playing first!" fired back Lake.

Before they could start quibbling, Lin raised up his hand. "You know you are only supposed to play them on the weekends, not the weekdays," said Lin in a stern tone.

Both became quiet. "Playing video games is a form of procrastination," continued Lin.

"Procrapnation?" asked River.

"Pro-cras-tin-ation," Lin spelled out. "To avoid doing homework, you play video games. So, when you avoid something by doing something else instead, you are procrastinating," explained Lin.

Both sons looked at Lin with a blank face. They weren't sure where he was going with this.

Lin sighed. "Alright look, next time you come home, finish your homework as soon as possible.

After that, help mom with the chores and then read with your remaining time," said Lin.

Lake made a serious face and nodded. River meanwhile flashed a mischievous grin and nodded eagerly. Lin knew who had started the video game shenanigans even before he walked through the front door.

The two brothers were very different. Lake was a smaller version of Lin. He was skinny as a stick, but overall healthy and had a modest character. River, on the other hand, took more after his mother, Manna. He was taller by about five inches and slightly bulkier. As for his character, he was a devil, more frequently getting into fights and arguments. For the most part, though, both were good kids. They usually got along and performed well in school.

*****

Lin began to walk over to the kitchen when he noticed a calendar hanging on the wall. "A calendar?" asked Lin. "I made it! We had to make something for Mother's Day," said River. Lin went closer and inspected the calendar. It said, "My mother's calendar" on the top and was a regular calendar, though the lines of the boxes weren't all that straight because they were handmade. The first couple of boxes were already filled in. It had Shuyu's signature marks, a mixture of numerals, geometric shapes, and small drawings. Lin was familiar with some of the drawings, as Shuyu used a diary as a to-do list. Also on the calendar, though, were some new marks he had not seen before, like the outline of a pen or pencil, which possibly stood for an appointment.

Lin chuckled. "Good job, River," he said, and then went to the kitchen.

*****

As he walked in, Lin saw his steaming dinner and hopped onto the chair. Shuyu was sitting directly opposite of him, eating her food while scrolling on her phone. Behind her, he saw the many things attached on the face of the fridge with magnets, such as a piece of paper serving as Shuyu's grocery list as well as a drawing done by Lake when he was about three.

Lin smiled when he thought of Lake's drawing. Lake was trying to draw the characters from his then-favorite show, Peppa Pig. There was an elephant named Gerald talking with a small pig named Piggie. Shuyu had drawn a dialogue bubble for Gerald and filled in "If I have to wait, I will wait." Shuyu was trying to teach the kids patience, especially River, who always wanted things done right away.

"The food is delicious," Lin remarked.

"Thanks," Shuyu stolidly replied.

Lin didn't take her tone to heart. She usually spoke this way when she was engrossed with the TV or phone. Shuyu wasn't always like this. In China, she was as obedient as a slave. When she came to America though, she dramatically changed. She still took care of him, but her attention was no longer on him. Instead, she was obsessed with social media. When she wasn't doing chores or running errands, she was always commenting on the latest tweet from her fashion idols or sharing a new recipe by her beloved cooks. But while social media did provide an outlet for boredom and served as an exciting hobby in her mundane life, Lin knew there was something deeper, a hidden pain in the real world, that made her escape into the virtual one.

"One of my comrades is planning to go to China in the fall," Lin said. Shuyu's finger, which was scrolling the phone's screen, froze. She then clicked the power button, turning off her phone and looked up at him. He waited for her to say something, but then realized she was waiting for him to continue, and so he did.

"Nothing is certain because of the virus going around. However, if it clears up by then, and the travel restrictions are removed, he will take a week off from work and go. I've asked him to visit our city, where Hua was last living with the family of her fiancé, and our village, too, so he can check up on Benshang," Lin said.

"I need to go with him," she pleaded. Lin finished chewing his food and put down the fork. "Shuyu, we've talked about this many times before, you know we don't have enough money saved to go there," Lin explained.

In the ten years that they had spent living in America, Shuyu had, on multiple occasions, insisted that they visit China. Unfortunately, for most of that time, Lin was working two or three jobs that had just barely covered their rent and basic necessities. In addition, he had only recently obtained his American medical degree and begun his residency. He got paid more than all his three jobs combined, but they still did not have enough saved to visit China.

Shuyu tried to hide her emotions by turning to her phone, but the anger and sadness were obvious. One of her reasons, if not her main reason for using social media, was to find Hua. He knew this because the first time she found a person with the name Hua on Facebook, she had become erratic, hugging Lin when he came home and enthusiastically telling him she had found their daughter. Unfortunately, while the girl did look like Hua, he knew it wasn't her, and he had a feeling Shuyu did too, but still, Shuyu desperately looked for his confirmation. He only hugged her and kissed her forehead. He knew there were hundreds of Huas on the internet, but none of them would be their Hua because of China's iron grip on its social media. He didn't tell Shuyu because he knew it would break her, and so she continued to spend countless hours of her day on social media, hoping to one day find her daughter.

Lin looked at his watch. It was 10 minutes before 4. He gobbled up the last few bites of his meal and then grabbed his white coat that hung on the rack next to the front door. "Goodbye Shuyu," he said as he exited and did not hear a reply.

*****

He smiled at the security guard as he approached the entrance of the hospital. The guard returned the smile and made a small gun with his right hand, pretending to shoot Lin as he entered the hospital. The hospital was bustling, much busier than this morning. In his office, he put on gloves and a facemask and then opened his computer and looked at the spreadsheet containing his remaining patients. It appeared that his first patient was a man named Martin, with no recorded last name. Perhaps it was a typo, Lin thought.

Nevertheless, Lin exited his office and went to meet his patient. He entered the lounge and looked around. There was an even mix of men and women, mostly white and hispanic from what he could tell. Some were on their phones, some watching TV, and others flipping through magazines. "Mr. Martin," Lin called out loud.

*****

A man who had his back hunched, palms pressed, and eyes closed, as if he was praying, lifted his head and stood up, staring Lin firmly in the eyes. Interestingly, he was black, and Lin realized he might be the first black patient he had ever had.

"Hello, Mr. Martin, my name is Dr. Kong, let's go to my office," Lin said.

Once inside, he looked over at Martin's patient file. It appeared that he was here for his yearly check-up. Suddenly he remembered that he didn't know his last name and decided to question him about it. "Your file doesn't state your last name, could you please tell me it?" Lin asked.

Martin smiled. "How are African-Americans doing in America, Doctor?" Martin asked. Lin was puzzled by the question. The question itself was unusual, but on top of that, he really had no answer because he rarely even encountered such people.

Martin could tell the doctor had no response, and so he continued, "At least they no longer live in fear, and that grown black men are no longer referred to as 'boys,'" he stated. Lin didn't know where Martin was going with any of this, and thus he decided to change the subject, "Uh, well, yes, I agree. Now for your check-up, let's get your blood pressure," Lin said.

He grabbed the sphygmomanometer off his table and walked over to Martin's chair.

"Do you believe in God, Dr. Kong?" Martin asked.

Lin paused as he was wrapping the inflatable cuff around Martin's arms. Lin wasn't too religious, and thus he didn't want to get into a religious debate. However, he knew some patients liked to talk during their check-ups, and he decided that the check-up might go faster if he talked to Martin rather than tried to avoid it.

"Uh, well no, I wasn't raised in a religious household," Lin said, as he resumed wrapping the cuff.

"I see. Well according to the Bible, in the Book of Genesis, it states that, "In the beginning God created the heaven and the earth. It then goes on to list God's creation," Martin said.

Meanwhile, the sphygmomanometer compressed and uncompressed Martin's arm and then it beeped. Lin checked the monitor. It said error where the numbers would usually appear.

"It took God seven days to create all the creations of this universe," continued Martin.

Lin unwrapped the cuff off of Martin's arm. "That's interesting, isn't God all powerful? Why did it take God seven days, why didn't he just snap his fingers and create everything?" Lin asked curiously.

Martin smiled. "We must trust God. If he created the universe in seven days, then there is wisdom in that," he explained.

Lin returned to his desk and placed the sphygmomanometer in the corner. He wasn't satisfied with the answer, but he had a few questions of his own. Back in China, he had a colleague who had visited Israel and bought a copy of a translated Hebrew Bible, saying that it was very inspiring. He let Lin borrow it, and in it, Lin read the story of Jacob and Rachel.

Lin did not think much of it then because at the time he had not met Manna. However, in retrospect, it seemed to parallel his life with Manna. "In the Bible, I've read a story about Jacob and Rachel. I'm curious, if two people love each other, why does God not allow them to be together, why do they have to wait so long to be with each other? And also, why do others interfere in the love between two people, why doesn't God protect their love?" Lin asked.

Lin and Manna had to wait twenty years to officially marry. In that time, Shuyu and Benshang repeatedly interfered in his efforts to get a divorce. Even after they got married, situations arose, such as Manna's sickness or the dysentery his children went through, that hampered Lin and Manna's love for each other. Where was God then? Floating on white clouds? Why was it so hard for an all-powerful God to let him be with the woman he loved in peace?

Martin closed his eyes and again seemed to be in a prayer position. He seemed to be pondering on how to respond. "I am a servant of God, not God himself," he finally said. "The questions you ask require knowledge that I don't have. But in the case of Jacob and Rachel, I can perhaps offer my perspective. When two people first meet each other and think they are in love, they are often driven by lust not love. Real love requires work, it requires sacrifice. We see this in Jacob's case. To prove he really loved Rachel, Rachel's father asked him to work for seven years. This transformed his spontaneous lust into love that qualified him for marriage. As for the interference by Rachel's father, it was for the purpose of tradition; her father could simply not ignore tradition and let his younger daughter marry before his older daughter for the sake of Jacob's love," Martin explained.

"In that case, why didn't he say that in the first place? Why didn't he tell Jacob that he needed to get his older daughter married before Rachel did?" Lin asked.

"Perhaps because he underestimated Jacob's love for Rachel. He thought that after waiting seven years of marriage, Jacob would be satisfied with the older daughter and not be patient enough to wait seven more years for Rachel," replied Martin.

Lin did not like this answer. It made it seem as if the story was a benefit for themselves. Rachel's father did not care about who Rachel married but rather that he benefited the most. In his case, he managed to get fourteen years of labor out of Rachel's marriage, and had there been another daughter older than Rachel, he probably would have gotten away with seven more.

Suddenly, he realized that he was supposed to be performing the check-up. Lin looked at the patient file and decided that height and weight would be the easiest to get. Martin, however, had his own plans. He suddenly stood up. "I'm sorry Dr. Kong, but I have to go," he said.

Lin was taken back. "Wait, what do you mean, we just started the checkup," Lin said. "I have places to be, so unfortunately I cannot stay much longer. Tell Mrs. Parker thanks," and left the room. Lin was stunned. He had never had a patient who abruptly walked out from their appointment. He felt like chasing after Martin and persuading him to finish his check-up, but he instead got up and closed the door. There was no point in trying to make a patient stay if they didn't want to. As he sat back down in his chair, he tried to figure out what he had done wrong. He realized that instead of performing the check-up, he had become sidetracked and talked about God.

God, Lin thought, as he chuckled. As far as he was concerned, God was an entity created by people to explain their beliefs. For instance, he could take anything he wanted, like the sun or moon, or even "time" as God and worship it. Yes, he thought, a faith based on time; after all, life could not exist without time.

*****

He could imagine people who worshipped time, gave the Time God daily gratitude for allowing them to live in it and permitting their movement within it. As a place of worship, they could use a church or temple. But the most sacred temple would be the Temple of Time, which would sanction the most venerated artifact, the Great Clock. Devotees would pay homage to it at least once a year. They would pray to it, bow to it, and completely submit themselves to it so that they may have a good life in this world as well as the next. What a religion it would be, Lin thought.

*****

Lin opened the door and Ben exited his office. "Take it easy with Gus," Lin said as Ben walked away from him. Ben waved the crumpled up newspaper in the air. "I got the memo Doc, goodbye," he said with his back toward Lin.

Ben had come in because he had a mild fever and he wanted to get tested for the new virus. While administering the test, small talk revealed that Ben was new in town. He had just come to this city with his longtime friend, Gus. They were both unemployed and thus frequently argued about money (though Ben pointed out they used to argue even when they were employed). He also revealed symptoms that he thought were minor, like headaches at night and chest pains during the day. Lin suspected he had high blood pressure and this was confirmed by the reading on the sphygmomanometer. He had prescribed a low dosage of Cozaar and Sectral, which were both covered by Ben's Medicare. He had also told him to avoid alcohol and salty foods. "I don't have money for either," replied Ben. "But thanks for the tip," he said.

Lin checked his watch. It was 10 minutes past seven. He had finished earlier than usual, most likely due to Martin's early exit.

*****

Suddenly, Lin's phone rang. Lin reached down into his coat pocket and took out his phone. The screen read "Unknown number." It could be a prank or possibly Shuyu. In the past, there were a few instances in which she had borrowed a stranger's phone to call him. He removed his facemask and accepted the call. "Hello?" he asked hesitantly.

"Charles! You said you would call at five, and it's now 7:10. Why haven't you called?"

"Where are you?" the woman on the other end of the phone asked.

Lin had no idea who this woman was.

"This is the—" Lin began.

But the woman continued as if she didn't hear Lin. "We haven't talked in three days — three whole days. Please, let's meet tonight. I know things haven't been good between us but please give me a chance," the woman pleaded.

"Ma'am, I'm sorry—" Lin said.

"DON'T MA'AM ME, YOU WEASEL," the woman exclaimed.

She then gathered herself, "I mean, I'm sorry Charles, I didn't mean that, you know that I love you. Just please, let's talk about this in-person. I'll fix everything, I'll change. I'll be sweet like I used to be. I won't cry. Please..." she begged.

"I'm sorry, this is the wrong number," Lin said.

There was a pause at the other end of the phone. "Oh," the woman finally said.

"This is Dr. Kong, not Charles," Lin explained.

"Doctor? As in a medical doctor?" she asked.

"Well, yes, I've just finished with my last patient. Now, if you'll excuse me I—" Lin said.

Lin was tempted to cut the call. He had already been through a lot today and wasn't in the mood to add to the list. But his shift was over now, and he was technically early, so he guessed there wasn't much to lose by assisting this woman.

"Yes, tell me, what's wrong?" he asked.

"I'm in love with a man named Charles. Our relationship was going well, but now it's going downhill. I don't know what to do, I don't know how to save our relationship," she said.

"Well, what do you mean it's going downhill?" Lin asked.

"It was perfect at first. We used to spend time at work, drink coffee together, and we once even saw a movie together. But now he's become more and more distant. It's driving me crazy," she explained.

"Well, maybe he just needs space," Lin suggested.

"Space? He's married for god's sake! Either he's spending time with his wife or he's dumping me for another woman, I can't leave him alone, he'll forget about me!" she said.

"Wait, he's married?" Lin asked.

"Oh, didn't I tell you? Both me and Charles are married to different people, but we're in love with each other," she explained.

"So you're having an affair? And you want me to help you sustain it?" Lin asked.

"It sounds wrong when you put it like that, but in reality, our marriages are stale. We married purely for financial reasons; it's easier to pay the rent when you have a husband or wife paying half of it for you. Thus we don't love our partners, we love each other," she explained.

Lin felt sympathetic for this woman because he realized that she was in the same position he had been when he was a young doctor in China. Lin had been married to Shuyu, who he didn't love at that time, and he had an affair with Manna, who he did love. So Lin was talking to a younger version of himself, and it was asking him for advice on what to do next. Lin had reflected on his life many times before, looking at what mistakes he made and what he would do differently to prevent them.

"Look Mrs.—," he began.

"Mrs. Parker, my name is Dorothy Parker," she stated.

Parker? Lin remembered that Martin had told him to tell Mrs. Parker "thanks" for something.

But now that Lin knew Mrs. Parker a bit better, he realized he probably shouldn't mention Martin. He was probably another man who she had an affair with and he was thanking her for it.

"Mrs. Parker, believe it or not, I too had an affair in my younger years," he said.

"Didn't we all, Dr. Kong?" she asked.

He wasn't sure how to respond to that. He hoped most people did not have affairs.

"Uh well, um, anyway, I ended up divorcing my wife and marrying the woman I had an affair with," he explained.

"Oh how romantic!" Mrs. Parker exclaimed.

"And she died a year later," he finished.

There was silence for a second or two. He then heard some muffled static and thought Mrs. Parker had cut the phone.

Finally, she whispered, "I'm sorry for your loss," in a hushed voice.

"Looking back, I regret having that affair. So I highly recommend that you stop yours. I understand that you're in love, but trust me, that feeling will pass," he explained.

There was a pause and then she said, "I understand Dr. Kong, thank you for your advice."

She didn't sound convinced, and she would most likely continue her affair. Nevertheless, he had done his job, and had given her guidance on what to do next, so he would leave it up to her as to whether she wanted to heed his advice or not.

"No problem. Take care of yourself. If things don't go well with Charles, don't punish yourself, move on and find someone else," he said.

"I will, goodbye Dr. Kong," she said and cut the phone.

*****

As Lin exited the hospital and walked home, he reflected on his day. By pure fate, he had been able to help many people, even those who were not his patients. One of them was even a younger version of himself. It made him happy that he could counsel people to prevent them from making the same mistakes he did.

He inhaled the refreshing night air and became aware of his environment. The city at night was chaotic, as if a yawning chasm was giving birth.

*****

He observed the people as they walked, talked, and laughed. Interestingly, he saw a small boy with a canvas bag on the corner of the street. The boy was shouting, "Saturday Evening Post!" at the motorists and pedestrians that passed by. Lin chuckled. He had a feeling that boy would grow up to be a writer.

*****

He then raised his eye level to observe the buildings. Yellow and white light emanated from the windows, and Lin could not see the people but only their silhouettes. In one, a couple bicker, the women telling her husband to go on a strike and the husband countering that it's too risky. In another, an applicant and employer both sit on chairs a few feet away from each other. The employer offers a job that pays well, but the applicant questions the morality of the job and refuses it. In yet another, a man buries his face in the lap of the woman he loves. Both yearn to be together, but they cannot due to the lack of financial stability.

Finally, Lin raised his gaze even higher and saw the pitch black sky dotted with white stars. In the center was the moon, it's light encapsulating the entire city. Maybe, just maybe, Lin thought, a God might exist.

Author Robert Eidelberg's Books With a Built-In Teacher

In addition to **Some Day: The Literature of Waiting – A Creative Writing Course With Time on Its Hands** all of the following "Books With a Built-In Teacher" by educator and author Robert Eidelberg are available through all online bookstores and from the author at the email on the copyright page

Hey, Professor: An Exhausting – But Not Remotely Exhaustive – Experiment in College Distance Learning (in collegial collaboration with 27 Hunter College undergraduate students)

"Who's There?" in Shakespeare's HAMLET – That is the Question!

Stanza-Phobia: A Self-Improvement Approach to Bridging Any Disconnect Between You and Poetry by Understanding Just One Poem (Yes, One!) and Winding Up Not Only Learning the Process Involved but Coming to Love at Least a Few More Poems (and Maybe Poetry Itself)

Good Thinking: A Self-Improvement Approach to Getting Your Mind to Go from "Huh?" to "Hmm" to "Aha!"

Playing Detective: A Self-Improvement Approach to Becoming a Mote Mindful Thinker, Reader, and Writer By Solving Mysteries

Detectives: Stories for Thinking, Solving, and Writing

So You Think You Might Like to Teach: 29 Fictional Teachers (for Real!) Model How to Become and Remain a Successful Teacher

Staying After School: 19 Student (for Real!) Have the Next What-if Word on Remarkable Fictional Teachers and Their Often Challenging Classes (in collegial collaboration with 19 Hunter College undergraduate students)

Julio: A Brooklyn Boy Plays Detective to Find His Missing Father (with John Carter)

ABOUT THE AUTHOR

A former journalist, Robert Eidelberg served thirty-two years as a secondary school teacher of English in the New York City public school system, nineteen and a half of those years as the chair of the English Department of William Cullen Bryant High School, a neighborhood high school in the borough of Queens, New York.

For several years after that he was an editorial and educational consultant at Amsco, a foundational school publications company; a community college and private college writing skills instructor; and a field supervisor and mentor in English education for the national Teaching Fellows Program on the campus of Brooklyn College of the City University of New York.

For the past twenty-one years, Mt. Eidelberg has been a college adjunct both in the School of Education at Hunter College of the City University of New York and in the English Department of Hunter College, where he teaches literature study and creative writing courses on "The Teacher and Student in Literature" and "The Literature of Waiting," both of which he expressly created for Hunter College undergraduate students.

Mr. Eidelberg is the author of ten educational "self-improvement" book, all of which feature "a built-in teacher" and two of which he collaborated on with his students in the special topics humanities courses her teaches at Hunter College on "The Teacher and Student in Literature" and on "The Literature of Waiting."

Robert Eidelberg lives in the historic Park Slope neighborhood of Brooklyn, New York, with his life partner of 47 years and their Whippet, Chandler (named, as was his predecessor, Marlowe, in honor of noir mystery writer Raymond Chandler).

CPSIA information can be obtained
at www.ICGtesting.com
Printed in the USA
BVHW031043090720
583344BV00001B/47